MANAGING AND SHARING RESEARCH DATA

A Guide to Good Practice

SAGE has been part of the global academic community since 1965, supporting high quality research and learning that transforms society and our understanding of individuals, groups, and cultures. SAGE is the independent, innovative, natural home for authors, editors and societies who share our commitment and passion for the social sciences.

Find out more at: **www.sagepublications.com**

Connect, Debate, Engage on Methodspace

 **Connect with other researchers and discuss your research interests**

Keep up with announcements in the field, for example calls for papers and jobs

Discover and review resources

Engage with featured content such as key articles, podcasts and videos

Find out about relevant conferences and events

Methodspace
Connecting the Research Community

www.methodspace.com

brought to you by

$SAGE

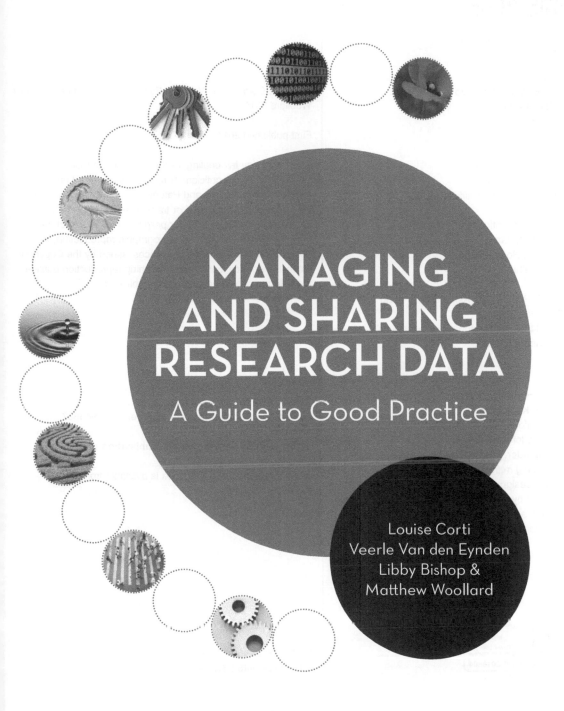

MANAGING AND SHARING RESEARCH DATA

A Guide to Good Practice

Louise Corti
Veerle Van den Eynden
Libby Bishop &
Matthew Woollard

Los Angeles | London | New Delhi
Singapore | Washington DC

Los Angeles | London | New Delhi
Singapore | Washington DC

SAGE Publications Ltd
1 Oliver's Yard
55 City Road
London EC1Y 1SP

SAGE Publications Inc.
2455 Teller Road
Thousand Oaks, California 91320

SAGE Publications India Pvt Ltd
B 1/I 1 Mohan Cooperative Industrial Area
Mathura Road
New Delhi 110 044

SAGE Publications Asia-Pacific Pte Ltd
3 Church Street
#10-04 Samsung Hub
Singapore 049483

Editor: Katie Metzler
Production editor: Ian Antcliff
Copyeditor: Christine Bitten
Proofreader: Kate Harrison
Marketing manager: Sally Ransom
Cover design: Francis Kenney
Typeset by: C&M Digitals (P) Ltd, Chennai, India
Printed and bound by CPI Group (UK) Ltd,
Croydon, CR0 4YY

Library of Congress Control Number: 2013945867

British Library Cataloguing in Publication data

A catalogue record for this book is available from the British Library

MIX
Paper from
responsible sources
FSC
www.fsc.org FSC® C013604

ISBN 978-1-4462-6725-7
ISBN 978-1-4462-6726-4 (pbk)

Contents

About the Authors

Louise Corti is an Associate Director of the UK Data Archive and Head of the Producer Relations and Collections Development teams. She also leads qualitative data activities at the Archive and directed UK Qualidata from 1998. She has 25 years of expertise in archiving, sharing and using social science data, and has particular expertise in the challenges of managing and sharing research data, standards for archiving qualitative data, and teaching with data. She has held numerous research awards in these areas focusing on best practice, training and tools.

Veerle Van den Eynden manages the Research Data Management team at the UK Data Archive. This team provides expertise, guidance and training on data management and data sharing to researchers, to promote good data practices and optimise data sharing. She leads research and development projects on various research data management aspects. Veerle has many years of experience researching interactions between people, plants and the environment, using a combination of social and natural science methods, and has experienced first-hand the benefits that data sharing brings to research.

Libby Bishop is a Manager in the Research Data Management team at the UK Data Archive where she provides guidance, support and training on data management, data management planning and data sharing to researchers and data producers. She has particular expertise in ethics and data sharing, including informed consent for archiving data and the ethics of re-using data. She also develops and delivers training for the User Support and Training section of the UK Data Service, with a focus on secondary analysis of qulitative data.

Matthew Woollard is Director of the UK Data Archive. He has practical and theoretical experience in all aspects of data service infrastructure, providing leadership in data curation, archiving and preservation activities. From 2002–2006 he was the Head of the History Data Service and from 2006–2010 an Associate Director and Head of Digital Preservation and Systems at the UK Data Archive. He currently provides leadership and strategic direction of the both the UK Data Archive and the ESRC-funded UK Data Service.

Acknowledgements

The authors would first like to thank the UK's Economic and Social Research Council (ESRC) for providing core funding for the UK Data Service, and its previous incarnations, since 1967. This continuity of support has enabled us to build one of the world's best national archiving centres and infrastructures, and to attract highly skilled researchers and support staff. This funding has also enabled us to play a leading role in developing proactive and capacity-building approaches to help researchers achieve better data curation practices. We would equally like to thank Jisc for providing more recent funding opportunities on research data management, from which we have benefited. These have inspired awareness and implementation of better local research data management practices, policies and infrastructure.

We thank Camille Corti-Georgiou, Sue Wood and Anne Etheridge for their help in proofing and preparing this manuscript. Other UK Data Archive staff members have contributed to specific exercises which have been adapted for this book: Laurence Horton, Bethany Morgan-Brett and Mus Ahmet.

We express our warmest thanks to the late Dr Alasdair Crockett, who co-authored the very first UK Data Archive *Managing and Sharing Data* guide back in 2006.

Finally thank you to all of our partners, Rob Lenart, Nick Snow, Allen Radtke and Penny Woollard, for bearing with our often highly antisocial hours spent writing, revising and editing.

Preface

Researchers' responsibilities towards their research data are set to change across all domains of scientific endeavour. Research funders are increasingly mandating open access to research data; governments internationally are demanding transparency in research; the economic climate is requiring much greater reuse of data; and fear of data loss calls for more robust information security practices. All these factors mean that researchers will need to improve, enhance and professionalize their research data management skills to meet the challenge of producing the highest quality shareable and reusable research outputs in a responsible and efficient way. The promotion of these skills offers a strategic contribution to the UK's and other countries' research capacity building programmes.

Robust research data management techniques give researchers and data professionals the skills required to deal with the rapid, and uneven, developments in the data management environment. Research funders in the UK, USA and across Europe are gradually implementing data management (and sharing) policies in order to maximize openness of data, transparency and accountability of research they support. Journal publishers increasingly require submission of the data upon which publications are based for peer review. Research funders and data users recognize the long-term value of well-prepared data. And institutions need good quality research information infrastructure to manage the ethical and security risks of their data assets.

This book contains up-to-date, easy-to-digest information about managing and sharing research data. It covers the full range of research data skills that feature in the research data lifecycle and includes case studies and practical activities that can assist in understanding the core concepts and applications. The detailed guidance presented results from many years of delivering best practice advice, guidance and training to a wide range of researchers. This has involved in-depth discussion around topical research projects and from working closely with researchers on developing solutions and tools that fit easily within standard research practices. We define research data as any research materials resulting from primary data collection or generation, qualitative or quantitative, or derived from existing sources intended to be analysed in the course of a research project. The scope covers numerical data, textual data, digitized materials, images, recordings or modelling scripts.

The book is aimed at researchers at all levels, from the novice Masters or PhD student to the experienced professor or research group leader. For the junior researcher the material helps to provide building blocks for a solid research knowledge base. For the experienced researcher the information can help plug some of the gaps in current knowledge; can refresh and update their knowledge in areas of rapid technological change, and can help them stay abreast of changes in legislation relating to the governance of research data or the ethics of research. It can also help reassure professional researchers that their practices are consistent with best practices. While this book has been written with the social science researcher in mind, many of the issues and practical strategies we set out are applicable more widely to any researcher creating or working with data.

The book is also aimed at the rapidly increasing group of research support staff, both in academic institutions and government departments, tasked with aspects of managing and sharing data, be it research grant and research governance, ethical review, IT services staff or library support.

While the information set out in this book is not necessarily sequential, we recommend reading the chapters in the order presented, so that knowledge is built incrementally. The exercises are intended to help consolidate knowledge and completing them will enable the reader to feel more confident in putting the skills into practice in a real-life research environment.

The following chapters of this handbook describe the key elements of data management that are essential in enabling the safe handling and sharing of research data. Chapter 1 introduces the key drivers for the practices of sharing data that have emerged, and considers arguments for why it is beneficial to share data and, more practically, how data can be shared. In Chapter 2 we introduce the concept of the research data lifecycle and how this extends the typical cycle of research. Chapter 3 deals with research data management planning, using a data management checklist, assigning roles and responsibilities, costing data management into a research project, and the resourcing of data management during research.

Chapter 4 describes documenting and providing context and provenance information for quantitative and qualitative data, examining in detail how to describe studies and files in a collection of research data. In Chapter 5 we cover formatting and organizing data, including file formats, data conversion, the organizing of files and folders, data quality assurance, version control and authenticity, data transcription and data digitization. Chapter 6 discusses the storing and transferring of data, setting out best practices in backing up data, providing information security, data transmission and encryption, data disposal, working with file-sharing and collaborative environments, and the long-term storage and preservation of data.

In Chapter 7 we discuss research ethics and privacy, dealing with legal and ethical issues that are relevant for data sharing, and consider pathways for providing access to data. These include informed consent, statistical disclosure control, anonymization of data and use of access control measures. Chapter 8 introduces Intellectual Property Rights in data, including copyright, database and other rights and the (re)use of existing data sources in compliance with such rights. Chapter 9 recommends data strategies for collaborative research, developing standard operating protocols, procedures and shared resources, coordinating data records and assigning data roles and responsibilities in a team. Chapter 10 covers how to make use of other people's research data, looking at opportunities for and challenges of reusing data, and provides six real-life case studies of data reuse. Finally, in Chapter 11 we examine publishing and citing data, including where to publish data and how to create citable data through the use of persistent digital identifiers.

Finally, the book has an accompanying website where additional exercises can be found plus links from the UK Data Service. The URL is: http://ukdataservice. ac.uk/manage-data/handbook

ONE
The Importance of Managing and Sharing Research Data

Research data are the cornerstone of scientific knowledge, learning and innovation and of our quest to understand, explain and develop humanity and the world around us. In the digital age, the generation of research data has not only grown exponentially, but data are nowadays very easily stored, kept and exchanged around the world. The demand for ensuring that the benefits of technological advances are employed to modernize how we treat and utilize research data is growing by the day.

Over 50 years ago, Watson and Crick (1953) published the structure of DNA in a single page article in *Nature*, with no raw data to underpin their findings. Recently, The 1000 Genomes Project Consortium (2010) accompanied their publication in *Nature* with 4.9 terabases of DNA sequences available through the project website and deposited in dbSNP, the database of single nucleotide polymorphisms (Kiermer, 2011). Genetics research is just one example that shows how the openness and exchange of information, including research data, can drive up rapidly the speed of research and discovery to our advantage. Just consider the medical benefits of our growing genetic understanding.

The period from 2000 has seen a boom in both the drivers of data sharing, as well as the development of human and material capability to do so. Research funders are increasingly mandating easy and/or open access to research data, and data plans to ensure maximum quality, sustainability, accessibility and openness of research data. Publishers of academic findings demand that the supporting data can be accessed for scrutiny or further exploration. Governments internationally are demanding transparency in research and the economic climate makes it desirable for much greater reuse of data to maximize the return on science investments. Many researchers themselves agree that lack of access to data impedes scientific progress.

Access to data means that scientific findings can be verified and scrutinized if needed. Society demands access to data: to enable businesses to employ new knowledge for the development of tools and applications; to allow organizations to question governmental policies and decisions; and for thousands of citizens to engage in research processes, or 'citizen science', to advance our collective scientific knowledge.

Researchers' responsibilities towards their research data are therefore changing across all domains of scientific endeavour. Researchers need to improve, enhance and professionalize their research data management skills to meet the challenge of producing the highest quality research outputs and sustainable data in a responsible and efficient way, with the ability to share and reuse such outputs. By data management we mean all data practices, manipulations, enhancements and processes that ensure that research data are of a high quality, are well organized, documented, preserved, sustainable, accessible and reusable. The promotion of data skills offers a strategic contribution to the UK's and other countries' research capacity building programmes. And institutions need high quality research data management to address the ethical and security risks of their data assets. Robust research data management techniques give researchers, data professionals and those involved in supporting research the skills that are required to deal with the rapid, and uneven, developments in the data management environment.

The Data Sharing Agenda

Researchers have always understood the importance of sharing: sharing findings in scientific publications; sharing expertise through peer networking; and collaboration via learned societies. Technological advances allow this sharing to be accelerated to a new level and applied in different ways: through open access to research publications and also to research data, tools, software and educational resources. The early 1990s saw a call for the opening up of published research articles to be available online, later coming to include a greater range of primary research materials.

Key drivers in the acceleration towards the opening up of research data have been the OECD *Principles and Guidelines for Access to Research Data from Public Funding* and the *Berlin Declaration on Open Access to Knowledge in the Sciences and Humanities*. The Organization for Economic Cooperation and Development (OECD) principles declared that publicly funded research data are a public good, produced in the public interest, and that it should be made openly available with as few restrictions as possible in a timely and responsible manner without harming intellectual property (OECD, 2007). The Berlin Declaration called for promoting knowledge dissemination through the open access paradigm via the internet, which requires the worldwide web to be sustainable, interactive and transparent, with openly accessible and compatible content and tools (Berlin Declaration, 2003).

At a European level the report of the High Level Expert Group on Scientific Data, noting the rising tide of data, proposed that we are on the verge of a great new leap in scientific capability, fuelled by data, with a need for a scientific e-infrastructure that supports seamless access, use, reuse and trust of data (European Commission, 2010). The report sketches the benefits and costs of accelerating the development of a fully functional e-infrastructure for scientific data. Open infrastructure, open culture and open content need to go hand in hand.

Recently, The Royal Society (2012) recommended that in order to benefit from the huge potential of the data boom, researchers and institutions should increase openness towards peer researchers and the public and should increase the recognition of research data. The adoption of common data standards is seen as crucial, as are mandates for data publishing. At a technical level the report stresses the need for data management experts in science and the need for tools to analyse large data streams in order to maximize the potential of data in science.

The prominence of data sharing is reflected in the exponential increase in data repositories. The Databib registry currently lists 518 data repositories, 42 of which are specific social science data repositories with nearly 200 having been created since 2000, as shown in Figure 1.1 (Databib, 2013).

Governments and organizations have also embraced open data to increase transparency of their activities. By opening up their information for anyone to access and use, the economic and innovation potential of public sector infor-mation can be harnessed. Since 2009, over 200 open data initiatives have been launched by governments, regional, national and international organizations worldwide (CTIC, 2013). High profile open data portals are the World Bank Catalog, the United Nations Catalog, UNdata and the EU Open Data Portal. Such portals open up organizational information to individuals, businesses and academia. The European Commission is also working with member states on data formats and interoperability between existing sites (European Commission, 2011).

In the UK the government's Open Data White Paper clearly explains what citizens, businesses and the public sector can expect from government and pub-lic services to reap the benefits of open data (Cabinet Office, 2012). The paper sets clear standards for the fast release of data in standardized, machine-readable and open formats, making data freely and easily accessible, with publishing being the default for government data. The government's data portal (data.gov.uk) holds over 9,500 datasets and also showcases how open government data have been used in innovative applications, reports, maps, policies and services. In the

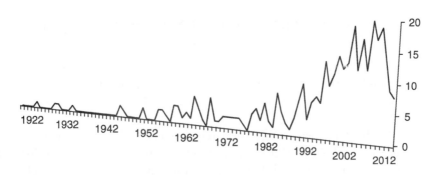

Figure 1.1 Growth in number of data repositories newly created each year

Source: Databib, 2013

USA, in summer 2013, the Obama administration showed a commitment to transparency with regards to non-classified federal government data by launching an Open Data project. The aim is to make far more data available to both the public and to private sector firms for innovation and commercial development (Higgins, 2013).

Whilst the open access agenda has been prompting academics to release and access more public data, we have also seen the rise of 'citizen science'. Citizen science involves lay members of the public gathering and analysing data through voluntary effort and amateur enthusiasm (CSA, 2012). Galaxy Zoo is possibly the best known, as shown in the case study below.

CASE STUDY — **The Citizen Science Alliance**

The Citizen Science Alliance (CSA) is a collaboration of scientists, software developers and educators, who collectively develop, manage and utilize internet-based citizen science projects in order to further science itself, and the public understanding of both science and of the scientific process.

The idea of citizen science projects is to engage citizens, with their available time, their interests and abilities, into scientific projects. The various projects in the 'Zooniverse' are inspired by teams of scientists who provide the initial ideas, some validation of contributions, and a user-oriented audience. Projects range from the classical sciences to climate science; from ecology to planetary science.

The most well-known, Galaxy Zoo at http://www.galaxyzoo.org/, asks its citizen researchers to classify galaxies according to their shapes. The Zoo started in 2007 with a dataset made up of a million galaxies imaged by the Sloan Digital Sky Survey. To their surprise, within 24 hours of launch almost 70,000 classifications an hour were being received. In the first year some 50 million classifications were received from 150,000 people.

The most recent challenge yet is to analyse the most distant 'ultra-deep' images from the Hubble Telescope making use of the new Wide Field Camera 3, installed during the final shuttle mission to Hubble.

Research Funder Data Management and Sharing Policies

In the UK, USA and EU, funders' and publishers' data sharing policies have been important drivers for data sharing, and with it for enhanced data management. They are based on the OECD principle that publicly funded research data are a public good, to be made openly available with as few restrictions as possible (OECD, 2007).

While in the UK some public research funders had adopted data sharing policies as early as the mid-1990s, a milestone was the adoption of the Common Principles on Data Policy by all Research Councils in 2011 (RCUK, 2011). This was followed by their Policy on Access to Research Outputs (RCUK, 2012). This requires that from April 2013, for all Council-funded research, peer-reviewed research papers are published in journals that are compliant with the Policy on Open Access, and include a statement on how the underlying research materials such as data, samples or models can be accessed. Knowing that across UK higher education institutions, 55% of research is funded by the research councils – an annual investment of about £3 billion – such policies strongly influence research practices (HESA, 2012).

At the time of writing, the following UK research funders have a data sharing policy:

- Arts and Humanities Research Council (AHRC)
- Biotechnology and Biological Sciences Research Council (BBSRC)
- British Academy
- Cancer Research UK (CRUK)
- Department for International Development (DFID)
- Department of Health
- Economic and Social Research Council (ESRC).
- Engineering and Physical Sciences Research Council (EPSRC)
- Medical Research Council (MRC)
- Natural Environment Research Council (NERC)
- Nuffield Foundation
- Science and Technology Facilities Council (STFC)
- Wellcome Trust

RCUK Common Principles on Data Policy (RCUK, 2011)

- Publicly funded research data are a public good, produced in the public interest, which should be made openly available with as few restrictions as possible in a timely and responsible manner that does not harm intellectual property.
- Institutional and project specific data management policies and plans should be in accordance with relevant standards and community best practice. Data with acknowledged long-term value should be preserved and remain accessible and usable for future research.
- To enable research data to be discoverable and effectively reused by others, sufficient metadata should be recorded and made openly available to enable other researchers to understand the research and reuse potential of the data. Published results should always include information on how to access the supporting data.
- RCUK recognizes that there are legal, ethical and commercial constraints on release of research data. To ensure that the research process is not damaged by inappropriate release of data, research organization policies and practices should ensure that these are considered at all stages in the research process.
- To ensure that research teams get appropriate recognition for the effort involved in collecting and analysing data, those who undertake Research Council funded work may be entitled to a limited period of privileged use of the data they have collected to enable them to publish the results of their research. The length of this period varies by research

(Continued)

(Continued)

> discipline and, where appropriate, is discussed further in the published policies of individual Research Councils.
>
> - In order to recognize the intellectual contributions of researchers who generate, preserve and share key research datasets, all users of research data should acknowledge the sources of their data and abide by the terms and conditions under which they are accessed.
> - It is appropriate to use public funds to support the management and sharing of publicly funded research data. To maximize the research benefit that can be gained from limited budgets, the mechanisms for these activities should be both efficient and cost-effective in the use of public funds.

While common principles provide the framework, each Research Council or funder has its own policy, with slightly different emphases. Some either mandate or encourage data sharing and many require that data management and sharing plans be submitted with grant applications, as discussed in Chapter 3. Most Councils place responsibility for managing and sharing research data with award holders, except for the EPSRC who place the responsibility with host research institutions. This is formulated in the EPSRC Policy Framework on Research Data (EPSRC, 2011). Research organizations receiving EPSRC funding will from May 2015 be expected to have appropriate policies and processes in place to preserve research data and to respond to access requests for such data. Researchers will also be expected to publish metadata for their research data holdings and preserve and provide access to research data securely for 10 years beyond the last data access. This policy is strongly influenced by the ethos of the Freedom of Information Act, which advocates openness and a timescale for publishing information. As a result, there is now an increase in universities and research organizations with institutional data policies, although there remain obstacles to implementation (DCC, 2013a). The Digital Curation Centre maintains a list of Research Council data policy requirements (DCC, 2012).

Research Councils also fund data sharing support services and infrastructure. Examples are:

- UK Data Service (ESRC) providing data management and sharing guidance and support to ESRC-funded researchers, as well as curation, preservation and dissemination of social science and economic research data;
- Network of designated NERC data centres (NERC) for the curation, preservation and dissemination, as well as value-adding for research data on the natural environment;
- MRC Data Support Service (MRC) that promotes data sharing for population health sciences;
- Atlas Petabyte Storage (STFC) providing medium- to long-term storage for scientific data;
- Archaeology Data Service (AHRC) preserving and disseminating digital archaeology data.

Some research funders, such as ESRC, NERC and STFC, also provide a publications repository for their funded researchers, which may provide temporary data storage and access facilities. BBSRC, Cancer Research UK, MRC and the Wellcome Trust are partners in UK PubMed Central.

In the USA the key data sharing policies that drive the data sharing agenda are those of the National Science Foundation (NSF) and the National Institutes of Health (NIH).

USA research funders with data policies (Dietrich et al., 2012) are:

- National Science Foundation (NSF)
- National Institutes of Health (NIH)
- United States Department of Energy (DoE)
- Office of Naval Research (ONR)
- United States Department of Education (DoE)
- United States Environmental Protection Agency (EPA)
- United States Agency for International Development (USAID)
- National Oceanographic and Atmospheric Administration (NOAA)
- American Heart Association (AHA)
- Alfred P. Sloan Foundation

In 2012 the European Commission (EC) published a communication and recommendations on access to, and preservation of, scientific information (European Commission, 2012a; 2012b). These called for coordinated actions across all member states to drive forward open access, long-term preservation and capacity building to promote open science, not just for EC-funded research, but also for national research funding. The EC funds 10% of all research across all member states. After further public consultation, an open access to data pilot is planned for Horizon 2020, the next framework programme.

Journals and Publishers

In line with the exponential growth in data sharing policies amongst research funders, publishers also increasingly have data policies that require research data underpinning findings published in peer-reviewed articles to be available for readers and reviewers. This is partly driven by prominent research funders urging publishers to adopt more stringent data policies to help drive the open data movement, and partly driven by the publishing community itself. The open access publisher, BioMed Central, has strongly pushed the adoption of journal data policies since 2010 through its open data statement, its cross-publisher working group on open data publishing, and its ongoing efforts on the copyright and licensing of data underpinning publications (Hrynaszkiewicz and Cockerill, 2012). The Joint Data Archiving Policy, adopted jointly by many leading journals in the field of evolution in 2011, and since adopted by numerous other journals across various disciplines, strongly influences the increase in journal data policies. This requires data that support the results described in a paper to be archived in an appropriate public archive as a condition for publication, often recommending Dryad as an appropriate repository (Dryad, 2013).

Journal policies vary, either expecting research data to be made available upon request, data to be submitted as a supplement to the publication, data to be deposited in a suitable public repository, or data to be deposited with a mandated repository as a condition of publication. The latter is the strongest possible form of publisher policy; an example of such a bidirectional relationship is between the publisher Elsevier and PANGAEA, the Publishing Network for Geoscientific and Environmental Data. Also *Nature* journals mandate specific repositories for particular disciplines and Dryad is the place of deposit for numerous journals, discussed further in Chapter 11.

An analysis of the quality and extent of data policies of 141 reputable economics journals showed that 20% have data availability policies, most of which are mandatory, requesting data submission prior to publication (Vlaeminck, 2013). The policy of the *American Economic Review*, adapted frequently by other economics journals, is considered as best in the field, only publishing papers if the data used in the analysis are readily available to any researcher for purposes of replication. Data files and user documentation have to be submitted before publication. In other social science disciplines, journals do not yet have mandatory data policies, but some such as the *Annual Review of Sociology* do accept data files as supplementary material. In the political sciences, the American Political Science Association (APSA) from 2012 included explicit statements about data access and research transparency in their revised ethics guidance (APSA, 2012). The APSA hosts, amongst other journals, the highly prestigious scholarly research journal, the *American Political Science Review*, and aims to incorporate these data sharing principles into journal submissions.

Policies alone do not increase data sharing if researchers remain reluctant to share their data with other researchers, as is suggested from studies by Savage and Vickers (2009) and Wicherts et al. (2006). The latter study requested research data from ten researchers publishing in the open access journals *PLoS Medicine* and *PLoS Clinical Trials*. Only one researcher made the original research data available. Wicherts et al.'s study had a 73% success rate (103 out of 141 research teams) for requesting research data for reanalysis from researchers publishing in four journals of the American Psychological Association. The requests involved repeated attempts and extensive assurances that the requested data would not be publicly released or reused.

More recently data journals have come into existence. Such journals publish data papers that describe a dataset, without going into the interpretation of the findings of the data. A data paper typically describes the methods to create the data, the structure and reuse potential of the dataset, as well as in which repository the dataset is available. Such data papers provide direct credit to the creation of research data. These are discussed in more detail in Chapter 11.

Researchers' Attitudes

Various surveys have recently found that the sharing of research data is still not as prevalent as it was expected to be, following the pump-priming support for the e-research infrastructure agenda in the mid-2000s. Furthermore, significant disciplinary differences prevail. A study in the UK by the Research Information Network (2008) of over 100 interviews with researchers across eight subject areas found significant variations in researchers' attitudes, behaviours and needs, in the availability of data infrastructure, and in the nature and effectiveness of funder policies across disciplines and subject areas. Only 37% of studied researchers shared their data with collaborators in their own circles and only 20% shared more widely outside of their own network. In a 2010 UK survey of social science researchers, only 17% of respondents reported to storing their data in their national data archive (Proctor et al., 2012).

The EU-funded Open Data Exchange (2011) project collected stories of successes, lessons learned and barriers of data sharing, reuse and preservation from leaders in scientific communities, research infrastructures, management and policy initiatives. The interviews provide perspectives on data sharing from many angles from funding policies, coordination and access to data infrastructure to position of leading-edge scientific research and data sharing.

In 2011 over 1,300 predominantly USA scientists participated in a survey exploring current data sharing practices and perceptions of the barriers and enablers for data sharing (Tenopir et al., 2011). While on the whole respondents were happy with their current processes for short-term data management, they were unhappy with facilities for longer-term data management and preservation, and support from their own institutions in this matter. Whilst stating to be overall in favour of data sharing, few research data were being actually shared. The scientists reported lack of time and money as barriers to data sharing, as well as a lack of relevant repository infrastructure and standards. The authors noted differences and approaches in data management practices based on primary funding agency, subject discipline, age, work focus and world region.

Youngseek and Stanton (2012) conducted a qualitative study of data sharing practices by interviewing 25 scientists across disciplines in USA universities. They found strong disciplinary influences, with data sharing being seen as critical for new science by biological, chemical and ecological scientists. Computer scientists, engineers, mathematicians and physical oncologists stated the opposite. A data sharing push by funders and journals, peer expectations and sharing practices within particular science disciplines, IT capability in the form of repositories and data standards, and a desire to showcase data quality were highlighted as the main motivators for data sharing. Main barriers to data sharing pointed to restrictions imposed by private funders, the cost of data preparation and sharing, a fear for reduced publication opportunities or being 'scooped' by others. Overall, researchers reported seeing an increase in data sharing practices within their communities. Sayogo and Pardo (2013) further reported for the earth and environmental sciences that key determinants to publishing data were data management skills, organizational support and acknowledgement received for data sharing.

Data sharing is particularly prominent in research domains characterized by large-scale international multi-institutional research projects, such as genomics, astronomy, high energy physics and climate science. In genomics, agreements for pre-publication data release such as the 1996 Bermuda Principles and the 2003

Fort Lauderdale agreement were essential for the success of the human genome project and other community resource projects (Marshall, 2001; Wellcome Trust, 2003). They led directly to journal policies requiring GenBank or EMBL data accession numbers prior to publication, and are proven to have enormously accelerated the progress of biomedical research.

Concerns about Sharing Data

Where researchers express concerns or have hesitations about sharing their research data, it is usually because of the unknown factor and a lack of understanding of what the process actually entails. Also importantly, lack of explicit career rewards for creating and sharing of data, as distinct from the publication of academic papers, are major disincentives. Most researchers wish to retain exclusive use of the data they have created until they have extracted all the publication value they can.

Table 1.1 lists some of the key worries about data sharing commonly voiced by researchers attending data management and sharing workshops, together with some arguments to mitigate these concerns. Here we have summarized the benefits of sharing data, because the benefits will, on the whole, outweigh the negatives.

Table 1.1   Concerns about data sharing voiced by researchers and arguments to counter these

Reasons not to share data	Counter arguments in favour of sharing
My data are not of interest or use to anyone else.	They are! Researchers want to access data from all kinds of studies, methodologies and disciplines. It is very difficult to predict which data may be important for future research. Who would have thought that amateur gardeners' diaries would one day provide essential data for climate change research? Your data may also be essential for teaching purposes. Sharing is not just about archiving your data but about sharing them amongst colleagues.
I want to publish my work before anyone else sees my data.	Data sharing will not stand in the way of you first using your data for your publications. Most research funders allow you some period of sole use, but also want timely sharing. Also remember that you have already been working with your data for some time so you undoubtedly know the data better than anyone coming to use them afresh.
I have not got the time or money to prepare data for sharing.	It is important to plan data management early in the research data lifecycle. Data management ideally becomes an integral part of your research practice, reduces time and financial costs and greatly enhances the quality of the data for your use too.
If I ask my respondents for consent to share their data then they will not agree to participate in the study.	Don't assume that participants will not participate because data sharing is discussed. Talk to them; they may be less reluctant than you might think, or less concerned over data sharing! Make it clear that it is entirely their decision, whereby they can decide whether their data can be shared, independent of them participating in the research. Explain clearly what data sharing means, and why it may be important. But they are still free to consent or not. You can always explain what data archiving means in practice for their data. If you have not asked permission to share data during the research, then you can always return to gain retrospective permission from participants.

Reasons not to share data	Counter arguments in favour of sharing
I am doing highly sensitive research. I cannot possibly make my data available for others to see.	The first thing is to ask respondents and see if you can get consent for sharing in the first instance. Anonymization procedures can help to protect identifying information. If these first two strategies are not appropriate then consider controlling access to the data or embargoing for a period of time.
I am doing quantitative research and the combination of my variables discloses my participant's identity.	Quantitative data can be anonymized through processes of aggregation, top coding, removal of variables, or controlled access to certain variables, for example, postcodes.
I have collected audiovisual data and I cannot anonymize them, therefore I cannot share these data.	Audiovisual data can be anonymized through blurring faces or distorting voices, but this can be time consuming and costly to carry out. It can mean losing much of the value of the data. It is better to ask for consent to share data from participants in an unanonymized form, and/or control access to the data.
I have made promises to destroy my data once the project finishes.	Why were such promises made? Always avoid making unnecessary promises to destroy data. There is usually no legal or ethical need to do so, except in the case of personal data. But that certainly would not apply to research data in general. Also consider where you have received this advice. You may need to negotiate with your ethics committee or Institutional review board about this agreement.
My data have been gathered under complete assurances of confidentiality.	Again why was such an assurance made? Was it essential? It is best to avoid unnecessary promises. Anonymization procedures can be implemented to protect identities, but confidentiality can never be completely guaranteed. You can also consider controlling access to the data.
It is impossible to anonymize my transcripts as too much useful information is lost.	Consult guidance on how to anonymize qualitative data. Alternatively, access controls on the data may be a better solution than anonymization if too much useful information would be lost.
My data collection contains data which I have purchased and it cannot be made public.	It is important to know who holds the copyright to the data you are using and to obtain the relevant permissions. You need to be aware of the license conditions of the data you are using and what you can and cannot do with the data.
Other researchers would not understand my data at all – or may use them for the wrong purpose.	Producing good documentation and providing contextual information for your research project should enable other researchers to correctly use and understand your data.
There is Intellectual Property in the data.	This should not be a problem if you seek copyright permission from the owner of the Intellectual Property rights. This is best done early on in the research project, but could be sought retrospectively.

Benefits of Data Sharing for Different Players in the Research Environment

Benefits for researchers:

- increases visibility of scholarly work;
- likely to increase citations rates, for example, open access journal articles are cited more;

(Continued)

(Continued)

- enables new collaborations;
- encourages scientific enquiry and debate;
- promotes innovation and potential new data uses;
- establishes links to next generation of researchers.

Benefits for research funders:

- promotes primary and secondary use of data;
- makes optimal use of publicly funded research;
- avoids duplication of data collection;
- maximizes return on investment.

Benefits for the scholarly community:

- maintains professional standards of open inquiry;
- maximizes transparency and accountability;
- promotes innovation through unanticipated and new uses of data;
- enables scrutiny of research findings;
- improves quality from verification, replication and trustworthiness;
- encourages the improvement and validation of research methods;
- provides resources for teaching and learning.

Benefits for research participants:

- allows maximum use of contributed information;
- minimizes data collection on difficult-to-reach or over-researched populations;
- allows participants' experiences to be understood as widely as ethically possible.

Benefits for the public:

- advances science to the benefit of society;
- adopts emerging norms such as open access publishing;
- to be, and appear to be, open and accountable;
- complies with openness laws and regulations.

Finally, a follow-up report by the EU-funded Open Data Exchange (2011) on data publishing found that integrating data sharing with the activity of publishing research, by formally joining publications with data, seemed to overcome researchers, major concerns (Reilly et al., 2011).

Skills

The drive towards increased access to and sharing of research data places data management practices in a prominent position within research practices. Knowing that data are the building blocks of all scientific knowledge and progress, the integrity of data is paramount. Data integrity translates as accuracy and consistency and is ensured through quality control. Data can only be shared if they are of high quality, well-curated, well-documented, and can be referenced and indexed.

This brings us to the skills researchers need to deliver such high quality data. While most university students get a good grounding in research methods and statistics, their studies rarely cover information management, the lifecycle of data and the practicalities of making data shareable for the longer term. As such, researchers tend to focus on the immediate activities needed to collect, interpret and report on analysed data.

We advocate the incorporation of the added-value skills needed to ensure well-managed, sustainable and shareable digital research data into research methods training, a plea also made by the journal *Nature*, to incorporate data management into every science course as one of the foundations of knowledge (Campbell, 2009).

Data management skills contribute to the development of professional skills, useful in academic pursuits, but also serving as transferable skills when moving into public sector and commercial workplaces. They also apply to the home environment, helping citizens look after and pass on their digital assets. As well as building up an individual's skills, good data management practices also bring efficiency gains for research teams or centres, by encouraging the use of standard, shared procedures and protocols, and by assigning roles and responsibilities.

In the UK the Jisc invested in a five-year Managing Research Data (MRD) programme to help develop data infrastructure, resources, tools and training materials across the higher education sector. The Digital Curation Centre (DCC) provides links to training materials developed in the course of this programme. These generic and subject specific training resources aim to equip researchers and data custodians such as library and research support staff with the skills they need to share and preserve data effectively (DCC, 2013b). The authors provided the first set of guidance and training materials in this field aimed at the social scientist (Corti et al., 2011; Van den Eynden et al., 2011).

There are also an increasing number of training courses on digital preservation, aimed at information professionals and archivists rather than researchers per se. These seek to provide hands-on knowledge and skills involving the collection, selection, management, long-term preservation, and accessibility of digital assets. They include, in the UK, the Digital Preservation Coalition (DPC) training courses and in the USA, the Library of Congress's Digital Preservation Outreach and Education Programme (DPOE) and their Train-the-Trainer workshops (DPC, 2013; Library of Congress, 2013).

Exercise 1.1   Reasons to share data

Write down five reasons why researchers may be most reluctant to share their research data.

Answers to Exercise 1.1

There are many reasons! Check Table 1.1 for key reasons given by researchers and note solutions provided for countering these arguments.

References

APSA (2012) *Ethics in Political Science*, American Political Science Association. Available at: http://www.apsanet.org/content_9350.cfm.

Berlin Declaration (2003) *Berlin Declaration on Open Access to Knowledge in the Sciences and Humanities*. Available at the Max Plank Society website at: http://oa.mpg.de/lang/en-uk/berlin-prozess/berliner-erklarung/.

Cabinet Office (2012) *Open Data White Paper: Unleashing the Potential*, UK Government Cabinet Office. Available at: http://data.gov.uk/sites/default/files/Open_data_White_Paper.pdf.

Campbell, P. (2009) 'Data's shameful neglect', *Nature*, 461: 145.

Corti, L., Van den Eynden, V., Bishop, L. and Morgan, B (2011) *Managing and Sharing Data: Training Resources*, UK Data Archive, University of Essex.

CSA (2012) Citizen Science Alliance. Available at: http://www.citizensciencealliance.org/.

CTIC (2013) *Public Dataset Catalogs Browser*, Asturias, Fundación CTIC. Available at: http://datos.fundacionctic.org/sandbox/catalog/faceted/.

Databib (2013) *Registry of Research Data Repositories*, Databib. Available at: http://databib.org/index.php.

DCC (2012) *Overview of Funders' Data Policies*, Digital Curation Centre. Available at: http://www.dcc.ac.uk/resources/policy-and-legal/overview-funders-data-policies.

DCC (2013a) *Institutional Data Policies*, Digital Curation Centre. Available at: http://www.dcc.ac.uk/resources/policy-and-legal/institutional-data-policies/uk-institutional-data-policies.

DCC (2013b) *Digital Curation Training for All*, Digital Curation Centre. Available at: http://www.dcc.ac.uk/training.

Dietrich, D., Adamus, T., Miner, A. and Steinhart, G. (2012) 'De-mystifying the data management requirements of research funders', *Issues in Science and Technology Librarianship*, Summer 2012. DOI: 10.5062/F44M92G2.

DPC (2013) *Digital Preservation Training Programme*, Digital Preservation Coalition. Available at: http://www.dpconline.org/training/digital-preservation-training-programme.

Dryad (2013) *Dryad*. Available at: http://datadryad.org/.

EPSRC (2011) *EPSRC Policy Framework on Research Data*, Engineering and Physical Sciences Research Council. Available at: http://www.epsrc.ac.uk/about/standards/researchdata/Pages/policyframework.aspx.

European Commission (2010) *Riding the Wave: How Europe can Gain from the Rising Tide of Scientific Data*, final report of the High Level Expert Group on Scientific Data, European Commission. Available at: http://cordis.europa.eu/fp7/ict/e-infrastructure/docs/hlg-sdi-report.pdf.

European Commission (2011) *Communication on Open Data*, European Commission. Available at: http://ec.europa.eu/information_society/policy/psi/docs/pdfs/directive_proposal/2012/open_data.pdf.

European Commission (2012a) *Communication Towards Better Access to Scientific Information: Boosting the Benefits of Public Investments in Research*, European Commission. Available at http://ec.europa.eu/research/science-society/document_library/pdf_06/era-communication-towards-better-access-to-scientific-information_en.pdf.

European Commission (2012b) *Recommendation on Access to and Preservation of Scientific Information*, European Commission. Available at: http://ec.europa.eu/research/science-society/document_library/pdf_06/recommendation-access-and-preservation-scientific-information_en.pdf.

HESA (2012) *Finances of UK Higher Education Institutions 2010/11*, Higher Education Statistics Agency. Available at: http://www.hesa.ac.uk/index.php?option=com_content&task=view&id=2404&Itemid=161.

Higgins, J.K. (2013) 'White House pulls back the curtains on big data project', *ECommerce Times*, 5 May. Available at: http://www.ecommercetimes.com/story/78088.html.

Hrynaszkiewicz, I. and Cockerill, M.J. (2012) 'Open by default: A proposed copyright license and waiver agreement for open access research and data in peer-reviewed journals', *BMC Research Notes*, 5: 494. DOI: 10.1186/1756-0500-5-494.

Kiermer, V. (2011) 'Innovation in scientific publishing, an editorial perspective', Nature Publishing Group. Available at: http://www.gracacarvalho.eu/xms/files/ACTIVIDADE_PARLAMENTAR/OUTRAS_ACTIVIDADES/2011/18-10-2011_STM/2011_10_Kiermer_Nature_STM_Roundtable_compressed.pdf.

Library of Congress (2013) *Digital Preservation Outreach and Education*, Library of Congress. Available at: http://www.digitalpreservation.gov/education/curriculum.html.

Marshall, E. (2001) 'Bermuda rules: Community spirit, with teeth', *Science*, 291(5507): 1192. Available at: http://www.sciencemag.org/content/291/5507/1192.full.

OECD (2007) *OECD Principles and Guidelines for Access to Research Data from Public Funding*, Organization for Economic Co-operation and Development. Available at: http://www.oecd.org/dataoecd/9/61/38500813.pdf.

Open Data Exchange (2011) *Ten Tales of Drivers and Barriers in Data Sharing*, Opportunities for Data Exchange Project. Available at: http://www.alliancepermanentaccess.org/wp-content/uploads/downloads/2011/10/7836_ODE_brochure_final.pdf.

Proctor, R., Halfpenny, P. and Voss, A. (2012) 'Research data management: Opportunities and challenges for HEIs', in G. Pryor (ed.), *Managing Research Data*. London: Facet Publishing. pp. 135–50.

RCUK (2011) *Common Principles on Data Policy*, Research Councils UK. Available at: http://www.rcuk.ac.uk/research/Pages/DataPolicy.aspx.

RCUK (2012) *Research Councils UK Policy on Access to Research Outputs*, Research Councils UK. Available at http://www.rcuk.ac.uk/research/Pages/outputs.aspx.

Reilly, S., Schallier, W., Schrimpf, S., Smit, E. and Wilkinson, M. (2011) *Report on Integration of Data and Publishing*, Opportunities for Data Exchange. Available at: http://www.alliancepermanentaccess.org/wp-content/uploads/downloads/2011/11/ODE-ReportOnIntegrationOfDataAndPublications-1_1.pdf.

Research Information Network (2008) *To Share or Not to Share: Publication and Quality Assurance of Research Data Outputs*, Research Information Network. Available at: http://www.rin.ac.uk/our-work/data-management-and-curation/share-or-not-share-research-data-outputs.

Savage, C.J. and Vickers, A.J. (2009) 'Empirical study of data sharing by authors publishing in PLoS journals', *PloSOne*, 4(9): e7078.

Sayogo, D.S. and Pardo, T.A. (2013) 'Exploring the determinants of scientific data sharing: Understanding the motivation to publish research data', *Government Information Quarterly*, 30(1): 19–31. DOI: 10.1016/j.giq.2012.06.011.

Tenopir, C., Allard, S., Douglass, K., Aydinoglu, A.U., Wu, L., Read, E., Manoff, M. and Frame, M. (2011) 'Data sharing by scientists: Practices and perceptions', *PlosOne*, 6(6): e21101. DOI:10.1371/journal.pone.0021101.

The 1000 Genomes Project Consortium (2010) 'A map of human genome variation from population-scale sequencing', *Nature*, 467:1061–73. DOI: 10.1038/nature09534.

The Royal Society (2012) *Science as an Open Enterprise*, The Royal Society Science Policy Centre Report 02/12. Available at: http://royalsociety.org/uploadedFiles/Royal_Society_Content/policy/projects/sape/2012-06-20-SAOE.pdf.

Van den Eynden, V., Corti, L., Bishop, L. and Horton, L. (2011) *Managing and Sharing Data; best practice for researchers*, UK Data Archive, University of Essex. Available at: http://www.data-archive.ac.uk/media/2894/managingsharing.pdf.

Vlaeminck, S. (2013) 'Data management in scholarly journals and possible roles for libraries – some insights from EDaWaX', *LIBER Quarterly*, 23(1): 48–79. Available at: http://liber.library.uu.nl/index.php/lq/article/view/URN%3ANBN%3ANL%3AUI%3A10-1-114595/8827.

Watson, J.D. and Crick, F.H.C. (1953) 'Molecular structure of nucleic acids – a structure for deoxyribose nucleic acid', *Nature*, 171(4356): 737–8.

Wellcome Trust (2003) *Sharing Data from Large-scale Biological Research Projects: A System of Tripartite Responsibility*, Wellcome Trust. Available at: http://www.sanger.ac.uk/datasharing/assets/fortlauderdalereport.pdf.

Wicherts, J.M., Borsboom, D., Kats, J. and Molenaar, D. (2006) 'The poor availability of psychological research data for reanalysis', *American Psychologist*, 61(7): 726.

Youngseek, K. and Stanton, J.M. (2012) 'Institutional and individual influences on scientists' data sharing practices', *Journal of Computational Science Education*, 3(1): 47–56.

TWO
The Research Data Lifecycle

Most data often have a much longer lifespan than the research project that creates them. Researchers may continue to work on data after funding has ceased, follow-up projects may analyse or add to the data, or data may be reused and repurposed by other researchers. If data are well managed during the course of a research project, and if they are properly preserved, curated and made accessible for the longer term, they will be able to be reused in future research.

During the 1990s and early 2000s the data lifecycle was promoted as a concept to support digital preservation and data curation practices. The notion of a data lifecycle is one that has gained popularity as the culture of data sharing becomes part of our everyday research language. The data lifecycle extends the typical research cycle. Table 2.1 sets out an overview of data-related activities typically undertaken in the research data lifecycle.

Table 2.1 Typical activities undertaken in the research data lifecycle

Activity	Key features
Discovery and planning	Designing research
	Planning data management
	Planning consent for sharing
	Planning data collection, processing protocols and templates
	Finding and discovering existing data sources
Data collection	Collecting data – recording, observation, measurement, experimentation and simulation
	Capturing and creating metadata
	Acquiring existing third party data
Data processing and analysis	Entering data, digitizing, transcribing and translating
	Checking, validating, cleaning and anonymizing data where necessary
	Deriving data
	Describing and documenting data
	Analysing data

(Continued)

Table 2.1   (Continued)

Activity	Key features
	Interpreting data
	Producing research outputs
	Authoring publications
	Citing data sources
	Managing and storing data
Publishing and sharing	Establishing copyright of data
	Creating discovery metadata and user documentation
	Publishing or sharing data
	Distributing data
	Controlling access to data
	Promoting data
Long-term management	Migrating data to best format
	Migrating data to suitable medium
	Backing up and storing data
	Gathering and producing metadata and documentation
	Preserving and curating data
Reusing data	Conducting secondary analysis
	Undertaking follow-up research
	Conducting research reviews
	Scrutinizing findings
	Using data for teaching and learning

The Data Documentation Initiative (**DDI**) is a popular documentation standard for social science data, and was one of the first initiatives to conceive the idea of a data lifecycle (DDI Alliance, 2013). The idea integrates research processes and activities with concepts of data curation, data preservation, data publishing and data sharing. Figure 2.1 shows this initial DDI lifecycle, which uses similar but not identical terminology to those concepts in Table 2.1. We will learn more about the DDI and its importance for describing social science data in Chapter 4 on documenting data.

Also in the domain of the social sciences, Humphrey set out a lifecycle model of research as it may be applied to the concept of 'e-science' (Humphrey, 2006). Shown in Figure 2.2, the chevrons in this diagram are discrete stages in research, each representing processes that generate information. The knowledge transfer (KT) stage in Humphrey's model deals with the wide variety of communications that flow from research, such as research outcomes, publications and so on.

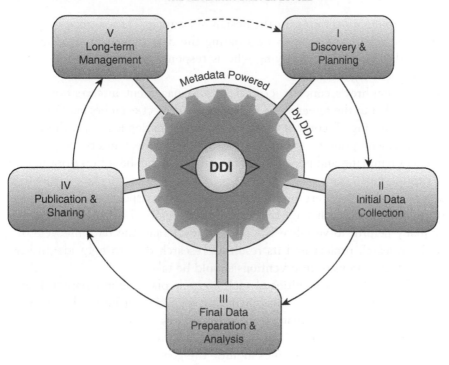

Figure 2.1 Data Documentation Initiative (DDI) lifecycle

Source: DDI, 2013

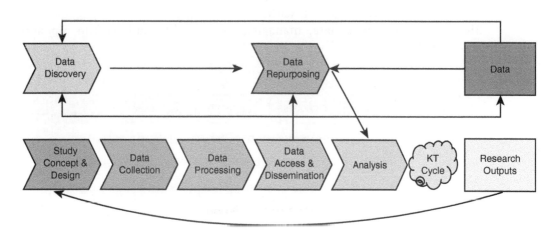

Figure 2.2 The lifecycle model of research knowledge creation

Source: Humphrey, 2006

The important point to note here are the gaps between chevrons: the transitions that occur in research as products are finished and pass to the next phase. Humphrey indicates that these transition points in the lifecycle are the places in a project's cycle that are most vulnerable to information loss, for example detailed sampling procedures for the design of a survey. These transition points are the most significant areas in negotiating the data management plan for a project, and in particular, clarifying who is responsible for the digital objects created at each stage.

Taking Humphrey's concern, critical data management intervention points can be grafted onto the research cycle before the project even begins. For example, formally signing off consent forms so that data sharing is not precluded can be a requirement prior to going into the field to collect interview data. Or spreadsheet templates and pre-set rules for data entry can be set up prior to data being captured.

As a researcher, it is very helpful to consider what aspects of data management might apply to each stage of your research before the project even starts. It is equally helpful to visualize the research cycle and the data lifecycle of a particular research project and its resulting research data to help identify the points at which actions or interventions should be taken.

We will cover the practicalities of such lifecycle planning in Chapter 3, with Exercise 3.1 illustrating how a sketched data lifecycle can be used to identify intervention points for data management procedures.

Since then other organizations have adapted the DDI lifecycle model to create their own version. Examples include the generic Data Curation Centre (DCC) Lifecycle Model (DCC, 2012) and the USA Geological Survey Data Lifecycle Diagram (USGS, 2013). This latter diagram (see Figure 2.3) clearly indicates the linear steps of planning, acquiring, preserving and publishing/sharing data, together with the ongoing processes throughout the lifecycle of describing data, managing their quality and backing up and securing them.

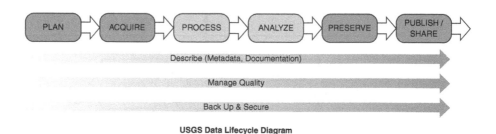

USGS Data Lifecycle Diagram

Figure 2.3   The USA Geological Survey data lifecycle model

Source: USGS, 2013

The **OAIS** reference model is a more formalized conceptual framework describing the environment, functional components, and information objects within a system responsible for the long-term preservation of digital materials. It provides a lifecycle model for data archives and is widely recognized in scientific, data management and archival communities (CCSDS, 2012).

In the case study below we give an example of a real-life research project, which shared its resulting data successfully, and its key data management intervention points.

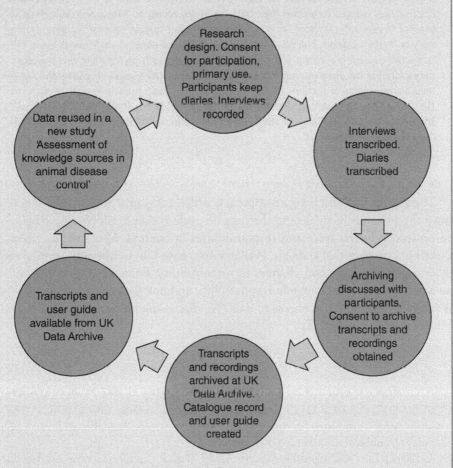

CASE STUDY	Data Lifecycle of the 'Health and Social Consequences of the Foot and Mouth Disease Epidemic in North Cumbria' Project (Mort, 2006)

The 2001 foot and mouth disease outbreak had an enormous effect on the economic, social and political life of rural areas in the UK. This research project, which was funded by the Department of Health, produced evidence about the human health and social consequences of the epidemic.

Research design. Consent for participation, primary use. Participants keep diaries. Interviews recorded

Interviews transcribed. Diaries transcribed

Archiving discussed with participants. Consent to archive transcripts and recordings obtained

Transcripts and recordings archived at UK Data Archive. Catalogue record and user guide created

Transcripts and user guide available from UK Data Archive

Data reused in a new study 'Assessment of knowledge sources in animal disease control'

Figure 2.4 Data lifecycle from the project 'Health and social consequences of the foot and mouth disease epidemic in North Cumbria, 2001–2003'

Source: Mort, 2006

(Continued)

(Continued)

The study recruited a standing panel of 54 local people from the worst affected area (North Cumbria). This panel wrote weekly diaries over a period of 18 months describing how their lives had been affected by the crisis and the process of recovery they observed around them. The panel was recruited to reflect a broad range of occupations including farmers and their families, workers in related agricultural occupations, those in small businesses including tourism, hotel trades and rural business, health professionals, veterinary practitioners, voluntary organizations and residents living near disposal sites.

The panel members produced 3,200 weekly diary entries of great intensity and diversity over an 18-month period. The data were supplemented by in-depth interviews with each respondent, focus group discussions, and 16 other interviews with stakeholders.

The research team gained consent from participants for primary participation in the project, but did not get consent for sharing or archiving their data. When the project was finished they wanted to archive their data for future reuse, so had to gain retrospective consent. As we will see later on, it is far more efficient to gain consent for data sharing early on in the fieldwork process. They consulted with the panel of participants about retrospective consent procedures and also sought expert advice from copyright law specialists to help draft terms of agreement that would give respondents a series of options about how their diaries, copies or portions of diaries, and/or their audio material would be archived. The research team gave respondents the choice to decide how their material was used. These data are now available to other researchers from the UK Data Service. Its data lifecycle is shown in Figure 2.4.

The significance of taking an approach which takes into account the whole of both the research lifecycle and the data lifecycle is that it allows all participants to understand their roles and responsibilities in context. Many of the pressure points in ensuring that data are available for reuse fall, temporally, immediately after significant tasks and changes in responsibility. Being clear that the end of an activity denotes a change in responsibility and not the end of a piece of work is vital for the long-term access to data. We discuss planning, roles and responsibilities next in Chapter 3.

References

CCSDS (2012) *Reference Model for an Open Archival Information System* (OAIS), The Consultative Committee for Space Data System Principles. Available at: http://public.ccsds.org/publications/archive/650x0m2.pdf.

DCC (2012) *The DCC Curation Lifecycle Model*, Digital Curation Centre. Available at: http://www.dcc.ac.uk/resources/curation-lifecycle-model.

DDI Alliance (2013) *Data Documentation Initiative*. Available at: http://www.ddialliance.org.

Humphrey, C. (2006) *e-Science and the Life Cycle of Research*, University of Alberta. Available at: http://datalib.library.ualberta.ca/~humphrey/lifecycle-science060308.doc.

Mort, M. (2006) *Health and Social Consequences of the Foot and Mouth Disease Epidemic in North Cumbria, 2001–2003* [computer file]. Colchester, Essex: UK Data Archive [distributor], November 2006. SN: 5407. Available at: http://dx.doi.org/10.5255/UKDA-SN-5407-1.

USGS (2013) *Data lifecycle Diagram*, USA Geological Survey. Available at: http://www.usgs.gov/datamanagement/why-dm/lifecycleoverview.php.

THREE
Research Data Management Planning

In research projects, early planning is essential to ensure that activities and actions are considered in detail, and are designed and organized in the best possible manner to ensure efficiency and successful completion of the work. The same applies to the planning of how research data will be managed over the length of a research project and beyond. Planning is best done using a data management plan.

A data management plan helps design, put into practice, and follow up on how research data are collected, organized, used and looked after to achieve the highest quality and long-term sustainability. The plan can consider both original uses intended by the primary researchers, as well as future uses, by those same researchers or by new users.

Planning helps focus on the resources and funding needed, and will clarify at an early stage individual and institutional roles and responsibilities.

In terms of data sharing, a plan can help to identify the specific factors that may promote, limit or prohibit data sharing, even before data have been collected. Potential limitations to data sharing could, for example, be the presence of personal information in data, uncertainties over intellectual property rights over data, proprietary file formats, or poorly documented data. As we will see in the following five chapters, there are strategies to overcome such limitations to data sharing.

One issue that can thwart timely data sharing is that of time constraints placed upon researchers, especially towards the end of a research project, when the pressures to publish and to secure continued research funding are at their highest. At that moment in the research cycle, the cost of implementing late data management and sharing measures can be prohibitively high. Putting in place data management strategies and activities during the planning and development stages of research will save time and effort in the short term and prevent panic and frustration at a later date. Many aspects of data management can be embedded in everyday aspects of research coordination and management and in research procedures, if planned early.

As we saw in Chapter 1, research funders increasingly require data management planning for research projects they fund to improve the longevity and quality of the data being generated and to ensure data can be shared beyond the primary research. Since the mid-2000s both UK and international research funders have introduced a requirement within their data policies for data management and/or sharing plans to be part of research grant applications. Tables 3.1 and 3.2 give an overview of such requirements for UK and USA research funders at the time of writing.

Table 3.1 Overview of UK research funders with data sharing policies and their requirements for data management and sharing plans

Funder	Plan required?	Required at application	Data topics in plan
Arts and Humanities Research Council (AHRC)	Yes	Technical plan	Standards, preservation, continued access and use
Biotechnology and Biological Sciences Research Council (BBSRC)	Yes	Data management and sharing plan	Type, format, standards, sharing methods, restrictions, sharing timeframe
Cancer Research UK (CRUK)	Yes	Data sharing plan	Volume, format, standards, metadata, documentation, sharing method, timescale, preservation, restrictions
Department for International Development (DFID)	Yes	Access and data management plan	Repositories, limits, timescale, responsibilities, resources, access strategy
Engineering and Physical Sciences Research Council (EPSRC)	No	Policy framework at institutional level (from 2015)	
Economic and Social Research Council (ESRC)	Yes	Data management plan	Volume, type, quality, archiving plans, difficulties sharing, consent sharing, IP rights, responsibilities
Medical Research Council (MRC)	Yes	Data management plan	Collection methods, documentation, standards, preservation, curation, security, confidentiality, sharing and access, timescale, responsibilities
Natural Environment Research Council (NERC)	Yes	Outline data management plan	Data management procedures, created data
Science and Technology Facilities Council (STFC)	Yes	Data management plan	Type, preservation, metadata, value, sharing, timescale, resources needed
Wellcome Trust	Yes	Data management and sharing plan	What data, when share, where share, how access, limits, how preserve, what resources

Source: Adapted from Knight, 2012

Table 3.2 Overview of USA funder requirements for data management and sharing plans

Funder	Data topics in plan
National Science Foundation (NSF) – includes Social, Behavioral and Economic Sciences Directorate; other directorates have different requirements	Expected data, retention, how share data, how manage data, legal/ethical restrictions on access, metadata, data storage and preservation, data format and dissemination, roles and responsibilities
National Institutes of Health (NIH) Data sharing plan required if funding is over $500,000	Data sharing

(Continued)

Table 3.2   (Continued)

Funder	Data topics in plan
Gordon and Betty Moore Foundation (GBMF)	Data description, data management, data sharing
Institute of Museum and Library Services (IMLS)	Data description, data restrictions, documentation, IP rights, metadata, storage, access, archiving and sharing
National Endowment for the Humanities (NEH)	Expected data, roles and responsibilities, data retention, data formats and dissemination, storage and preservation
National Oceanic and Atmospheric Administration (NOAA)	Data description, stewardship, documentation, data sharing, contact, storage, protection, archiving and preservation
Bill and Melinda Gates Foundation (Data access plan if funding over $500,000)	Expected data, data access, timeframe for sharing, storage and dissemination
National Institute of Justice	Data management and archiving process, confidentiality protections, tasks associated with data preparation and archiving, costing
Institute of Education Sciences	Expected data, data management, confidentiality of private information, roles and responsibilities, schedule for data sharing, format, documentation, how to share, limitations to sharing

Source: California Digital Library, 2013a

While each funder specifies particular requirements for the content of a plan, common topics in a plan are:

- What data will be created during research.
- Which policies might apply to the data, such as legal, institutional and funding requirements.
- Which data standards will be used, including metadata standards.
- How data will be documented.
- Ownership, copyright and intellectual property rights in data.
- Data security aspects.
- Data storage and backup measures and required equipment or infrastructure.
- Plans for sharing data, who will have access and whether there are any embargoes or restrictions.
- Data management roles and responsibilities.
- Costing or resources needed over and above usual research and dissemination activities to enable data sharing (certainly for the shorter term following the end of any funded research project).

In funding applications, a data management plan should not be treated as a simple administrative task for which standardized text can be pasted in from model templates, with little intention to implement the planned measures early on, or without considering what is really needed to enable data sharing. Instead, it should be, and indeed is, a strategic plan for research data on which all future publication and dissemination activities depend. Besides funder requirements, a data management plan is good practice for any research project that will be generating data.

Good data management does not end with planning. It is critical that measures are put into practice in such a way that issues are addressed when needed before minor inconveniences become insurmountable obstacles. Researchers who have developed data management and sharing plans have found it beneficial to think about and discuss data issues within the research team as research progressed.

Key issues to think about at the start of data management planning are:

- know your legal, ethical and other obligations regarding research data, towards research participants, colleagues, research funders and institutions;
- know your institution's policies and services, such as storage and backup strategy, research integrity framework, Intellectual Property rights policy, and any data sharing facilities like an institutional repository;
- assign roles and responsibilities to relevant parties;
- design data management according to the needs and purpose of the research;
- aim to incorporate data management measures as an integral part of your research cycle;
- implement and review management of data as part of continued research progression and review.

Using a Data Management Checklist

A checklist, such as the one below, can help you identify what to put in place for good data practices, and which actions to take to optimize data sharing.

Data Management Checklist (Based on UK Data Service, 2013a)

Planning

- Who is responsible for which part of data management?
- Are new skills required for any activities?
- Do you need extra resources to manage data, such as people, time or hardware?
- Have you accounted for costs associated with depositing data for longer-term preservation and access?

Documenting

- Will others be able to understand your data and use them properly?
- Are your structured data self-explanatory in terms of variable names, codes and abbreviations used?
- Which descriptions and contextual documentation explain what your data mean, how they were collected and the methods used to create them?
- How will you label and organize data, records and files?
- Will you be consistent in how data are catalogued?

(Continued)

(Continued)

Formatting

- Are you using standardized and consistent procedures to collect, process, transcribe, check, validate and verify data, such as standard protocols, templates or input forms?
- Which data formats will you use? Do formats and software enable sharing and long-term sustainability of data, such as non-proprietary software and software based on open standards?
- When converting data across formats, do you check that no data, annotation or internal metadata have been lost or changed?

Storing

- Are your digital and non-digital data, and any copies, held in multiple safe and secure locations?
- Do you need to securely store personal or sensitive data? If so, are they properly protected?
- If data are collected with mobile devices, how will you transfer and store the data?
- If data are held in multiple places, how will you keep track of versions?
- Are your files backed up sufficiently and regularly and are backups stored safely?
- Do you know which version of your data files is the master?
- Who has access to which data during and after research? Is there a need for access restrictions? How will these be managed after you are dead?
- How long will you store your data for and do you need to select which data to keep and which to destroy?

Confidentiality, ethics and consent

- Do your data contain confidential or sensitive information? If so, have you discussed data sharing with the respondents from whom you collected the data?
- Are you gaining written consent from respondents to share data beyond your research?
- Do you need to anonymize data, for example, to remove identifying information or personal data, during research or in preparation for sharing?

Copyright

- Have you established who owns the copyright in your data? Might there be joint copyright?
- Have you considered which kind of license is appropriate for sharing your data and what, if any, restrictions there might be on reuse?
- If you are purchasing or reusing someone else's data sources have you considered how that data might be shareable, for example negotiating a new licence with the original supplier?
- Can you preserve for the long term, personal information so that it can be used in the future?

Sharing

- Do you intend to make all your data available for sharing or how will you select which data to preserve and share?
- How and where will you preserve your research data for the longer term?
- How will you make your data accessible to future users?

Other organizations have produced their own comprehensive checklists (Atkinson et al., 2012; MIT Libraries, 2013; University of Edinburgh, 2013; University of Oxford, 2013), which are all useful and may probe you to ask additional questions relevant to your project.

Roles and Responsibilities

Data management is not always simply the responsibility of the researcher who has collected the data. Various parties are involved in the research process and may play a role in ensuring good quality data, safeguarding them and facilitating data sharing. *It is crucial that roles and responsibilities are assigned and not just presumed.* For collaborative research, assigning roles and responsibilities across partners is important.

People involved in data management and sharing can include:

- the project director designing and overseeing the research;
- research staff designing research, collecting, processing and analysing data, thereby taking account where data will be held and who will have access;
- laboratory or technical staff generating metadata and documentation;
- a database designer;
- external contractors involved in data collection, data entry, transcribing, processing and / or analysis, where standard protocols should be agreed in advance and documented;
- support staff managing and administering research and research funding, providing ethical review and assessing Intellectual Property rights;
- institutional IT services staff providing data storage, security and backup services;
- external data centres or web archives that facilitate data sharing.

Also consider whether any particular training may be needed for any staff involved. Your institution or specialist organizations may coordinate or provide training in various aspects of research data management (DCC, 2013b).

Costing Data Management into Your Research

Two generic approaches in costing research data management and sharing in advance of a research project starting, can be taken. Either can be used in a data management plan or can inform a funding application.

On the one hand, all data-related activities and resources for the entire datacycle – from data creation, through processing, analyses and storage, to sharing and long-term preservation – can be priced to calculate the total cost of all data generation, data sharing, data access and preservation activities. This will document the full costs of data creation from start to finish and subsequent sharing.

Alternatively, the resources that would be needed to preserve and make research data shareable beyond the primary research team can be identified; that is, selecting only those costs that are above and beyond the planned research procedures and practices. Resources needed may include people, equipment, infrastructure and tools to manage, document, organize, store and provide access to data.

Research applications are often seeking to establish the costs of these additional activities, yet it is not always simple to disentangle them from more standard research activities. There is no hard and fast rule, as some projects will pay more attention to detailed data documentation, organization and formatting than others as part of routine fieldwork or data preparation before analysis. National surveys run by national statistics institutes are usually seen as setting the standards for the highest quality in data planning, collection, documentation and dissemination. Much also depends on the long-term storage, preservation and publications plans beyond the duration of the research itself. When data are deposited with a professional data centre or repository, such as the UK Data Archive, data preservation and dissemination activities may be covered by the data centre or repository, or the repository may have a charging model. Your institution may have a system of internal recharging for long-term storage and preservation.

Costs can be calculated by listing all data management activities and steps required to make data shareable, based on a data management checklist. This is followed by pricing each activity in terms of people's time or physical resources needed, such as hardware or software. Resourcing and costing should be coordinated with your institution, research office and with institutional IT services, as you need to know which resources, e.g. for data storage and backup, are available to you from your institution.

The UK Data Archive has developed a simple checklist tool that can be used for the latter option of costing data management (UK Data Service, 2013b). The tool lists a series of 18 data management activities and topics considered to be pertinent for data sharing, such as describing and documenting data, data cleaning, digitization, storage, security, or data anonymization. Comments and suggestions are given for each topic to help you decide whether you need additional resources for a particular data management activity. For each relevant activity the additional time and/or other resources needed can then be estimated, calculated and costed as people's time or physical resources such as hardware or software needed.

Online Planning Tools

As funders have adopted data policies with varying data management planning requirements, there have been some collective efforts to develop tools to support researchers when preparing relevant plans. Examples include the DMP Online and the DMPTool.

DMP Online

The Digital Curation Centre's (DCC) DMP Online is a web-based tool designed to help researchers and other data stakeholders develop data management plans according to the requirements of major research funders, publishers or institutional requirements. Using the tool, researchers and their colleagues can create, store, update and share multiple versions of a data management plan at the grant application stage and during the research lifecycle. The tool combines the DCC's comprehensive 'Checklist for a Data Management Plan' with an analysis of research funder requirements. Plans can be customized according to funder or institutional requirements, and exported in a variety of formats. Funder- and institution-specific best practice guidance is provided to users via a range of tailored templates, which have been developed in conjunction with universities and research funders including the Economic and Social Research Council, the Medical Research Council and the Wellcome Trust (DCC, 2013a).

DMPTool

In the USA, in response to similar demands for data management plans from funding agencies such as the National Science Foundation (NSF) and the National Institutes of Health (NIH), a group of research institutions collaborated to create a flexible online tool to help researchers generate the plans. The tool allows researchers to select their institution and research funder and presents a plan template according to that funder's requirements. Funder-specific and institution-specific guidance and resources for each topic are included. Plans can be exported as .txt or .rtf files, or shared online in PDF format (California Digital Library, 2013b).

We suggest this data management planning exercise is undertaken when you have had a chance to study all the chapters in this book and have gained knowledge of specific approaches, practices and techniques.

Exercise 3.1   Data management planning and the data lifecycle

Read the following research project scenario, then:

1. Sketch a data lifecycle diagram, such as shown in Chapter 2, for this research project and annotate the points at which you think data management procedures should be implemented. Identify any differences between standard research planning and explicit planning for sharing data at the end of the project.
2. Develop a data management plan starting from the data management checklist set out in this chapter.

(Continued)

(Continued)

Research scenario: You are a researcher at a UK university and plan to carry out research on the public understanding of climate change and associated risks in the UK. Understanding what people think about climate change is important for developing better communication and dialogue between the science community, policy-makers and various sectors of the public.

Your planned research consists of:

- An online survey with 2,000 invited members of the public in the UK to assess their under-standing of climate change and climate change risks, as well as their sources of information.
- Interviews with 20 key stakeholders in climate policy and science communication.
- Qualitative content analysis of secondary data taken from newspapers and popular science journals, evaluating reporting about climate change in the media.

Data resulting from the online survey will be transferred to the statistical software package SPSS for analysis.

Interviews will be audio-recorded and transcribed into MS Word. Transcripts will be imported into NVivo for content analysis.

Secondary textual data from newspapers and journals will be imported into NVivo for content analysis.

Exercise 3.2   Discussion

1. A data lifecycle diagram with data management intervention points for the project might look something like that in Figure 3.1.
2. The data management plan based on checklist items would include the following kinds of information:

Planning

- Who is responsible for which part of data management?

   Me: creating, processing, documenting and analysing all data.

   Transcriber: transcribe audio into text.

   University IT services: provide storage and backup, long term access/sharing.

Documenting

- Are your structured data self-explanatory in terms of variable names, codes and abbreviations used?

   Survey data: make sure that SPSS file contains full question text for each variable; include both code and category labels, and ensure variable names are independently understandable.

- Which descriptions and contextual documentation can explain what your data mean, how they were collected and the methods used to create them?

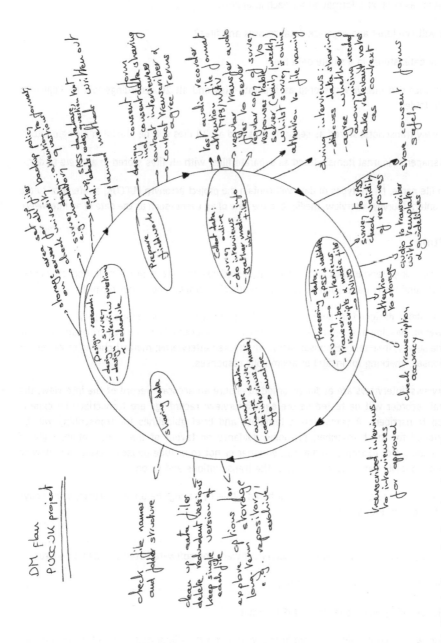

Figure 3.1 Data lifecycle diagram for discussion of research scenario in Exercise 3.1

(Continued)

(Continued)

The research methodology will be written out during the research planning stages, and augmented at relevant times during the research, for later use in publications and documentation for the data files. Background notes will be handwritten during interviews. These will be typed out later as context information for each interview.

- How will you label and organize data, records and files?

    Survey data: stored in a single data file.

    Audio-recorded interviews: stored as separate files and all 20 recordings will be kept in a single folder.

    Interview transcripts: stored as separate files and all 20 files will be placed in a single folder.

    Newspaper or journal items: stored as separate files, with all files stored in a single folder.

    Each file name, for all types of data will contain the project acronym PUCCUK; a reference to the file content (survey, interview, media) and the date of an event (such as the date of an interview).

Formatting

- Are you using standardized and consistent procedures to collect, process, transcribe, check, validate and verify data, such as standard protocols, templates or input forms?

    Survey data: designed in such a way that all questions in the online survey need to be answered, avoiding missing responses; responses are submitted directly by participants into the online survey; free-text responses are spell-checked afterwards; manual checks of validity of responses, checking for invalid or anomalous responses.

    Interviews: interviews are audio-recorded to ensure an accurate record of the interview; the digital recorder will be tested before each interview; recordings are transcribed by experienced transcribers. A transcription template and brief guidelines for transcribing will be developed for the transcriber, providing guidance on layout of the transcription, style of transcribing (for example, verbatim), whether or not to include pauses/hesitations, how to record inaudible parts, how to transfer the transcriptions and so on.

    Media articles: relevant articles are gathered either by saving the original article, or by copying the content into a file.

- Which data formats will you use? Do formats and software enable sharing and long-term sustainability of data, such as non-proprietary software and software based on open standards?

    Survey data will be stored in SPSS format.

    Audio recordings will be stored in **MP3** format.

    Interview transcripts will be stored in MS Word and will be imported into an NVivo database.

    Media extracts will be stored as **PDF** documents or copied into MS Word documents.

    These are all well-established standard formats.

- When converting data across formats, do you check that no data, annotation or internal meta-data have been lost or changed?

I will check each transcript for accuracy by comparing original recording with transcript for two randomly chosen extracts in each interview.

Storing

- Are your digital and non-digital data, and any copies, held in a safe and secure location?

All data files will be stored on the university server that is backed up nightly. The university's computing network is protected from viruses by a firewall and anti-virus software. Digital recordings will be copied to the server after each day of interviews.

- Do you need to securely store personal or sensitive data?

Signed consent forms will be stored in a locked cabinet in the office. Interview recordings and transcripts, which may contain personal information, will be password-protected at file-level and stored on the server.

- If data are collected with portable devices, how will you transfer and store the data?

Audio-recorded interviews will be copied from the recorder to the server after each day of interviews.

- If data are held in multiple places, how will you keep track of versions?

Original versions of files will always be kept on the server. If copies of files are held on a laptop and edits made, their file name will be changed.

- Are your files backed up sufficiently and regularly and are backups stored safely?

The University has a backup policy with nightly backup.

- Do you know which version of your data files is the master?

Those will be kept on the server.

- Who has access to which data during and after research? Are various access regulations needed?

The transcriber will have access to the interview files. Only I have access to data files during research. The transcriber will have access to transcribe interviews. After transcription the transcriber will be asked to delete all locally held files, and sign a destruction form as the data are personal.

Confidentiality, Ethics and Consent

- Do your data contain confidential or sensitive information? If so, have you discussed data sharing with the respondents from whom you collected the data?

(Continued)

(Continued)

Interviews may contain some sensitive information related to employment. This will be discussed with interviewees (see next question).

- Are you gaining written consent from respondents to share data beyond your research?

Yes, consent to share the data will be discussed with interviewees. Interviewees will decide whether their information can be shared and whether or not it needs anonymizing.

The introduction to the survey will state that the data (which will be anonymized) may be shared with other researchers. Participants will be given an optional opt-out at the end of the questionnaire.

- Do you need to anonymize data, for example, to remove identifying information or personal data, during research or in preparation for sharing?

Survey data will be anonymized before sharing. Interviews may need anonymizing. This will be discussed with interviewees. Information which might identify an individual could be used in analysis but would not remain in the anonymized version of the data. A non-sharable version of the research data will be kept by the project investigator for x years. The introduction to the survey will state that the data (which will be anonymized) may be shared with other researchers.

Copyright

- Have you established who owns the copyright of your data? Might there be joint copyright, for example, because your research is collaborative, or because you are reusing or repurposing existing third party data where copyright is held by another party? Copyright may also be joint in detailed interviews between you as the researcher and the respondent as the speaker and owner of the words.

I own the copyright of the newly created research data. I will use a copyright transfer clause in my consent form to enable me to use extracts of the qualitative interviews in my publications.

The media information is copyright of the respective publishers and will be attributed accordingly.

- If you are purchasing or reusing someone else's data sources have you considered how that data might be shareable?

The media information is the copyright of the respective publishers. The original articles may not be shared. Extracts may be used in publications and will be attributed to the source.

Sharing

- How and where will you preserve your research data longer term?

When the research finishes I will store a single version of each file on the server. If publishers require data as supplement for articles I will supply those. I will explore whether there exists a relevant data repository to hold the data for the longer term, and what, if any, special requirements or costs may apply.

- How will you make your data accessible to future users?

I will indicate in publications that interested researchers can request access to the data. I will explore whether there exists a relevant data repository to hold the data long term.

References

Atkinson, S., Blanchette, A., Bremner, P., Farrar, R., Wright, D. and Wylie, L. (2012) *Research Data Management Survival Guide for New PhD Students*, University of Exeter. Available at: https://eric.exeter.ac.uk/repository/handle/10036/3738?show=fullhttp://hdl.handle.net/10036/3738.

California Digital Library (2013a) *DMPTool - Funder requirements*, California Digital Library, University of California. Available at: https://dmp.cdlib.org/pages/funder_requirements.

California Digital Library (2013b) *DMPTool*, California Digital Library, University of California. Available at: https://dmp.cdlib.org/.

DCC (2013a) *DMP Online*, Digital Curation Centre. Available at: https://dmponline.dcc.ac.uk/.

DCC (2013b) *Data Management Courses and Training*, Digital Curation Centre. Available at: http://www.dcc.ac.uk/training/data-management-courses-and-training.

Knight, G. (2012) *Funder Requirements for Data Management and Sharing*, London School of Hygiene and Tropical Medicine. Available at: http://researchonline.lshtm.ac.uk/208596/.

MIT Libraries (2013) *A Data Planning Checklist*, MIT Libraries, Massachusetts Institute of Technology. Available at: http://libraries.mit.edu/guides/subjects/data-management/checklist.html.

UK Data Service (2013a) *Data Management Checklist*, UK Data Archive, University of Essex. Available at: http://ukdataservice.ac.uk/manage-data/plan/checklist.aspx.

UK Data Service (2013b) *Data Management Costing Tool*, UK Data Archive, University of Essex. Available at: http://ukdataservice.ac.uk/manage-data/plan/costing.aspx.

University of Edinburgh (2013) *Data Management Planning Checklist*, University of Edinburgh. Available at: http://www.ed.ac.uk/schools-departments/information-services/services/research-support/data-library/research-data-mgmt/planning.

University of Oxford (2013) *Data Management Planning Checklist*, University of Oxford. Available at: http://www.admin.ox.ac.uk/rdm/dmp/checklist/.

FOUR
Documenting and Providing Context for Data

A crucial part of ensuring that research data can be used, shared and reused by a wide range of researchers for a variety of purposes, is by taking care that those data are accessible, understandable and usable. Original researchers wishing to return to their data some time later, or new users wanting to use data, need sufficient contextual and explanatory information to make sense of those data. This requires clear and detailed data description and annotation. Besides information that is needed for reuse of data, data also need to be accompanied by information for citing and discovering the data.

The collective term 'data documentation' includes information on why and how data were created, prepared or digitized, what they mean, what their content and structure are, and any alterations or coding that may have taken place. Good documentation is critical for understanding data in the short, medium and longer term; and is vital for successful long-term data preservation. There is a growing interest in well-documented high quality datasets gaining recognition and acknowledgement as valuable published research outputs.

Creating comprehensive data documentation is easiest when begun at the outset of a research project and continued throughout the life of the research. It should be considered as part of best practice in creating, organizing and managing data.

Data documentation requires descriptive material at two levels. The high-level information, commonly known as study-level or data collection-level information, describes the research project, the data creation processes, rights and general contexts. The lower level information covers descriptions and annotations at the file and within-file level. This hierarchy of description prevents significant duplication. Qualitative researchers will probably value more detailed and descriptive contextual information about the research process and fieldwork approaches.

Metadata are a specific subset of data documentation, which provide standardized, structured information explaining the purpose, origin, time references, geographic location, creating author, access conditions and terms of use of a data collection. Metadata provide structured searchable information that helps users to find existing data resources and provide a bibliographic record for citing data.

Study-Level Documentation

Study-level documentation for a data collection or dataset provides high-level information on the research context and design, the data collection methods used, any data preparations and manipulations and summaries of findings based on the data.

Study-Level

Good study-level data documentation should include information on:

- research design and context of data collection: project history, aims, objectives and hypotheses, investigators and funders;
- data collection methods: data collection protocols, sampling design, sample structure and representation, work flows, instruments used, hardware and software used, data scale and resolution, temporal coverage and geographic coverage, and digitization or transcription methods used;
- structure of data files, with number of cases, records, files and variables, as well as any relationships among such items;
- secondary data sources used and provenance, for example, for transcribed or derived data;
- data validation, checking, proofing, cleaning and other quality assurance procedures carried out, such as checking for equipment and transcription errors, calibration procedures, data capture resolution and repetitions, or editing, proofing or quality control of materials;
- modifications made to data over time since their original creation and identification of different versions of datasets;
- for time series or longitudinal surveys, changes made to methodology, variable content, question text, variable labelling, measurements or sampling, and how panels were managed over time and between waves;
- information on data confidentiality, access and any applicable conditions of use;
- publications, presentations and other research outputs that explain or draw on the data.

Much of this information is usually already included in publications, final reports to funders, working papers and lab books. At the UK Data Service, all useful sources of information that are provided by the data producer are gathered and combined into a bookmarked **PDF/A** user guide accompanying a data collection, as shown in Figures 4.1 and 4.2. For surveys this includes important documentation such as original questionnaires, show cards or visual aids, interviewer instructions, interview topic guides or experimental protocols.

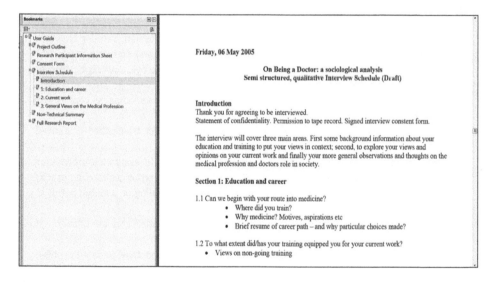

Figure 4.1   Documentation files for a survey data collection held at the UK Data Service

Source: UK Data Service, 2013a

Figure 4.2   User guide for a qualitative data collection at the UK Data Service

Source: UK Data Service, 2013b

Data-Level Documentation

Data-level documentation provides information about individual databases or data files, for example interview transcripts or pictures, as well as documentation for elements within the files, for example describing variables within an SPSS file.

Quantitative Data

Data documentation can be embedded within data files, such as variable and code descriptions in databases. Many data analysis software packages have facilities for data annotation and description, as variable attributes, data type definitions, table relationships and so on. Alternatively, information about data items can be recorded in a structured document such as a codebook. File names and the organization of files can also provide important context about a data collection, as discussed in the section on file-naming in Chapter 5.

Documenting Structured Tabular Data

Structured tabular data should have cases or records and variables adequately documented with:

- **Names, labels and descriptions** for variables and/or records; variable labels should be brief with a maximum of 80 characters and where applicable indicate the unit of measurement or reference the question number of a survey or questionnaire.

  Example: variable 'q11hexw' with label 'Q11: hours spent taking physical exercise in a typical week' – the label gives the unit of measurement and a reference to the question number (Q11b).

- **Value code labels**

  Example: variable 'p1sex' = 'sex of respondent' with codes '1 = female', '2 = male', '8 = don't know', '9 = not answered'.

- **Coding and classification schemes fully explained**

  Example: Standard Occupational Classification 2000 – a series of codes to classify respondents' occupations; ISO 3166 alpha-2 country codes – an international standard of 2-letter country codes. Note that some 'standard' codes change over time. If possible include original codes and label in documentation.

- **Codes for missing values**: blanks, system-missing, or '0' values are best avoided.

- **Derived data** created after collection, with code, algorithm or command files used to create them. For simple derivations, such as grouping age data into age intervals, variable and value labels can be used to explain them; complex derivations can be described by providing the algorithms, logical statements or functions used to create derived variables, such as the SPSS or Stata command files.

- **Weighting and grossing variables** created and guidance on how to use them.

- **Deviating universe information** for variables in case of skipped cases or questions.

Uncoded, ungrouped and underived raw data can provide further opportunities for reuse in addition to data where coding, grouping or derivation has already been applied. In many cases coding reduces the granularity of information for reuse, as other researchers may wish to re-code original data for different analyses. If original responses, such as responses to open-ended questions, can be kept, this is advantageous.

Examples of How Documentation can be Embedded in Different Software Packages

- **SPSS file:** variable descriptions and attributes, such as codes, data type, missing values, for each variable in the data file can be documented in 'Variable View' or via syntax, whereby embedded data documentation is then contained in the SPSS command file. At the UK Data Service, a data dictionary is created for each archived SPSS data file at the data processing stage, as shown in Figure 4.3.
- **MS Access database:** variable descriptions and attributes can be documented in 'Design View' and relationships between tables and files can be created, as shown in Figure 4.4.
- **ArcGIS geodatabase:** shapefiles, or layers, and tables can be organized in a geo-database with rich metadata created in ArcCatalog.
- **MS Excel spreadsheets:** an additional worksheet within the data file can contain data-related documentation.

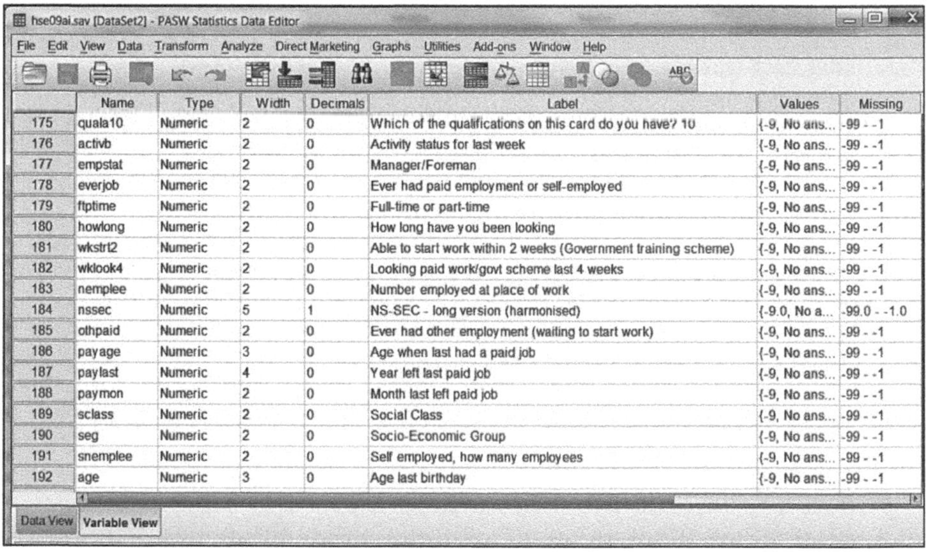

	Name	Type	Width	Decimals	Label	Values	Missing
175	quala10	Numeric	2	0	Which of the qualifications on this card do you have? 10	{-9, No ans...	-99 - -1
176	activb	Numeric	2	0	Activity status for last week	{-9, No ans...	-99 - -1
177	empstat	Numeric	2	0	Manager/Foreman	{-9, No ans...	-99 - -1
178	everjob	Numeric	2	0	Ever had paid employment or self-employed	{-9, No ans...	-99 - -1
179	ftptime	Numeric	2	0	Full-time or part-time	{-9, No ans...	-99 - -1
180	howlong	Numeric	2	0	How long have you been looking	{-9, No ans...	-99 - -1
181	wkstrt2	Numeric	2	0	Able to start work within 2 weeks (Government training scheme)	{-9, No ans...	-99 - -1
182	wklook4	Numeric	2	0	Looking paid work/govt scheme last 4 weeks	{-9, No ans...	-99 - -1
183	nemplee	Numeric	2	0	Number employed at place of work	{-9, No ans...	-99 - -1
184	nssec	Numeric	5	1	NS-SEC - long version (harmonised)	{-9.0, No a...	-99.0 - -1.0
185	othpaid	Numeric	2	0	Ever had other employment (waiting to start work)	{-9, No ans...	-99 - -1
186	payage	Numeric	3	0	Age when last had a paid job	{-9, No ans...	-99 - -1
187	paylast	Numeric	4	0	Year left last paid job	{-9, No ans...	-99 - -1
188	paymon	Numeric	2	0	Month last left paid job	{-9, No ans...	-99 - -1
189	sclass	Numeric	2	0	Social Class	{-9, No ans...	-99 - -1
190	seg	Numeric	2	0	Socio-Economic Group	{-9, No ans...	-99 - -1
191	snemplee	Numeric	2	0	Self employed, how many employees	{-9, No ans...	-99 - -1
192	age	Numeric	3	0	Age last birthday	{-9, No ans...	-99 - -1

Figure 4.3 Embedding data-level metadata in a SPSS file: variable labels, values and missing value codes

Source: UK Data Service, 2013c

Qualitative Data

A collection of qualitative data, such as a combination of interview transcripts, audio or video recordings or images, benefits from a single at-a-glance finding aid. File-level attributes can be detailed in a number of ways, including providing a summary at the top of a text file, attaching descriptive information

Figure 4.4   Embedding data-level metadata in a MS Access database

Source: UK Data Service, 2013d

to a file in a different document, or setting out file-level information for all data files in a collection in a single document. A data list provides information to easily identify and locate relevant items within a data collection. It typically contains descriptive attributes or biographical characteristics of participants or entities studied, such as age, gender, occupation or location; and identifying details of the data items, such as file name, description, file format and size.

Each item in the list should have a unique identifier, which should be consistently named so that links can be made between related data items such as interview transcripts, interview recordings and field notes. Information included in the data list should be detailed enough to enable sub-setting and filtering, but not detailed enough to enable identification of participants where confidentiality has been promised. Pseudonyms can be used instead of real names, places and occupations. A data list should indicate where parts of the data might be missing,

Study Number 6377
Integrated Floodplain Management, 2006-2008
Morris, J.

Floodplain farm survey

Interview ID	Farmer code	Age	Farm scheme	Farm type	Size of farm (hectare)	Number of holdings	Date of interview	Interviewer name	No of pages	Text file name	Audio file name
1	Be1	35-45	Beckingham	Beef	360	1	04.12.2006	Helena	28	6377int001	6377int001
2	Be2	45-55	Beckingham	Arable	364	1	05.12.2006	Helena	21	6377int002	6377int002
3	Be3	45-55	Beckingham	Arable	372	2	06.12.2006	Helena	22	6377int003	6377int003
4	Be4	45-55	Beckingham	Arable	194	3	06.12.2006	Helena	18	6377int004	6377int004
5	Be5	55-65	Beckingham	Arable	108	1	07.12.2007	Helena	21	6377int005	6377int005
6	Be6	45-55	Beckingham	Arable	1254	2	01.02.2008	Helena	19	6377int006	
7	Bu1	55-65	Bushley	Mixed	101	2	13.02.2007	Quentin	29	6377int007	6377int007
8	Bu2	>65	Bushley	Mixed	97	1	15.02.2007	Quentin	15	6377int008	6377int008
9	Bu3	>65	Bushley	Arable	194	4	13.02.2007	Quentin	21	6377int009	6377int009
10	Bu4	55-65	Bushley	Mixed	202	1	15.03.2007	Helena	19	6377int010	6377int010
11	Cu1	35-45	Cuddyarch	Dairy	64	1	08.05.2007	Helena	19	6377int011	6377int011
12	Cu2	55-65	Cuddyarch	Dairy	189	2	08.05.2007	Helena	18	6377int012	6377int012
13	Cu3	55-65	Cuddyarch	Mixed livestock	76	1	08.05.2007	Helena	13	6377int013	6377int013
14	Cu5	45-55	Cuddyarch	Mixed livestock	198	1	09.05.2007	Helena	24	6377int014	6377int014
15	Cu6	55-65	Cuddyarch	Dairy	89	1	09.05.2007	Helena	14	6377int015	6377int015
16	Cu7	>65	Cuddyarch	Mixed livestock	190	4	11.05.2007	Helena	20	6377int016	6377int016
17	Cu8	55-65	Cuddyarch	Mixed livestock	109	2	11.05.2007	Helena	22	6377int017	6377int017
18	Id1	55-65	Idle	Arable	158	3	07.02.2007	Quentin	17	6377int018	6377int018a
18	Id1	55-65	Idle	Arable	158	3	07.02.2007	Quentin	17	6377int018	6377int018b
19	Id1b	55-65	Idle	Arable	158	3		Quentin	22	6377int019	
20	Id2	45-55	Idle	Dairy	150	1	08.02.2007	Quentin	17	6377int020	6377int020

Figure 4.5   Example data list for a qualitative data collection in the UK Data Service catalogue, providing key characteristics of interviewed farmers

Source: UK Data Service, 2013e

such as partial transcripts or those completely missing from a collection. An example of a data list used by the UK Data Service is given in Figure 4.5. A MS Excel spreadsheet is the preferred format for the data list as it enables sorting and filtering and is a widely used format.

For text-based qualitative data, any biographical or other contextual information relating to the interview or interviewee can be detailed at the beginning of a file either as a header or as a summary page. Clear speech demarcation and the use of speaker tags are crucial when transcribing interviews and focus groups. Examples can be seen in the UK Data Service's model transcription template, as shown in Chapter 5 in the section on data transcription.

Non-digital materials such as reports, photographs, transcriptions, hand-written fieldwork notes and analogue audio-visual recordings should also be consistently labelled with appropriate identifiers and filed in an organized way.

Qualitative Software Tools for Documenting Data

Many researchers use computer assisted qualitative data analysis software (**CAQDAS**) for handling and managing qualitative research data even if they do not always take advantage of the more complex analysis features of the software (Fielding and Lee, 2002). While the software can be invaluable, applications vary and each package has distinctive requirements for handling and exporting data and outputs. The UK Data Archive recently developed best practice guidelines and recommendations for documenting and annotating qualitative data when using NVivo 9 as a software package to organize, code and analyse data, as set out in the case study below.

| CASE STUDY | Documenting Data in NVivo 9 |

Researchers using qualitative data analysis packages, such as NVivo 9, to analyse data can use a range of the software's features to describe and document data. Constructing documentation during analysis can support the analytic process and also results in richer contextual information when data are shared; they can be exported from the project file together with the data at the end of research.

Researchers can create classifications for: persons, such as interviewees; data sources, such as interviews; and codes. Classifications can contain attributes such as the demographic characteristics of interviewees, pseudonyms used, or the date, time and place of interview. If researchers create generic classifications beforehand, attributes can be standardized across all sources or persons throughout the project. Existing template and pre-populated classification sheets can be imported into NVivo 9.

Documentation files, such as the description of methodology, project plan, interview guidelines and consent form templates can be imported into the NVivo 9 project file and stored in a 'documentation' folder in the Memos folder or linked from NVivo 9 externally. Additional documentation about analyses or data manipulations can be created in NVivo 9 as memos. An event log that is date- and time-stamped can record all project events carried out during the NVivo 9 project cycle. Additional descriptions can be added to all objects created in, or imported to, the project file, such as the project file itself, data, documents, memos, nodes and classifications.

All textual documentation compiled during the NVivo 9 project cycle can later be exported as text files; classifications and event logs can be exported as spreadsheets to document preserved data collections. The structure of the project objects can be exported in groups or individually. Summary information about the project as a whole or groups of objects can be exported via project summary extract reports as a text, MS Excel or XML (Extensible Markup Language) file. (Chatsiou, 2011)

Metadata for Cataloguing Collections

For the purposes of cataloguing, citing, discovering and retrieving data collections, metadata are a subset of core data documentation providing standardized, structured information that explains, amongst other things, the purpose, origin, time references, geographic location, creator, access conditions and terms of use of a data collection.

Metadata for online data catalogues or discovery portals are often structured to international standards or schemes such as Dublin Core, **ISO** 19115 for geographic information, Data Documentation Initiative (**DDI**), Metadata Encoding and Transmission Standard (**METS**) or General International Standard Archival Description (**ISAD(G)**). For the purposes of citing data, a limited metadata 'kernel' promoted by DataCite is widely in use for data catalogues (See Chapter 11 on data citation).

'DataCite Metadata Schema for Publication and Citation of Research Data' (DataCite, 2011)

DataCite mandatory metadata elements are:

- identifier
- creator
- title
- publisher
- publication year.

DataCite optional elements are:

- subject
- contributor
- date
- language
- resource type
- alternate identifier
- related identifier
- size
- format
- version
- rights
- description.

DataCite administrative metadata elements are:

- date of last metadata update
- metadata version number.

Metadata records are typically viewed through library systems or web browsers. The advantage of having such highly structured systematic information about similar items is that web-based analysis engines can search them easily using specific fields. Disparate catalogues can be federated and shared and interactive browsing tools can be applied. Metadata can also be harvested for data sharing through the Open Archives Initiative Protocol for Metadata Harvesting (OAI-PMH).

The **DDI** is an international **XML**-based descriptive metadata standard for social science data used by most social science data archives in the world, including the UK Data Archive (Vardigan et al., 2008). The use of standardized records in **XML** brings key data documentation together into a single document, creating rich and structured content about the data. **DDI** catalogue records contain mandatory and optional metadata elements relating to:

- study description: information about the context of the data collection such as bibliographic citation of the study and data; scope of the study such as topics, geography, time; method of data collection; sampling and processing; data access information; and information on accompanying materials;
- data file description: information on data format, file type, file structure, missing data, weighting variables and software;
- variable descriptions.

An example of a **DDI**-structured catalogue record is given in Figure 4.6.

Metadata of this type is usually collected via a form, provided by a data repository, though increasingly software can be used to generate selected information from data files. The data producer is the most appropriate person to complete this information, usually being closest to the research and the data. Repository staff then quality assure and enhance information from accompanying documentation to create a coherent, consistent and complete metadata record. Where researchers can provide detailed and meaningful data collection titles, descriptions, keywords, contextual and methodological information, richer

Figure 4.6   Metadata record for a single data collection in the UK Data Service data catalogue

Source: UK Data Service, 2013f

resource-discovery metadata are generated for their deposited collections. Some form of indexing using controlled vocabularies is usually carried out by repository staff to help classify data.

The UK Data Archive hosts a thesaurus, the Humanities and Social Science Electric Thesaurus (HASSET), to index its data collections (UK Data Archive, 2013). HASSET's subject coverage reflects the subject content of the UK Data Archive holdings focusing on the social sciences and humanities. Coverage is most comprehensive in the core subject areas of social science disciplines: politics, sociology, economics, education, law, crime, demography, health, employment, and, increasingly, technology and environment.

```
1   <?xml version="1.0" encoding="UTF-8"?>
2   <?oxygen RNGSchema="esds.rnc" type="compact"?>
3 ▽ <TEI xmlns="http://www.tei-c.org/ns/1.0">
4 ▽   <teiHeader>
5 ▽     <fileDesc>
6 ▽       <titleStmt>
7           <title>Family Life and Work Experience Before 1918</title>
8           <title type="collection">Edwardians</title>
9         </titleStmt>
10 ▽      <publicationStmt>
11          <authority>Paul Thompson</authority>
12          <distributor>ESDS Qualidata</distributor>
13          <idno type="intNum">esds2000int004</idno>
14        </publicationStmt>
15 ▽      <sourceDesc>
16          <bibl><!-- Bibliographic Information concerning the transcript --></bibl>
17        </sourceDesc>
18      </fileDesc>
19 ▽    <profileDesc>
20 ▽      <particDesc>
21 ▽        <listPerson>
22 ▽          <person xml:id="subject">
23 ▽            <persName type="unanonymised">
24                <roleName type="honorific">Mr</roleName>
25                <forename>Gus</forename>
26                <surname>Knifton</surname>
27              </persName>
28              <birth date="1887">1887</birth>
29              <occupation>General Omnibus Co.</occupation>
30              <sex value="1">Male</sex>
31 ▽            <persState type="marriage">
32                <p>Married</p>
33              </persState>
34            </person>
35 ▽          <person xml:id="interviewer">
36              <!-- Information about interviewer?  Same name as depositor? -->
37            </person>
38          </listPerson>
39        </particDesc>
40 ▽      <settingDesc>
41 ▽        <setting>
42 ▽          <locale>
43              <placeName>London</placeName>
44            </locale>
45          </setting>
46        </settingDesc>
47      </profileDesc>
48    </teiHeader>
49 ▽  <text>
50 ▽    <body>
51 ▽      <div>
52          <u who="#interviewer" xml:id="u1">Now, you were born in .. in</u>
53          <u who="#subject" xml:id="u2">Britannia Street, Hoxton</u>
```

Figure 4.7   An example of a qualitative interview transcript marked up with XML tags

Source: UK Data Archive, 2006

There are an increasing number of stand-alone tools becoming available for helping create structured metadata for survey data. Two tools allow the easy creation of **DDI** metadata files: Nesstar Publisher and Survey Documentation and Analysis (SDA) both allow researchers to publish an SPSS file to create and edit a **DDI** record for that dataset based on the SPSS set-up information, without the need to know **XML** (Nesstar, 2013; SDA, 2013).

In the case of publishing textual data there is a need to provide a framework to enable forward-looking data searching, data sharing, anonymization, publishing to the web, and data preservation. This is provided by **XML**, which has a powerful role in helping mark-up qualitative data via the use of **XML** elements. The UK Data Service uses a very limited set of **XML** elements for marking-up interview transcripts. Essentially, the mark-up consists of distinguishing turns of speech and using tags to identify basic demographic characteristics of an interviewee if they are known and can be used. Examples include gender, year of birth, occupation and place of residence. An example of a marked-up text file is shown in Figure 4.7. The Text Encoding Initiative (**TEI**) element or tag set is useful as an **XML** reference standard, and more complex mark-up can be done including adding thematic coding, geo-spatial references and researcher annotations (UK Data Archive, 2006).

The Challenges of Providing Context for Qualitative Data

Data archives have to make some pragmatic assumptions about the degree to which data documentation enables data to be understood and used independently. Because qualitative data tend to be less structured and more varied than quantitative data, reusers can benefit from a wide range of contextual materials. These help guide reusers in understanding and taking into account the intentions of the primary researchers who collected the data.

As we will see in Chapter 10, reusing qualitative data is not as commonplace as secondary analysis of surveys, and some qualitative researchers have claimed that it is difficult to divorce research data from context (Mauthner et al., 1998). For them, context can be viewed as more than static information about persons, actions or situations, but also factors resulting from everyday interaction and interpretive processes. For example, looking at a single interview benefits from situating it within the larger research narrative, or examining a turning point in someone's life requires some details about their biography (Holstein and Gubrium, 2004; Neale and Bishop, 2012). Original data creators do benefit from having 'been there' when data were collected and having access to original context, yet there are equally examples whereby principal investigators who are not directly engaged in fieldwork must rely upon their co-workers or fieldworkers' notes and documentation of the research process and data being generated. While documentation can help recover a degree of context, field notes, letters and memos documenting the research can help open up the original fieldwork experience to others. Making available audio-visual recordings of interviews can also significantly enhance the capacity to reuse data.

It is useful to consider providing documentation at different levels of context, including: annotations within interview transcripts; notes about the fieldwork

Table 4.1 Levels of context for qualitative research

Level of context	Data type	Description	Example
Data-level	Transcribed interview	Annotation to provide context about intonation, emotions, facial expressions and so on, during a conversation. Can use Jeffersonian transcription, using symbols to indicate intonation and emotion (Jefferson, 1984).	– I'm sorry [sounds upset] I'm a little bit emotional today – Hh (0.2) u:m (0.1) →I'm sorry I'm a little bit← emo:ˉtional tod[ayˉ .hih]
Data-level	Interview event	Background information about participants	Living circumstances, biography, key life course changes, or family or household context
Study-level	Interview event	Information about the fieldwork setting	Who was present at the interview, description of the interview location and the environment
Study-level	Data collection	Detail about research planning and fieldwork implementation	Sampling methodology, consent process, topic guide, interview recording process, transcription process
Study-level	Institutional/ cultural context	Documentation of the wider political and social climate or time-bound issues that may influence the research	Political situation, capturing any key events or actors, e.g. a Government's White Paper on food policy that gave rise to a study of food and eating behaviour indicating the public policy climate of personal responsibility for obesity at the time of research; or the role of the Peace Process in a study of young peoples' lives in Northern Ireland

situation; and notes about the broader social, cultural or economic context within which the research takes place (Bishop, 2006; Corti, 2006). Table 4.1 sets out these different levels.

The project 'Health and social consequences of the foot and mouth disease epidemic in North Cumbria' provides an excellent overview and detailed descriptions about the challenges of and steps taken to enable the archiving of data to make them available to other researchers in their user guide (Mort, 2006). Equally, the Timescapes project team on the Siblings and Friends Project produced a comprehensive future-facing guide for their project (Weller et al., 2011). They took particular care that the documentation was made accessible to a diverse audience, including the young people who participated in their research. The guide includes standard context such as project description, research questions and methodology; as well as extensive detail on the ethics of working with young people. This includes documenting the processes of consent, anonymization and enabling access, discussed further in Chapter 7.

The labour involved in preparing detailed contextual materials for research data needs to be taken into account and balanced with the notion of providing sufficient context.

Exercise 4.1   Scenario for documenting research data resulting from a survey and interviews

You carry out research on the public understanding of climate change and associated risks in the UK. Understanding what people think about climate change is important in the development of better communication and dialogue between the science community, policy-makers and various sectors of the public.

Your research consists of:

- An online survey with 2,000 invited members of the public in the UK to assess their understanding of climate change and climate change risks, as well as their sources of information.
- Interviews with 20 key stakeholders in climate policy and science communication.
- Qualitative content analysis of secondary data taken from newspapers and popular science journals, evaluating reporting about climate change in the media.

Data resulting from the online survey are transferred to SPSS for analysis.

Interviews are audio-recorded and transcribed into MS Word. Transcripts are imported into the NVivo software for content analysis.

Secondary textual data from newspapers and journals are also imported into NVivo for content analysis.

How would you document your resulting research data, to enable their future use by other researchers?

Exercise 4.2   Creating structured metadata

When submitting an article on young adult smokers' responses to tobacco warnings in the Netherlands to the journal *BMC Public Health*, you are encouraged to publish the supporting data for readers to consult. You can submit your data with DANS EASY, the online archiving system of Data Archiving and Networked Services (DANS) (DANS, 2013). What kinds of structured metadata would you need to describe your data collection when submitted to DANS EASY, as supplementary material for your article? Register and login to DANS EASY at https://easy.dans.knaw.nl and proceed to a 'New deposit'.

Exercise 4.3   Fun quiz

1. XML stands for (choose one option only):

   (a) EXtra Mash-up Language

   (b) EXtensible Mark-up Language

   (c) EXample Mark-up Language

   (d) X Mark-up Library

2. DDI stands for (choose one option only):

   (a) Data Destruction Inventory

   (b) Data Documentation Initiative

(Continued)

(Continued)

    (c) Demographic Data Instance

    (d) Data Detection Instrument

3. TEI stands for (choose one option only):

    (a) Text Entity Inventory

    (b) Text Explanation Initiative

    (c) Text Enrichment Inventory

    (d) Text Encoding Initiative

4. Data documentation is essential for (choose all that apply):

    (a) me to understand my research data in 15 years time

    (b) illustrating my doctoral thesis with pictures

    (c) a reviewer to understand the findings in my article under review

    (d) a researcher who uses my archived data for new research

5. For a study on sustainable travel to work schemes using choice experiments with 100 staff members at a university, data documentation for the resulting numerical dataset can be (choose all that apply):

    (a) the list of participants

    (b) the choice cards used in the experiment

    (c) the instructions given to participants

    (d) the invitation sent to staff members, seeking participants

    (e) a news item about the research in the university's newsletter

    (f) the ethical review application submitted to the university's Research Ethics Committee

    (g) a government white paper on future options for sustainable travel-to-work

    (h) a published article describing the methodology and findings

6. For variable 'Cperil' of the British Crime Survey, how could its data-level documentation be improved?

    Variable 'Cperil': How crime in your local area compares to the country as a whole.

    Value 1 Higher than average
    Value 2 Lower than average
    Value 3 About average
    Value 9

(choose all that apply)

    (a) use a more logical variable name, for example 'CrimeLocalVsCountry'

    (b) specify that Value 9 means 'missing' value, better still, using various missing value categories that can indicate the reason why the information is missing

    (c) refer to the crime measurement classification scheme

7. Appropriate context that can be gathered to help understand a shared data collection from a qualitative study comprising transcribed interviews with 40 senior politicians includes (choose all that apply):

    (a) a copy of the topic guide that was used by the interviewer

    (b) a copy of the original audio-recordings

(c) the weather report for the day of each interview

(d) information about the political make-up of the parliament at the time of the research study

(e) a list of the interviewees and their position in the government

(f) a link to their biographical entry in *Who's Who*

Discussion for Exercise 4.1

For the survey data file, ensure that the SPSS file contains the full question text as variable label for each corresponding variable, or as detailed a description of the question text as possible. Variable names should consist of meaningful codes. Variable attributes are clearly defined, complete and without any abbreviations, explaining codes, categories and missing data values for each variable.

The online survey questionnaire is exported as a **PDF** file to complement the SPSS data file.

Each interview transcript contains an introductory paragraph providing the context and setting for the interview. The collection of 20 transcripts is accompanied by a data list. Alternatively in NVivo a classification is created for all relevant demographic and background characteristics such as gender, age, profession, organization and communication medium used; and for interviews, date, place and interviewer name. The topic guide used in the interviews is exported to PDF for reference.

A list or table of bibliographic references contains all sources of information used for the secondary analysis of media content.

A published article provides background information on the research methods used, sampling, fieldwork, data collection and so on.

Answer to Exercise 4.2

Metadata to describe your data collection in the DANS EASY repository, that underpin your *BMC Public Health* article, would have as required, recommended and additional elements:

- Creator name and organization
- Title of data collection or research
- Description
- Date created
- Access rights (unrestricted or restricted access)
- Date data are available
- Target audience for the data
- Subject / keywords
- Spatial coverage (geographical location)
- Temporal coverage (time period)
- Format of data files
- Related article or other resources
- Language

Answers to Exercise 4.3

1. XML stands for:

   (b) EXtensible Mark-up Language

2. DDI stands for:

   (b) Data Documentation Initiative

3. TEI stands for:

   (d) Text Encoding Initiative

4. Data documentation is essential for:

   (a) me to understand my research data in 15 years time – Correct. You would otherwise find it very difficult to understand your data after so much time.

   (b) illustrating my doctoral thesis with pictures – Incorrect. Although you could document your pictures with interesting metadata such as creator, date, place, topic, etc.

   (c) a reviewer to understand the findings in my article under review – Correct. This presumes your data are available to the reviewer.

   (d) a researcher who uses my archived data for new research – Correct. This presumes you have archived your data for future use.

5. For a study on sustainable travel to work schemes using choice experiments with 100 staff members at a university, data documentation for the resulting numerical dataset can be:

   (a) the list of participants – Incorrect. This is confidential information and is not needed to understand the data.

   (b) the choice cards used in the experiment – Correct. This is essential to be able to understand the numerical data.

   (c) the instructions given to participants – Correct. This is essential to understand the data collection methodology fully.

   (d) the invitation sent to staff members, seeking participants – Correct. Not essential, but can provide interesting methodological context.

   (e) a news item about the research in the university's newsletter – Correct. Not essential, but provides interesting context for the research.

   (f) the ethical review application submitted to the university's Research Ethics Committee – Incorrect. This is probably confidential information, and is not needed to understand the data. However, the consent form used is useful documentation.

   (g) a government white paper on future options for sustainable travel-to-work – Correct. Although not essential, it provides interesting political context for when the research was carried out.

   (h) a published article describing the methodology and findings – Correct. This provides good information on research methods used.

6. For variable 'Cperil' of the British Crime Survey, how could its data-level documentation be improved?

   Variable 'Cperil': How crime in your local area compares to the country as a whole.

Value 1 Higher than average
Value 2 Lower than average
Value 3 About average
Value 9

(a) use a better variable name, for example 'CrimeLocalVsCountry' – Incorrect. That would not add any additional information to the user.

(b) specify that Value 9 means 'missing' value, better still, using various missing value categories that can indicate the reason why the information is missing – Correct. Not mentioning what exactly Value 9 means is bad practice, plus detailing reasons for missing information helps to carry out better analyses of data.

(c) refer to the crime measurement classification scheme – Incorrect. No such classification scheme exists; this question asks for an interviewee's opinion about the local level of crime.

7. Appropriate context that can be gathered to help understand a shared data collection from a qualitative study comprising transcribed interviews with 40 senior politicians includes:

(a) a copy of the topic guide that was used by the interviewer – Correct. This provides a guide to questions asked and the flavour of the interview.

(b) a copy of the original audio-recordings – Correct. While these are strictly data, and not documentation, the original audio material would help to provide greater context to hear speech intonation.

(c) the weather report for the day of each interview – Incorrect. This is not relevant!

(d) information about the political makeup of the parliament at the time of the research study – Correct. This provides interesting political context for when the research was carried out.

(e) a list of the interviewees and their position in the government – Correct. This provides interesting context about their role in government at the time of interview.

(f) a link to their biographical entry in *Who's Who* – Correct. This provides context about the individual and their background.

References

Bishop, L. (2006) 'A proposal for archiving context for secondary analysis', *Methodological Innovations Online*, 1(2): 10–20. DOI: 10.4256/mio.2006.0008. Available at: http://ukdataservice.ac.uk/media/262210/miobishop_pp10_20.pdf.

Chatsiou, A. (2011) *Data Handling in NVivo9, MANTRA Research Data Management Training*, Edina, University of Edinburgh. Available at: http://datalib.edina.ac.uk/mantra/nvivomodule.html.

Corti, L. (2006) 'Editorial', *Methodological Innovations Online* [Special Issue: Defining context for qualitative data], 1(2): 1–9. DOI: 10.4256/mio.2006.0007. Available at: http://ukdataservice.ac.uk/media/262207/miocortieditorial_pp1_9.pdf.

DANS (2013) *DANS EASY system*, Data Archiving and Networked Services (DANS), The Hague. Available at: https://easy.dans.knaw.nl/.

DataCite (2011) *DataCite Metadata Schema for the Publication and Citation of Research Data Version 2.2*, DataCite. Available at: http://schema.datacite.org/meta/kernel-2.2/.

Fielding, N. and Lee, R. (2002) 'New patterns in the adoption and use of qualitative software', *Field Methods*, 14(2): 197–216.

Holstein, J.A. and Gubrium, J.F. (2004) 'Context: Working it up, down and across', in C. Seale, G. Gobo, J.F. Gubrium and D. Silverman (eds). *Qualitative Research Practice*. London: Sage.

Jefferson. G. (1984) 'Transcription Notation', in J. Atkinson and J. Heritage (eds), *Structures of Social Interaction*. New York: Cambridge University Press.

Mauthner, N., Parry, O. and Backett-Milburn, K. (1998) 'The data are out there, or are they? Implications for archiving and revisiting qualitative data', *Sociology*, 32(4): 733–45.

Mort, M. (2006) *Health and Social Consequences of the Foot and Mouth Disease Epidemic in North Cumbria, 2001–2003* [computer file]. Colchester, Essex: UK Data Archive [distributor], November. SN: 5407. Available at: http://dx.doi.org/10.5255/UKDA-SN-5407-1.

Neale, B. and Bishop, L. (2012) 'The Timescapes Archive: A stakeholder approach to archiving qualitative longitudinal data', *Qualitative Research*, 12(1): 53–65. Available at: http://qrj.sagepub.com/content/12/1/53.

Nesstar (2013) *Nesstar Publisher*, Norwegian Social Science Data Services. Available at: www.nesstar.com/software/publisher.html.

SDA (2013) *SDA Survey Documentation and Analysis*. Available at: http://sda.berkeley.edu/.

UK Data Archive (2006) *Searching and Sharing Qualitative Data: The Uses of XML*, UK Data Archive. Available at: http://ukdataservice.ac.uk/media/262231/xml.pdf.

UK Data Archive (2013) *Our Hasset Thesaurus*, UK Data Archive, University of Essex. Available at: http://www.data-archive.ac.uk/find/hasset-thesaurus.

UK Data Service (2013a) Documentation table in catalogue record for SN 6986. Available at: http://discover.ukdataservice.ac.uk/catalogue/?sn=6986.

UK Data Service (2013b) User guide in catalogue record for SN 6124. Available at: http://discover.ukdataservice.ac.uk/catalogue/?sn=6124.

UK Data Service (2013c) SPSS file for SN 6732. Available (after download) at: http://discover.ukdataservice.ac.uk/catalogue/?sn=6732.

UK Data Service (2013d) MS access file for SN 6377. Available (after download) at: http://discover.ukdataservice.ac.uk/catalogue/?sn=6377.

UK Data Service (2013e) Data list for SN 6377. Available at: http://discover.ukdataservice.ac.uk/catalogue/?sn=6377.

UK Data Service (2013f) Catalogue record for SN 6986. Available at: http://discover.ukdataservice.ac.uk/catalogue/?sn=6986.

Vardigan, M., Heus, P. and Thomas, W. (2008) 'Data Documentation Initiative: Toward a standard for the social sciences', *International Journal of Digital Curation*, 3(1): 107–13. DOI:10.2218/ijdc.v3i1.45.

Weller, S., Edwards, R. and Stephenson, R. (2011) *Timescapes: Your Space! Siblings and Friends Project Guide*, Timescapes, University of Leeds. Available at: www.timescapes.leeds.ac.uk/assets/files/P1-Project-Guide-FINAL.pdf.

FIVE
Formatting and Organizing Data

Data form the basis of, and are the result of, empirical research. Research data exist in many different forms: textual data, numerical data, databases, geospatial data, images, audio-visual recordings, and data generated by machines or instruments.

All digital data exist in specific file formats; the form in which information is coded so that a software programme can read and interpret those data. A particular file format is usually linked to a specific software programme. If the same file is to be read by a different programme it may need to be converted. Using standard and interchangeable or open 'lossless' data formats ensures longer-term usability of data.

Quality control of data is an integral part of all research and takes place at various stages – during data collection, data entry or digitization, and data checking. It is vital to develop suitable procedures before data gathering starts in order to adhere to any conventions, instructions, guidelines or templates that will help to ensure quality and consistency across a data collection.

High quality data are well organized, structured, named and versioned and the authenticity of master files identified. It is important to ensure that different copies or versions of files, files held in different formats or locations, and information that is cross-referenced between files are all subject to version control.

File Formats

There are important things to consider when choosing a file format for digital data, and the choice should be planned early in the research cycle to ensure that the format suits all purposes that might be necessary. The points to consider are:

- format best suited for data creation;
- format best suited for data analyses and other planned uses;
- format best suited for long-term sustainability and sharing of data;
- open versus proprietary format;
- format lossy or not;
- format suitable for conversion.

The format and software in which research data are created usually depend on how researchers choose to collect and analyse data, on the hardware being used or the availability of software. It can also be determined by discipline-specific standards and customs. For example:

- **Image, audio and video data formats** may be determined by the kind of camera or recording equipment being used. Unless high quality data are initially recorded, one cannot go back and upgrade those later. It may be wise to collect data in maximum fidelity as they can always be downgraded and reduced in size, but not the other way around. Also consider which format would be best suited in view of all the planned uses and conversions.
- **Numerical data** are typically placed in spreadsheets or databases, where cases or records are plotted against variables or measurements. For social science surveys the standard file format of choice is often SPSS due to its statistical analysis ability. In ecological research CSV or MS Excel are more widely used, being the standard data input format for many analytical packages.
- **Qualitative research data**, like interviews, may initially be collected as digital audio recordings, such as in **WAV** or **MP3** format, and then be transcribed as textual files, such as in MS Word. Such data are frequently analysed using computer assisted qualitative data analysis software (**CAQDAS**) such as NVivo or ATLAS.ti, whereby textual files are imported into the **CAQDAS** database.

When thinking about long-term accessibility and usability of research data, sustainable digital file formats and software are needed. For many formats, there is a danger that they will become obsolete in the future, which would make the data impossible to read and interpret. Despite the backward compatibility of many software packages to import data created in previous software versions and the interoperability between competing popular software programs, the safest option to guarantee long-term data access is to convert data to standard or open formats. Not only can most software packages interpret these, they are also suitable for data interchange and transformation, and are likely to stand a better chance of being reused well into the future.

Standard formats include the widely used proprietary Microsoft Office software products, MS Word, Rich Text Format and MS Excel, or the popular SPSS format. These are likely to have a long-term sustainability as they are so widely used.

File formats can be proprietary or open; proprietary formats are owned by a company that claims intellectual property rights for the use of the software by granting licenses. Examples of open file formats are **PDF/A**, **CSV**, **TIFF**, Open-Document Format (**ODF**), **ASCII**, tab-delimited format, comma-separated values and **XML**. File formats can also be lossy or lossless. Lossy formats save space by removing detailed information that is assumed to be unimportant. For example, the lossy format **JPEG** removes fine detail in images, whilst the lossless format **TIFF** keeps all the detail. Also, repeatedly editing and saving files in a lossy format results in a greater loss of information.

While researchers will use the most suitable data formats and software according to planned analyses during their research, once data analysis is completed and data are to be prepared for long-term storing, data conversion must be considered. Using open, standard, interchangeable and longer lasting formats, avoids being unable to use the data in the future. This is also recommended for any backups of data, as discussed in Chapter 6 in the section on backing up data.

For long-term digital preservation, data centres and archives hold data in open and standard formats. File formats recommended by the UK Data Archive for long-term preservation, at the time of writing (2013) are set out in Table 5.1.

Table 5.1 Examples of recommended file formats

Type of data	Recommended file formats for sharing, reuse and preservation
Quantitative tabular data with extensive metadata a dataset with variable labels, code labels, and defined missing values, in addition to the matrix of data	SPSS portable format (.por) delimited text and command ('setup') file (SPSS, Stata, SAS, etc.) containing metadata information some structured text or mark-up file containing metadata information, such as DDI XML file
Quantitative tabular data with minimal metadata a matrix of data with or without column headings or variable names, but no other metadata or labelling	Comma-separated values (CSV) file (.csv) tab-delimited file (.tab) including delimited text of given character set with SQL data definition statements where appropriate
Geospatial data vector and raster data	ESRI Shapefile (.shp, .shx, .dbf, .prj, .sbx, .sbn optional) geo-referenced TIFF (.tif, .tfw) CAD data (.dwg) tabular GIS attribute data
Qualitative data textual	eXtensible Mark-up Language (XML) text according to an appropriate Document Type Definition (DTD) or schema (.xml) Rich Text Format (.rtf) Plain text data, ASCII (.txt)
Digital image data	TIFF version 6 uncompressed (.tif)
Digital audio data	Free Lossless Audio Codec (FLAC) (.flac)
Digital video data	MPEG-4 (.mp4) motion JPEG 2000 (.jp2)
Documentation	Rich Text Format (.rtf) PDF/A or PDF (.pdf) OpenDocument Text (.odt)

Source: UK Data Archive, 2013

Table 5.2 sets out some advantages and disadvantages of various file formats for storing a text document.

Table 5.2   Considerations in file format choice for storing text documents

Text format	Representation and encoding	Readability and constraints	Information on formats/encoding	Preservation and storage
Plain Text (.txt)	• Individual characters (letters, punctuation, new lines) each encoded into bytes using ASCII encoding, or another character encoding such as UTF8 or ISO 8859-1 • Stored in a simple sequence. Only the text is stored with no information about formatting, fonts, page size, etc.	• Portable across all computer systems • Can be read and modified by a huge range of software applications	• Freely available and standardized	• If storage media are damaged, any undamaged sections can be recovered without problems
Microsoft Word document (.doc, docx)	• Text plus formatting, page size, fonts and so on are stored in a complex encoding	• Only runs on Windows and Macintosh, not on Linux • Other software applications have been written that can read and edit, but not fully reliable	• Owned by Microsoft and not freely available	• Only Microsoft Word software can recover and edit the contents with complete fidelity • No guarantee that Microsoft will always ensure that new versions of the software can open documents stored in older versions
PDF (Portable Document Format) (.pdf)	• Text plus formatting, page size and similar information are stored in a moderately complex encoding	• Viewed and printed on all major platforms, using free software provided by Adobe or others • Cannot be readily edited	• Freely available but owned by Adobe and can be changed by them at any time, for any reason	
HTML (HyperText Mark-up Language) (.html)	• Text plus simple formatting is stored in a simple encoding based on the plain text file format • Plain text mark-up is interspersed with the text	• Viewed in any web browser • Edited in a text editor, in any 'rich text' editor, word processor or an HTML editor	• Freely available and controlled by a public-interest standards body	

Text format	Representation and encoding	Readability and constraints	Information on formats/encoding	Preservation and storage
A structural mark-up language like DocBook XML (.xml or .dbk) or the Text Encoding Initiative (TEI)	• Stored in a simple encoding • No specification of how the document should appear when viewed on-screen or printed on paper • DocBook is an XML language for describing documents and their logical structure	• Can be read and edited on any platform • Easy transformation into other formats for viewing (e.g. HTML) or printing (e.g. PDF) • Structural mark-up also assists with indexing for discovery		• Good preservation formats
Image format JPEG (.jpg) or TIFF (.tif)	• Preserves appearance but loses all structure	• Can be viewed on any modern platform using a wide range of software • Editing the content of the document such as the sequence of characters and words is cumbersome		• Good option for documents that only exist in paper format

Source: adapted from ANDS, 2013

CASE STUDY	File Formats

The Wessex Archaeology Metric Archive Project brought together metric animal bone data from a range of archaeological sites in England into a single database format (Grimm, 2008). The dataset contains a selection of measurements commonly taken during Wessex Archaeology zoo-archaeological analysis of animal bone fragments found during field investigations. The dataset was created by the researchers in MS Excel and MS Access formats and deposited with the Archaeology Data Service (ADS) in the same formats. The ADS preserved the dataset in Oracle and in comma-separated values format (**CSV**) and disseminate the data via both an Oracle/Cold Fusion live interface and as downloadable CSV files.

Various initiatives aim to preserve and share modelling software and code. In biology, the BioModels Database of the European Bioinformatics Institute (EBI) is a repository for peer-reviewed, published, computational models of biological processes and molecular functions (Li et al., 2010). All models are annotated and linked to relevant data resources. Researchers are encouraged to deposit models written in an open source format, the Systems Biology Mark-up Language (**SBML**); and models are curated for long-term preservation.

Data Conversion

Data may need to be converted between file formats, for example, to convert for data analysis purposes or to convert to a preferred data preservation format in preparation for long-term storage or archiving. Both data transcription from audio-visual to text form, and digitization from non-digital to digital format are common types of format conversions.

When data are converted from one format to another, through export or by using data translation software, certain changes may occur to the data. After conversion, data should be checked for errors or changes that might be caused by the export process such as:

- **for data held in statistical packages, spreadsheets or databases, some data or internal metadata such as missing value definitions, decimal numbers, formulae or variable labels may be lost during conversion to another format, or data may be truncated;**
- **for textual data, editing such as highlighting, bold text or headers and footers may be lost;**
- **for images, detailed information may be lost when converting from a lossless format such as TIFF to a lossy format such as JPEG, affecting resolution and colour representation; equally, loss of sound quality may occur in conversion from WAV to MP3.**

When carrying out file format conversions it is sensible to check that the 'significant properties' of the data are retained. If you use MS Excel try saving a spreadsheet as **CSV** and then importing it back. Is it the same? If not, why not?

Figure 5.1 shows how data that use highlighting for annotation in MS Excel (a) are at risk of losing the highlighting when converted to another simpler format such as tab-delimited text (b).

Qualitative data analysis software packages such as NVivo, ATLAS.ti and MAXQDA, have export facilities that enable a whole 'project' consisting of the raw data, coding tree, coded data, and associated memos and notes to be saved. These are typically saved in the system's own proprietary formats, so are less useful for longer-term accessibility. However, access to coding schemes used in these systems can be valuable for teaching and replication or for recoding data.

(a) MS Excel version

	A	B	C	D	E	F
1		Timber volumes in m3				
2	Year	1994	1995	1996	1997	1998
3	Date recorded	20/01/1995	23/01/1996	11/01/1997	16/01/1998	14/12/1998[1]
4	Logging private land	20346.345	47005.223	26001.754	11468.897	0.000
5	Logging forest reserves	4060.567	1777.783	804.997	0.000	3329.653
6	Logging state land	0.000	1200.000	559.162	2077.567	358.935
7	Total	61119.912	87065.006	64802.913	51354.464	5686.588
8						
9		Data missing				
10		Estimate				
11						
12	[1] temporary volumes					
13						

(b) tab-delimited version

	A	B	C	D	E	F
1		Timber volumes in m3				
2	Year	1994	1995	1996	1997	1998
3	Date recorded	20/01/1995	23/01/1996	11/01/1997	16/01/1998	14/12/19981
4	Logging private land	20346.345	47005.223	26001.754	11468.897	0
5	Logging forest reserves	4060.567	1777.783	804.997	0	3329.653
6	Logging state land	0	1200	559.162	2077.567	358.935
7	Total	61119.912	87065.006	64802.913	51354.464	5686.588
8						
9		Data missing				
10		Estimate				
11						
12	1 temporary volumes					
13						

Figure 5.1   Loss of highlighting used for annotation during conversion from MS Excel spreadsheet (a) to tab-delimited text (b) tab-delimited text

These can often be exported from the system as individual files in accessible formats, such as plain text, Rich Text Format, MS Excel or **XML**. See the case study in Chapter 4 on documenting data using NVivo9.

Data Transcription

Transcription is a translation between forms of data. In the social sciences this is most commonly converting audio recordings of interviews or discussions to text format. Whilst audio-transcription is often part of the analysis process it also enhances the sharing and reuse potential of qualitative research data.

High quality and consistent transcription that matches the analytic and methodological aims of the research is part of good data management planning. Attention needs to be given to transcribing conventions needed for the research, transcription instructions or guidelines for transcribers, and a template to ensure uniformity across a collection.

How transcription is carried out depends very much upon the theoretical and methodological approach and can vary between disciplines. A typical sociological research project that is looking for emergent themes from the data usually requires a 'denaturalized' (most like written language) approach to transcription (Bucholtz, 2000). A project using conversation analysis would use a 'naturalized' approach where transcription would try to capture all the sounds made using a range of symbols to represent particular features of speech, such as length of pauses, laughter, overlapping speech, or intonation (Jefferson, 1984). Care should be taken not to 'correct' grammar or vocabulary as it was spoken in the recording.

Transcription work is a time-consuming process and is frequently outsourced to external transcribers. It is vital to develop a standard transcription template for transcribers to follow and to provide written instructions or guidelines indicating the required transcription style, layout and editing, to ensure uniformity across the transcriptions. A good rule of thumb is to make sure transcriptions:

- each have a unique identifier such as a name or number;
- have a uniform layout throughout a research project or data collection;
- use speaker tags to indicate turn-taking or question / answer sequence in conversations;
- carry line breaks between turn-takes;
- are page numbered;
- have a document cover sheet or header with brief interview or event details such as date, place, interviewer name and interviewee details;
- show clearly whether amendments have been made, for example, translation to lay words or real names changed. Anonymization edits are best placed between brackets.

The following sample transcript suggests a standard layout including contextual and identifying information. This template is used by the UK Data Service as its recommended transcription template (UK Data Service, 2013).

Standard Transcription Template

Study Title: Immigration Stories	Interview number: 12
Depositor: K. Clark	Interview ID: Yolande
Interviewer: Ina Jones	Date of interview: 12 June 2009

Information about interviewee:

Date of birth: 4 April 1957	Marital status: married
Gender: female	Occupation: catering assistant
Geographic region: Essex	Ethnicity: Chinese

Y: I came here in late 1968.

I: You came here in late 1968? Many years already.

Y: 41 years already. 41 years already.

I: (laugh) It is really a long time. Why did you choose to come to England at that time?

Y: I met my husband and after we got married in Hong Kong, I applied to come to England.

I: You met your husband in Hong Kong?

Y: Yes.

I: He was working here [in England] already?

Y: After he worked here for a few years -- in the past, it was quite common for them to go back to Hong Kong to get a wife. Someone introduced us and we both fancied each other. At that time, it was alright to me to get married like that as I wanted to leave Hong Kong. It was like a gamble. It was really like a gamble.

When considering designing the format for transcription, best practice is to:

- consider compatibility of your transcription format with the import features of qualitative data analysis software before developing a template or guidelines. Document headers and textual formatting, such as italics or bold, may be lost when transcripts are imported. Text formatted in two columns indicating speakers and utterances may also be problematic;

- draft transcriber instructions or guidelines, indicating your required transcription style, layout and editing, especially if multiple transcribers carry out work;
- either anonymize data during transcription, or mark sensitive information for later anonymization;
- provide a translation, or at least a summary of each interview in your national language or in English (if text is not in your national language) in addition to transcriptions in the original language.
- Various software packages designed to automatically transcribe text from an audio source are available. These automatic speech recognition (ASR) software require significant training and calibration to be able to recognize a particular voice, accent and dialect. They can be useful if interviews are similar and avoid any peculiar jargon. It is best to use them with caution and always ensure checking of the whole text.

CASE STUDY — **Automatic Speech Recognition (ASR)**

ASR is a well-funded richly researched area, mainly because of its application in many areas of life. These include smart phone functionality such as: Apple's Siri; military flight and air traffic control activities; intelligence gathering; in the workplace for capture and analysis of customer calls; or for professional dictation, used by courts and doctors. There are various methods used to analyse and process speech: acoustic or waveform methods; artificial intelligence approaches; and statistical learning and modelling of human speech based on mathematical models or algorithms. Every year there are large-scale speech recognition conferences held and there have also been government-sponsored evaluations such as the GALE project (GALE, 2010).

A good introduction to this topic is provided by Oard (2012) investigating the application of ASR for oral history research. However, ASR systems are likely to make mistakes due to problems such as:

- an ASR system might not recognize a particular word in its dictionary, such as jargon;
- the interviewee might have an unusual accent;
- colloquial phrases used may be made up of existing words that are not commonly used in English. Examples are: all hat and no cattle; like nailing jello to the wall; put your John Hancock there.

Pieraccini (2012) provides the more interested reader with a look across six decades of work in science and technology to develop computers that can interact with humans using speech

---

Finally, attention should be paid to data security when transmitting recordings and transcripts that contain personal and confidential information to transcribers, and back to the researcher. It is essential to establish data security procedures for the transcriber to follow when handling the data; a non-disclosure agreement can be drawn up with transcribers and files can be encrypted before transfer.

Additional information on transcription is available from the *Transcribing Your Own Data Toolkit* produced by the Real Life Methods project and from the *Learning Qualitative Data Analysis on the Web* resource (Gibbs, 2010; Real Life Methods, 2011).

Here we use the term digitization to refer to converting paper-based sources to digital form, such as into a database. Historians often use the term transcription for this process.

Digitizing Data

Data sharing is made easier when research data and accompanying documentation are in digital format. Non-digital data can be converted to the digital source in a variety of ways, depending on their format and condition. Information can be entered manually by keyboard into a text or database template. Image scans can be created via a document scanner or by digital photography; and text can be digitized via optical character recognition from image scans.

Research data collected in the past might be available in a variety of media and formats. We consider the most common ones here:

- text-based materials, such as handwritten diaries, field notes, tables, diagrams, annotated printed questionnaires or typewritten text. These are usually in paper format;
- images of people, places or objects, such as from ethnographic work. These are usually photographs or slides;
- audio-visual recordings of interviews or observation, typically held as analogue audio cassettes, microcassettes, video tapes or reel-to-reel tapes;
- Diagrams, such as maps, plans or blueprints, usually paper-based.

Textual data can be digitized to different levels depending on the quality of the writing or typeface:

1. Scanning as an image file and saving as a TIFF image file. This is the best method for information in poor typeface, readable handwritten text or text with multiple tables and graphs. If information needs to be anonymized, black marker black-out is used on a copy (not the original), prior to scanning. Precious materials should be photocopied before feeding into any multi-feed scanner, in case they get damaged. If using a digital camera to capture images, it should have sufficient resolution capability, measured in megapixels. The camera should be secured with a horizontal mount and ensure that there is good overhead or dedicated lighting. Camera images should be transferred to safe media, and files well-organized.
2. If there are multiple pages in the original document, resulting scanned TIFF files can be collated into a searchable PDF/A file using 'Paper Capture' in Adobe Acrobat. The PDF/A file can be bookmarked to aid navigation, with contents page and headings.
3. Text with good typeface can be scanned as an image file and then processed using 'optical character recognition' (OCR) software that recognizes text. Some training of the system may be required to enable it to recognize non-standardized words, such as technical terminology. Checking and proofing of the resulting OCR text against the original text source

is necessary as errors do occur. This can be rather time-consuming work. The resulting file can be saved and formatted as a word-processed file.

4. Text can be manually transcribed by keyboard from the original source. In this process the new source should be kept as close to the original as possible and if changes are made, such as correcting typos, they should be indicated in brackets.

5. Images can be scanned or photographed and saved in **TIFF** file format. Audio is best digitized to **WAV** file format and video to **MPEG** or motion **JPEG 2000** format.

Maps can be digitized into raster format through scanning or into vector format by digitizing map features, such as lines, points, shapes, with a digitizing tablet or via on-screen digitization from a scanned image.

Finally, when considering digitization of sources where the content is not your own, attention needs to be paid to the copyright of the original material, discussed in Chapter 8 on rights. You should also document the digitization process as this provides important information on the data quality, data source and purpose of the digitization. Remember that there is already some useful metadata within these files.

Organizing Data Files in a Logical Manner

The ease of reading, retrieving and using data is also strongly determined by how data are organized and structured, both within data files, for example, within a database, and how data files are named and organized in a file structure, such as a directory or folder.

File Names

Sensible file names and well-organized folder structures make it easier to find and keep track of data files. A file name is a principal identifier for a file. Develop a naming system that works for your project and use it consistently. Good file names can provide useful cues to the content, status and version of a file, can uniquely identify a file and can help in classifying and sorting files. File names that reflect the file content also facilitate searching and discovering files. In collaborative research, it is essential to keep track of changes and edits to files via the file name. File names should be independent of the location of the file on a computer.

File names can have as elements:

- a project acronym;
- content description;
- file type information;
- date;
- creator name or initials;
- version number, such as using ordinal and decimal version numbers;
- status information, for example draft vs. final.

Best practice for file-naming is to:

- create meaningful but brief names;
- use file names to classify broad types of files;
- do not use spaces, dots and special characters such as & or ? or !;
- use hyphens '-' or underscores '_' to separate logical elements in a file name;
- avoid very long file names;
- reserve the 3-letter file extension for application-specific codes that represent file format, such as .doc, .xls, .mov and .tif.

Whilst computers add basic information and properties to a file, such as file type, date and time of creation and modification, this is not reliable data management. It is better to record and represent such essential information in the file name, in the file itself or through a folder structure.

Examples of good file names are:

- FG1_CONS_12-02-2010.rtf (Interview transcript of the first focus group with consumers that took place on 12 February 2010.)
- Int024_AP_05-06-2008.doc (Interview with participant 024, interviewed by Anne Parsons on 5 June 2008.)
- BDHSurveyProcedures_00_04.pdf (Version 4 of the survey procedures for the British Dental Health Survey.)

Examples of poor file naming might be:

- SrvMthdDraft.doc, SrvMthdFinal.doc, SrvMthdLastOne.doc and SrvMthdFridaynight.doc.
- Focus group consumers 12 Feb?.doc.
- Health&Safety Procedures1.

Batch or bulk renaming of files can be done with the help of dedicated software such as Ant Renamer, RenameIT or Rename4Mac.

File Structure

Thinking carefully how best to structure files in folders will make is easier to locate and organize files and versions. When working in collaboration, the need for an orderly structure is even higher. It is good practice to organize files relating to a particular project within a folder whose name contains the project name or acronym and a date, for example, the year. Within that top-level folder, consider the best hierarchy for files, deciding whether a deep or shallow hierarchy is preferable. This will make it easier to create copies and backups.

Research project files could be organized according to:

- research activity, such as interviews, surveys or focus groups;
- data type, such as images, text or database;
- kind of material, for example, publications, deliverables or documentation.

Related items should be linked to one another in common folders or via file names. For example, note files may be linked to corresponding data files. Besides data files, include folders for project management and administration, literature review and methodology, promotion and dissemination.

Figure 5.2 shows a recommended file structure and file-naming convention for a research project. Note that data and documentation files are held in separate folders. Data files are further organized according to data type and then according to research activity. Documentation files are also organized according to type of documentation and research activity.

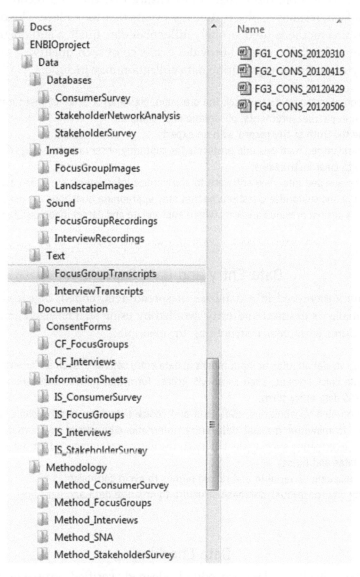

Figure 5.2   Example file structure and file-naming for a research project

Quality Assurance

Quality control of data is an integral part of all research and takes place at various stages, during data collection, data entry or digitization, and data checking. It is vital to assign clear roles and responsibilities for data quality assurance at all stages of research and to develop good procedures before data gathering starts.

Data Collection

During data collection, researchers must ensure that the data recorded reflect the actual facts, responses, observations or events that took place. The quality of data collection methods used strongly influences data quality, and documenting in detail how data are collected provides evidence of such quality.

Quality control measures during data collection may include:

- calibration of instruments to check the precision, bias and/or scale of measurement;
- taking multiple measurements, observations or samples;
- checking the truth of the record with an expert;
- using standardized methods and protocols for capturing observations, alongside recording forms with clear instructions;
- computer-assisted interview software to standardize interviews, verify response consistency, route and customize questions so that only appropriate questions are asked, confirm responses against previous answers where appropriate and detect inadmissible responses.

Data Entry and Data Capture

When data are entered in a database or spreadsheet, coded, digitized or transcribed, quality is ensured and error avoided by using standardized and consistent procedures with clear instructions, for example:

- setting up validation rules or input masks in data entry software, such as for entry of dates;
- using data entry screens, such as an MS Access form that mimics a questionnaire form, or an SPSS data entry form;
- using controlled vocabularies, code lists and choice lists from which values need to be selected, to minimize manual data entry. Internationally agreed conventions exist for recording information such as the ISO 8601, the format recommended for the representation of dates and times;
- detailed labelling of variable and record names to avoid confusion;
- designing a purpose-built database structure to organize data and data files.

Data Checking

During data checking, data are edited, cleaned, verified, cross-checked and validated. Checking typically involves both automated and manual procedures, such as:

- double-checking coding of observations or responses and out-of-range values;
- checking data completeness;
- verifying random samples of the digital data against the original data;
- double entry of data;
- statistical analyses such as frequencies, means, ranges or clustering to detect errors and anomalous values;
- proof-reading transcriptions;
- peer review.

Quality Control of Data at the UK Data Archive

At the UK Data Archive various quality control checks are applied to all research data while they are prepared for archiving in the data collection. Controls include: checking the number of cases and variables against the documentation; checking the completeness of variable and value labels; checking categorical variables for out-of-range values or wild codes; checking interval variables for improbable values; checking that data and documentation do not breach confidentiality rules and ensuring documentation is in digital format.

The level of quality control depends on how much additional value is to be added to the data, based on anticipated future usage (UK Data Archive, 2010). One of four standards of data processing is applied to each incoming study (A*, A, B, C), dependent on anticipated future usage and the condition of the data and documentation. Standard A* represents full enhanced data processing reserved for the highest used studies, such as regular government series or key longitudinal studies. Processing activities include preparing full question text for surveys and converting interview text to XML to display in online data browsing systems. Standard C represents the lowest level of processing for data that are less likely to be reused and where the deposited materials are in very poor condition with little improvement possible, or are in a software-dependent format with no alternatives available. Processing activities at all levels involve disclosure and copyright checks. A study can be elevated from standard C to A* if it becomes in demand.

Version Control and Authenticity

A version of a file is where a file has been changed and is closely related to another file in terms of its content. It is important to keep track of changes to files and therefore of different versions of files and to know which is the master or most recent version of a file, whether files are held in the same or in different locations. After some time it is often difficult to locate a correct version or to know how versions differ.

A suitable version control strategy depends on whether files are used by single or multiple users, are in one or multiple locations and whether or not versions across users or locations need to be synchronized or not, so that if information in one location is altered, the related information in other locations is also updated. The London School of Economics provides a useful version toolkit for researchers (London School of Economics and Political Science Library, 2008).

Another reason for keeping track of changes being made to data files during research is to be able to document the history or provenance, or lineage, of data.

This forms part of good data documentation as described in Chapter 4. For example, one can document how research data have been derived, manipulated, cleaned or updated, especially if different people or organizations are involved.

Best Practice in Version Controlling Files

The version of a file can be identified by:

- the date recorded in the file name or within the file, for example: HealthTest-2008-04-06
- version numbering in the file name, for example, HealthTest-00-02; HealthTest_v2
- a file history, version control table or notes included within a file, where versions, dates, authors and details of changes to the file are recorded, as shown in Table 5.3.

Table 5.3   Examples of a version control table

Title	Vision screening tests in Essex nurseries
File Name	VisionScreenResults_00_05
Description	Results data of 120 Vision Screen Tests carried out in 5 nurseries in Essex during June 2007
Created By	Chris Wilkinson
Maintained By	Sally Watsley
Created	04/07/2007
Last Modified	25/11/2007
Based on	VisionScreenDatabaseDesign_02_00

Version	Person responsible	Notes	Last amended
00_05	Sally Watsley	Version 00_03 and 00_04 compared and merged by SW	25/11/2007
00_04	Vani Yussu	Entries checked by VY, independent from SK	17/10/2007
00_03	Steve Knight	Entries checked by SK	29/07/2007
00_02	Karin Mills	Test results 81-120 entered	05/07/2007
00_01	Karin Mills	Test results 1-80 entered	04/07/2007

Version control can also be maintained through:

- version control facilities within software used; MS Word has the ability to keep track of different versions of a file (File→Versions), whereby for each version created the author, date and any comments annotated are kept in a versions list;
- using versioning software, such as Subversion (SVN);
- using file-sharing software such as Dropbox, Google Docs, which keeps a revision history, or Amazon S3. See Chapter 9 for a discussion on collaborative work spaces and the legal and sustainability implications of using cloud services;
- controlling rights to file-editing;
- manual merging of entries or edits by multiple users.

Best practice is to:

- decide how many versions of a file to keep, which versions to keep, for how long and how to organize versions;
- identify milestone versions to keep, e.g. major versions rather than minor versions (keep version 02–00 but not 02–01);
- uniquely identify different versions of files using a systematic naming convention, such as using version numbers or dates;
- record changes made to a file when a new version is created;
- record relationships between items where needed, for example: between code and the data file it is run against; between data file and related documentation or metadata; or between multiple files;
- track the location of files if they are stored in a variety of locations;
- regularly synchronize files in different locations, such as using MS SyncToy software;
- identify a single location for the storage of milestone and master versions.

As digital information can be copied and altered so easily, it is important to be able to demonstrate the authenticity of digital data and to be able to prevent unauthorized access to data that may potentially lead to unauthorized changes.

Best practice to ensure authenticity is to:

- save files with a new version number *before* editing;
- keep a single master file of data;
- assign responsibility for master files to a single project team member;
- regulate write access to master versions of data files;
- record all changes to master files;
- maintain old master files in case later ones contain errors;
- archive copies of master files at regular intervals;
- develop a formal procedure for the destruction of master files.

Exercise 5.1   Scenario for formatting and organizing research data resulting from a survey and interviews

You carry out research on the public understanding of climate change and associated risks in the UK. Understanding what people think about climate change is important to be able to develop better communication and dialogue between the scientific community, policy-makers and various sectors of the public.

Your research consists of:

- An online survey with 2,000 invited members of the public in the UK to assess their understanding of climate change and climate change risks, as well as their sources of information.

(Continued)

(Continued)

- Interviews with 20 key stakeholders in climate policy and science communication.
- Qualitative content analysis of secondary data taken from newspapers and popular science journals, evaluating reporting about climate change in the media.

Which file formats would you use for your resulting research data? How would you organize your data files and your data? Which file name convention might you apply?

Exercise 5.2   Fun quiz

1. Organizing my file names and folder structures consistently is (choose all possible answers):

   (a) a waste of precious time

   (b) not necessary until I finish my project

   (c) important for sharing and future use of the data

   (d) good practice for my research project

2. Systematic and logical file naming (choose all possible answers):

   (a) makes it easier to keep track of data files

   (b) provides useful cues to the content and status of a file

   (c) can help in classifying files

   (d) is not necessary as I am the only person using my data

3. In order to guarantee safe and long-term access to your research data and resources, it is best to convert them into a standard format. Which standard formats are most appropriate for textual files? (choose all possible answers)

   (a) Rich Text Format (.rtf)

   (b) PDF/A (.pdf)

   (c) OpenDocument Text (.odt)

   (d) Notepad (.txt)

4. Proprietary software is software that is (choose one answer only):

   (a) the best option for keeping my data safe

   (b) going to be around forever

   (c) a safe and stable way to store my data

   (d) not recommended for long-term storage of my data

5. Digital information can easily be copied, changed or deleted. How can you ensure your data are authentic? (choose all possible answers)

   (a) keep master files of data

   (b) regulate write access to master files

   (c) assign responsibility for master files

   (d) record changes to master files

6. Transcription of data (choose one answer only):

   (a) should always be carried out by the researcher

   (b) should only ever be carried out by a professional transcriber

(c) can be carried out by either a researcher or a professional transcriber as long as there is consistency within the transcripts

(d) should always be carried out in full

7. When digitizing textual data (choose one answer only):

(a) a flat bed scanner should always be used to image scan

(b) a digital camera will scan images well, provided lighting is adequate

(c) OCR stands for Optical Character Recording

(d) when re-keying always ensure grammatical errors are corrected in an interview transcript

Exercise 5.3   transcribing qualitative data

Figure 5.3 shows a transcribed interview from a PhD project on ageing and midlife. The researcher gave the audio recordings to different transcribers with varying ranges of transcription experience. Some transcribers were students and some were secretaries who all agreed to do the work informally, cheaply and quickly. The transcribers were not given any guidance by the researcher on prescribed transcription conventions or on how the transcript should look.

Read through the transcript. What do you notice about the transcript? What might you have done differently?

[Interview_2_with_Penny [1][1]]

Interview with Penny
Interview 2
In her office
6th November 2007

The first set of questions is about aging mostly and the experiences of aging. Um first of all, if you could tell me your date of birth actually?

Fifteenth of the fifth forty eight.

Ok could you start by describing yourself and telling me a few words about yourself

About myself, oh my god, I'm 55 and the mother of 3 daughters, um I therefore dye my hair constantly, I have still got one daughter still living at home and I am happily married. I have been married for 31 years, I know I don't seem like it [said in a breathy jokey voice].

Mmm

I was a late mother, I didn't have children till I was 30 and we were married for 6 years and I just didn't want to be a mother, but then again I didn't want to get married, so, and then all of a sudden I wanted it like yesterday. I work everyday, but not full time at the moment and I am very happy with my lot.

(Continued)

Figure 5.3   (Continued)

Sorry how old did you say you were?

55, botox is a wonderful thing

(Clears throat)

So starting wherever you like can you tell me about your life?

I had a charmed early life, my mum and dad, I was brought up in the east end.

Mmm

My mum didn't work, I had a sister and my sister is two years older than me and I had an idyllic childhood, even though I had a tragedy, I had a brother, John, who died in a car accident when he was 9 and obiously it affected my parents greatly because he was the boy, but we all got through it and I think that made me probably, I don't know if it affected my life in the way that I lived my life but I never felt that when someone said to me, Oh their Granny died it didn't affect me as greatly because they were quite old really, and so I suppose death affected me and how I thought about people dying affected me.

Mmm

If someone has lasted to this age I would still be very upset for that person but to be honest I wouldn't be upset that that person has gone because that person was old. But I have since lost my mum and she was 80, had a good life and all the rest of it, but she had a good life. [cough]. Yes so I had a wonderful life and yeah I count myself very lucky.

You said something about the way it made you think about other people's deaths, but did it make you think about your own death?

No, not me no, no I wouldn't think about my own death.

Mmm

I don't think about death much, I have to say, because apart from my brother dying and my mum dying no death has affected me, you know, that's what I mean I don't think a death would affect me as much as my brother's did because he was so young and it was so tragic and it was my dad who backed a car into him, so he had to live with that and it was a pure accident. The car went that way and my brother instead of going that way went backwards you know in a garage and um at the time my mum went a bit, I wouldn't say doolally, but she went to normal it was abnormal, you know so, at the time it was awful really and me and my sister would go out and my dad was so upset because he thought we blamed him, which we didn't, and we just felt for him you know. He had to live with that for all of his years, but he said thank god it was me, because if it had been anyone else he would have killed them, he would have had such anger. Yeah so that was the worse case we could have thought about.

Figure 5.3   Transcript from PhD ageing project

Source: Morgan, 2010

Exercise 5.4 Transcribing qualitative data

In this second exercise on transcription, you are about to carry out 30 in-depth interviews with women on a sensitive topic. You want to transcribe these and have decided that you will use a local transcription service. You need to develop guidance notes for transcribers and a transcriber confidentiality agreement. What kinds of clauses would you put in this agreement and what areas would it need to cover? Try to come up with some appropriate wording, including setting the scene using a brief introduction to the project for the transcribers.

Discussion for Exercise 5.1

The responses to the online survey can be exported directly from the survey into SPSS format, which is the software that will most likely be used to analyse the responses. Should the online survey package used not provide direct export to SPSS, then the responses can be exported in MS Excel or **CSV** format and imported into SPSS. Once the project is finished the data file can be stored long-term in SPSS portable format (.por), which can be generated from SPSS. All survey data will be kept in a single data file.

The interviews are audio-recorded with a digital recorder. Each interview is kept in a separate file and all 20 recordings are kept in a single folder. A good format in which to record them is **MP3** or **WAV**. The audio files can also be stored long-term in these formats, or can be converted to **FLAC** format. Audio recordings can be transcribed into MS Word and stored long-term as **RTF**. Each interview transcript is kept in a single file and all 20 files are placed in a single folder. MS Word transcripts can be imported into qualitative data analysis packages for content analyses, creating a single **CAQDAS** database.

Secondary textual data from newspapers and journals may be available as **PDF** documents or can be copied into MS Word documents. Both formats can be imported into qualitative data analysis packages for content analysis. These items can be imported into the same **CAQDAS** database as the interviews. Each newspaper or journal item is kept in a separate file, with all files stored in a single folder.

A suitable file structure and file-naming convention for the data files could be:

PUCC

    01-Survey

      Archive

        PUCC-Survey2013-01-00.sav

        PUCC-Survey2013-02-00.sav

      Current

        PUCC-Survey2013-03-00.por

    02-Interviews

      01-Audio

        PUCC-Interview01-2013-01-07.mp3

        PUCC-Interview02-2013-01-08.mp3

(Continued)

(Continued)

  02-Text

    PUCC-Interview01-2013-01-07.rtf

    PUCC-Interview02-2013-01-07.rtf

  03-Media

    PUCC-Media01-2009-05-18.pdf

    PUCC-Media02-2012-12-03.pdf

  04-Database

    PUCC-Database-01-00.nvp

Answers to Exercise 5.2

1. Organizing my file names and folder structures consistently is:

   (a) a waste of precious time – Incorrect. It's definitely not a waste of time. Having well-organized file names and folder structures makes it easier to keep track of your data files, provides useful cues to the content and status of a file and can aid the classification of files.

   (b) not necessary until I finish my project – Incorrect. You should organize your folders along the way as part of good research practice; then there will be very little reorganization to be done at the end of a project.

   (c) important for sharing and future use of the data – Correct. Good organization of your files and formats is essential for sharing your data and for understanding your own data in the future.

   (d) good practice for my research project – Correct. Make good file-naming and folder structuring part of your everyday research practice.

2. Systematic and logical file naming:

   (a) makes it easier to keep track of your data files – Correct. Especially if your file names contain clear information about their content, date, author, type of file, and project or activity they belong to.

   (b) provides useful cues to the content and status of a file – Correct. As long as your file names describe the file content and its version.

   (c) can help in classifying files – Correct. As long as your files names contain different elements of information, including a project, an activity such as a meeting or survey, or a time period.

   (d) is not necessary as I am the only person using my data – Incorrect. A good system really helps, especially when returning to data later on.

3. In order to guarantee safe and long-term access to your research data and resources, it is best to convert them into a standard format. Which standard formats are most appropriate for textual files?

   (a) Rich Text Format (.rtf) – Correct. This is one option that retains some degree of text formatting.

   (b) PDF/A (.pdf) – Correct. This is one option, but you may not have full access to edit the text and this is still a proprietary format.

(c) OpenDocument Text (.odt) – Correct. This is one option that retains formatting and acts as a universal document format.

(d) Notepad (.txt) – Correct. This format has longer-term accessibility, but may lose formatting and other relevant information when converted from a richer text format.

4. Proprietary software is software that is:

(a) the best option for keeping my data safe – Incorrect. Proprietary software formats are far less likely to have longer-term accessibility than open formats.

(b) going to be around forever – Incorrect. Proprietary software may be around for a long time, but there are no guarantees about how long that will be, and whether it will always be usable.

(c) a safe and stable way to store my data – Incorrect. It may well be safe and stable at the present moment and for the near future, but there are no long-term guarantees. It is better to use non-proprietary software for long-term storage and security of your data.

(d) not recommended for long-term storage of my data – Correct. See answer to option (b).

5. Digital information can easily be copied, changed or deleted. How can you ensure your data are authentic?

(a) keep master files of data – Correct. Keep master files of your research data in a safe and backed up location, separate from your working files, updating master files whenever major changes have been made to them.

(b) regulate write access to master files – Correct. Making master files 'read-only' ensures that no accidental changes can be made to them.

(c) assign responsibility for master files – Correct. If numerous people can access and edit master files and there is not one person with clear responsibility, the chances are high that unexpected changes can be made to the files without anyone noticing.

(d) record changes to master files – Correct. This can be done via a version control table within the files. All the solutions above can help ensure the authenticity of your data.

6. Transcription of data:

(a) should always be carried out by the researcher – Incorrect. Not necessarily. Researchers may want to carry out their own transcription to save money, to immerse themselves in the data, or to use the transcription process as part of their methodology, such as in conversation analysis, but it is also common to use professional transcribers.

(b) should only ever be carried out by a professional transcriber – Incorrect. Not necessarily. Some researchers may want or need to do the transcription themselves.

(c) can be carried out by either a researcher or a professional transcriber as long as there is consistency within the transcripts – Correct. It doesn't really matter whether the transcription is carried out by the researcher themselves or by a professional transcriber. Regardless of who does the task, the most important thing is to maintain consistency across the transcripts. This can be achieved through developing a short set of transcription guidelines that all transcribers should follow.

(d) should always be carried out in full – Incorrect. Transcription does not always have to be carried out in full, but full transcripts are optimal for future sharing and reuse.

7. When digitizing textual data:

(a) a flat bed scanner should always be used to image scan – Incorrect. A flatbed, feed scanner or digital camera mounted on a stand can all be used to image scan text on paper.

(b) a digital camera will scan images well, provided lighting is adequate – Correct. Provided the camera gives sufficient resolution and a horizontal mount and lighting are provided, this will produce high quality image scans.

(Continued)

(Continued)

(c) OCR stands for Optical Character Recording – Incorrect. It stands for Optical Character Recognition.

(d) when re-keying always ensure grammatical errors are corrected in an interview transcript – Incorrect. Keep the new data as close to the original source as possible. Changes should only be made to obvious errors, clearly indicating between brackets that the original source has been altered.

Discussion for Exercise 5.3

Look at the ageing and midlife project transcript that we have annotated with specific comments, in Figure 5.4. You might notice that there does not seem to be any particular convention here. As multiple transcribers were used, transcripts were returned in varying formats using different conventions. In this particular case, where each 'umm' and 'ahh' was recorded, lengthening the document. However, conversation analysis would require a high level of annotation where pauses as fillers would need to be recoded. Spelling was not always correct so the transcripts needed careful proofing, and no page or line numbers were used. Finally, it is important to consider the

File was labelled [Interview_2_with_Penny [1][1]]

Interview with Penny
Interview 2
In her office
6th November 2007

The first set of questions is about aging mostly and the experiences of aging. Um first of all, if you could tell me your date of birth actually?

Fifteenth of the fifth forty eight

Ok could you start by describing yourself and telling me a few words about yourself

About myself, oh my god. I'm 55 and the mother of 3 daughters, um I therefore dye my hair constantly, I have still got one daughter still living at home and I am happily married. I have been married for 31 years, I know I don't seem like it [said in a breathy jokey voice].

Mmm

I was a late mother, I didn't have children til I was 30 and we were married for 6 years and I just didn't want to be a mother, but then again I didn't want to get married, so, and then all of a sudden I wanted it like yesterday. I work everyday, but not full time at the moment and I am very happy with my lot.

Sorry how old did you say you were?

55, botox is a wonderful thing

(Clears throat)

So starting wherever you like can you tell me about your life?

I had a charmed early life, my mum and dad, I was brought up in the east end.

Mmm

My mum didn't work, I had a sister and my sister is two years older than me and I had an idyllic childhood, even though I had a tragedy, I had a brother, John, who died in a car accident when he was 9 and obiously it affected my parents greatly because he was the boy, but we all got through it and I think that made me probably, I don't know if it affected my life in the way that I lived my life but I never felt that when someone said to me, Oh their Granny died it didn't affect me as greatly because they were quite old really, and so I suppose death affected me and how I thought about people dying affected me.

Mmm

If someone has lasted to this age I would still be very upset for that person but to be honest I wouldn't be upset that that person has gone because that person was old. But I have since lost my mum and she was 80, had a good life and all the rest of it,

Comment [b1]: The original file was labelled like this. This is poor version control. What does the [1][1] stand for? Might be better as Int.001_final.

Comment [b2]: Might an ID be useful too?

Comment [b3]: Is this the second interview with this particular respondent or the second interview in the study as a whole?

Comment [b4]: Would more contextual information be beneficial?

Comment [b5]: It would be easier to read dates if they were written numerically. It would also make it easier to search for dates in a transcript if written numerically.

Comment [b6]: Clear speech demarcation and speaker tags are crucial in transcripts. They are not used here.

Comment [b7]: How much description of intonation should be included and what are the rules for assigning it?

Comment [b8]: Are all sounds like 'mmm's going to be represented? Conversation analysis may be very interested in capturing them, and gaps. These 'mmms' have been put into the turn taking sequence which makes the transcript overly long.

Comment [LC9]: Are round or square brackets to be used when noting sounds?

Comment [b10]: At what point should pseudonyms be added? If they are repeat interviews then it might be best to do it after fieldwork is completed. The researcher could brief interviewees to avoid using names when referring to people so it would reduce the burden on the anonymisation process.

Comment [b11]: Need to double check spelling.

> but she had a good life. [cough]. Yes so I had a wonderful life and yeah I count myself very lucky.
>
> *Comment [b12]: Is it necessary to include addition noises?*
>
> You said something about the way it made you think about other people's deaths, but did it make you think about your own death?
>
> No, not me no, no I wouldn't think about my own death.
>
> Mmm
>
> I don't think about death much, I have to say, because apart from my brother dying and my mum dying no death has affected me, you know, that's what I mean I don't think a death would affect me as much as my brother's did because he was so young and it was so tragic and it was my dad who backed a car into him, so he had to live with that and it was a pure accident. The car went that way and my brother instead of going that way [left or right] went backwards you know in a garage and um at the time my mum went a bit, I wouldn't say doolally, but she went so normal it was abnormal, you know so, at the time it was awful really and me and my sister would go out and my dad was so upset because he thought we blamed him, which we didn't, and we just felt for him you know. He had to live with that for all of his years, but he said thank god it was me, because if it had been anyone else he would have killed them, he would have had such anger. Yeah so that was the worse case we could have thought about.
>
> *Comment [b13]: What does the ellipse mean? Pause, missing words?*
>
> *Comment [b14]: Here context is required. The original interviewer would have had to have recorded the body language here.*
>
> *Comment [b15]: Need consistency with spelling certain words. Should it be capitalised or not?*
>
> *Comment [b16]: Page number should be at the bottom. Possibly even line numbers.*

Figure 5.4   Annotated transcript from PhD ageing project

Source: Corti et al., 2011

formatting of this transcript, in that the transcript used two columns for speaker tags and utterances, rendering it almost impossible to import into a **CAQDAS** package without major reformatting. Finally, if you have carried out research requiring transcription of interviews did you use any kind of templates or give thought to or guidance on any protocol for transcribing?

Discussion for Exercise 5.4

Your transcriber agreement and guidelines for transcription may look something like the following documents taken from a real life PhD project on recovery from bulimia nervosa. The research incorporated a series of in-depth qualitative interviews, which contained highly sensitive data. The researcher asked her transcribers to follow a set of transcribing conventions that she clearly set out in a short guide, shown below in Figure 5.5. She also issued a sample transcription. She prepared a confidentiality agreement that she asked her transcribers to sign, as shown in Figure 5.6. Read through these.

> **A Qualitative Exploration of Recovery from Bulimia Nervosa:**
> **Transcription Guidance Note**
>
> **Background to the Research**
> Bulimia is very difficult to overcome, so how and why some people manage to recover is not very well understood. The term recovery also means different things to different people; clinicians have suggested various criteria but there is currently little attention to what recovery means to those who have actually lived and experienced the recovery process.
>
> The purpose of my research is to look at recovery from the point of view of former sufferers of bulimia. After conducting a number of in-depth interviews, I hope to yield a rich collective account of the difficulties encountered and the insights gained during the journey of recovery.

(Continued)

Figure 5.5 (Continued)

I am conducting this research as part of a PhD in the Department of Sociology at the University of London, under the supervision of Professor Jane Woodstock. My research is being funded by the Economic and Social Research Council (ESRC) and has been granted full ethical approval by the Research and Enterprise Office (REO) at the University of London.

Due to the sensitive nature of this research, you will be required to sign a Confidentially Agreement which confirms you will adhere to the principles of anonymity and confidentiality and will not speak about the content or nature of the interviews to anyone apart from myself.

Theoretical Approach: Verbatim Transcription

Decisions about how transcription should be carried out are intimately connected with the type of analysis that is intended. Transcription of speech is always a compromise: greater detail gives more material for interpretation, yet too much detail can slow up the reading of the text in an artificial manner. This project requires **full verbatim transcription**. Taking a full verbatim transcription approach means that as well as preserving the actual words which were spoken, extra verbal material captured on the recording – such as the speaker's use of intonation, pauses, rhythm and hesitation – is also preserved. This keeps some of the additional meaning that was conveyed in the original interview, thereby providing contextual information as to the manner in which words were spoken. In addition, verbatim transcription requires that the character of the conversational exchange is apparent, so the words of the researcher must also be included.

General Notes:

- Document should include a header on every page with the serial number of the interview on the left hand side and your name on the right hand side
- Insert page numbers at the bottom of each page, in the centre
- Use Times New Roman, font size 12, type what the interviewer says in **bold** and justify the text
- Identify the interviewer and the respondent separately and indicate the gender of the respondent. Use; for the Interviewer and either F1: or M1: for the respondent depending on whether they are male or female (see attached example)
- Although I request that a record of what the interviewer says be included, the one exception to this concerns 'back channel utterances', i.e. where I can be heard in the background saying words such as "right", "yeah", "I see" or utterances such as "mmhhmm" whilst the interviewee is speaking. These function to encourage the respondent to continue speaking and reassure them that they are being listened to. It is not necessary to break up the respondent's speech by including them
- Use punctuation as for normal written prose. Grammar should not be altered or "tidied up". Do not use 'eye spellings' (e.g. "enuff" for 'enough')

Things to Include in Full:

- Unfinished questions or statements that trail off – indicate these with ellipses ( ), for example: "I never did understand her approach, the way she saw it, or"
- False sentence starts
- Repeated phrases, words, statements or questions
- Discussion that continues after the interview appears to be 'formally' finished
- Non-lexical utterances or 'fillers' such as 'umms' and 'errs' and 'uhs'
- Hesitations and Pauses – indicate these with ellipsis ( ), for example: "well recovery to me sort of means err"
- To indicate an exclamation of surprise, shock or dismay, use the standard exclamation mark
- Emphases – indicate any emphasis on a word or phrase by putting it in italics

Things to Include in Brackets

- Noises in background-for example (loud banging) or (door slams) or (muffled voices)
- The tone of the respondent. Here I am happy for you to include any comments on mood, feeling, passion, emotion and paralinguistics – for example: (laughs loudly) or (mumbles slowly) or (sounds angry) or (falters slightly) or (sighs)
- Unclear words or phrases must be marked where they occur within the text by placing the word "inaudible" in brackets and in bold e.g. **(inaudible)**. PLEASE DO NOT GUESS AT ANYTHING WHICH YOU CANNOT UNDERSTAND.

After Transcription

When you have completed transcribing an interview, please email it to me at (email address). On receipt of the transcript I will confirm that you then delete and destroy both the interview recording and the interview transcript in all its forms of storage – e.g. CD, WAV file, Word Document.

Thank you for agreeing to take part in this research project. Attached is a sample interview, indicating how I would like the interviews for this research to be transcribed. If there are large parts of the recording which you cannot understand or decipher, then please contact me immediately. Likewise, if you are concerned with any aspect of the transcription or these guidelines are unclear, then please do not hesitate to contact me on (mobile number) or at (email address)

Alice Jackson

Figure 5.5 Guidance notes for transcribers, Recovering from bulimia PhD project

Source: Jackson, 2010

University of London

An Exploration of Recovery from Bulimia Nervosa
Transcriber Confidentiality Agreement

This research is being undertaken by Alice Jackson, PhD candidate in the Department of Sociology, University of London. The purpose of the research is to explore recovery from bulimia nervosa from the point of view of former sufferers.

As a transcriber of this research, I understand that I will be hearing recordings of confidential interviews. The information on these recordings has been revealed by interviewees who agreed to participate in this research on the condition that their interviews would remain strictly confidential. I understand that I have a responsibility to honour this confidentially agreement.

I agree not to share any information on these recordings, about any party, with anyone except the Researcher of this project. Any violation of this and the terms detailed below would constitute a serious breach of ethical standards and I confirm that I will adhere to the agreement in full.

I, _____ agree to:

1. Keep all the research information shared with me confidential by not discussing or sharing the content of the interviews in any form or format (e.g. WAV files, CDs, transcripts) with anyone other than the Researcher.

2. Keep all research information in any form or format (e.g. WAV files, CDs, transcripts) secure while it is in my possession.

(Continued)

Figure 5.6 (Continued)

3. Return all research information in any form or format (e.g. WAV files, CDs, transcripts) to the Researcher when I have completed the transcription tasks.

4. After consulting with the Researcher, erase or destroy all research information in any form or format regarding this research project that is not returnable to the Researcher (e.g. CDs, information stored on my computer hard drive).

Transcriber:

_____   _____   _____
(print name)   (signature)   (date)

Researcher:

_____   _____   _____
(print name)   (signature)   (date)

This study has been reviewed and ethically approved by the Research and Enterprise Office (REO) at the University of London.

Figure 5.6   Transcriber confidentiality agreement, Recovering from bulimia PhD project

Source: Jackson, 2010

They are examples of excellent documents, but note a couple of matters that could be improved upon:

- providing advice on how to store information safely, for example backing up data in a password-controlled area or keeping paper in a locked filing cabinet;
- explaining how to send data, such as audio recordings and transcripts, safely between the researcher and transcriber, making use of encrypted files or USBs by recorded delivery.

References

ANDS (2013) *File Formats. ANDS Guides: Awareness level*, Australian National Data Service. Available at: http://ands.org.au/guides/file-formats-awareness.pdf.

Bucholtz, M. (2000) 'The politics of transcription', *Journal of Pragmatics*, 32: 1439–65.

Corti, L., Van den Eynden, V., Bishop, L. and Morgan, B. (2011) *Managing and Sharing Data: Training Resources*, UK Data Archive, University of Essex.

GALE (2010) *Global Autonomous Language Exploitation (GALE)*, Linguistic Data Consortium, University of Pennsylvania. Available at: http://projects.ldc.upenn.edu/gale/.

Gibbs, G. (2010) *Transcription Section. Learning Qualitative Data Analysis on the Web resource*. Available at: http://onlineqda.hud.ac.uk/resources.php#T.

Grimm, J. (2008) *Wessex Archaeology Metric Archive Project (WAMAP)*, Archaeology Data Service. Available at: ads.ahds.ac.uk/catalogue/resources.html?abmap_grimm_na_2008.

Jackson, A. (2010) Research data from PhD on *A Qualitative Exploration of Recovering from Bulimia* project. Unpublished data, University of London.

Jefferson, G. (1984) 'Transcription notation', in J. Atkinson and J. Heritage (eds), *Structures of Social Interaction*. New York: Cambridge University Press.

Li, C., Donizelli, M., Rodriguez, N. et al. (2010) 'BioModels Database: An enhanced, curated and annotated resource for published quantitative kinetic models', *BMC Systems Biology*, 4(92). Available at: www.ebi.ac.uk/biomodels-main/.

London School of Economics and Political Science Library (2008) *Versions Toolkit for Authors, Researchers and Repository Staff*, LSE. Available at: www2.lse.ac.uk/library/versions/VERSIONS_Toolkit_v1_final.pdf.

Morgan, B. (2010) Research data from PhD on *The Negotiation of Midlife: Exploring the Subjective Experience of Ageing*. Unpublished data, University of Essex.

Oard, D. (2012) 'Can automatic speech recognition replace manual transcription?' in D. Boyd, S. Cohen, B. Rakerd and D. Rehberger (eds), *Oral History in the Digital Age*, Institute of Library and Museum Services. Available at: http://ohda.matrix.msu.edu/2012/06/automatic-speech-recognition/.

Pieraccini, R. (2012) *The Voice in the Machine: Building Computers That Understand Speech*. Cambridge: MIT Press.

Real Life Methods (2011) *Transcribing your own Qualitative Data Toolkit*, Real Life Methods Project, University of Manchester. Available at: http://www.socialsciences.manchester.ac.uk/realities/resources/toolkits/transcribing-your-data/.

UK Data Archive (2010) *Our Quality Control*, UK Data Archive, University of Essex. Available at: http://www.data-archive.ac.uk/curate/archive-quality.

UK Data Archive (2013) *File Formats Table*, UK Data Archive, University of Essex. Available at: http://www.data-archive.ac.uk/create-manage/format/formats-table.

UK Data Service (2013) *Model Transcription Template*, UK Data Service, University of Essex. Available at: http://www.data-archive.ac.uk/media/136055/ukdamodeltranscript.pdf.

SIX
Storing and Transferring Data

Looking after and protecting research data from unwanted loss requires having in place good strategies for securely storing, backing up, transmitting and disposing of data. Collaborative research brings challenges for shared storage of, and access to, data.

There have been some examples of public data losses and mishaps that demonstrate the sometime disastrous consequences of human error or negligence.

In the UK, in 2008 a memory stick lost by a contractor from the Department of Work and Pensions in the UK containing personal details of 12 million people was found in a pub car park (Burns, 2008). Also in 2008, the UK Home Office lost data containing confidential information on 130,000 serious offenders. These were lost on a memory stick used by Home Office consultants (Winnett, 2008). In the academic sector, where research scientists amass gigabytes of data, a fire at the University of Southampton caused significant damage to scientific facilities and loss of data, not all of which were backed up (Curtis, 2005).

According to the Boston Computing Network (2013) the picture of data loss is of concern to those of us who store precious digital data:

- 6% of all PCs will suffer an episode of data loss in any given year, which for the year 1998 in the USA amounted to some 4.6 million data loss episodes in USA businesses;
- in the USA 140,000 hard drives crash every week;
- 31% of PC users have lost all of their files due to events beyond their control;
- 60% of companies that lose their data will shut down within six months of the disaster;
- 30% of all businesses that have a major fire go out of business within a year, and 70% fail within five years;
- 34% of companies fail to test their tape backups, and of those that do, 77% have found tape backup failures.

Ensuring your data are *safe* is crucial to any information-based activity. A good storage and backup strategy will prevent data loss. This in turn will prevent having to replicate research, maintain the privacy of data subjects and keep reputational risk at bay.

Storing Data

Digital storage media are inherently unreliable and all file formats and physical storage media will ultimately become obsolete. The accessibility of any data files depends on the quality of the storage medium and the availability of the relevant data-reading equipment for that particular medium.

Media currently available for storing data files are optical media and magnetic media. All optical media, such as **CDs** and **DVDs** are vulnerable to damage by poor handling, changes in temperature and relative humidity, poor air quality and lighting conditions. The UK's National Preservation Office has published guidelines on caring for **CDs** and **DVDs** (Finch and Webster, 2008). Optical media are best stored vertically, in jewel (**CD** storage) cases, in a dark environment, at 30–50% relative humidity, avoiding high (above 23°C), low (below 10°C) and fluctuating temperatures. Rewritable discs, **CD-RW** and **DVD-RW**, are not recommended for long-term storage.

Magnetic media, such as hard drives and tapes, are also subject to physical degradation. A personal computer is more likely to suffer from a fatal crash in a stiflingly hot office than in a temperature-controlled environment.

Printed paper-based materials and photographs are subject to degradation from sunlight and acid, for example, from sweat or acid found in some kinds of paper. High quality materials should be used for long-term storage of paper, for example using acid-free paper, folders and boxes and non-rust paperclips rather than staples.

Best Practice in Storing Data

- store data uncompressed in non-proprietary or open standard formats for long-term software readability (see Table 5.1 on file formats);
- copy or migrate data files to new media every two to five years, since both optical and magnetic media are subject to physical degradation;
- use a storage strategy, even for a short-term project, with two different forms of storage, for example, on hard drive and on **CD**;
- check the data integrity of stored data files at regular intervals. We describe the checksum method under the section on backing up data later in this chapter;
- organize and label stored data clearly so they are easy to locate and physically accessible;
- ensure that areas and rooms for storage of digital or non-digital data are fit for the purpose, structurally sound and free from the risk of flood and fire;
- create digital versions of paper-based data or information in **PDF/A** format for long-term preservation and storage.

Professional digital archives have preservation policies which provide guidance on looking after data (National Archives of Australia 2011; UK Data Archive, 2011).

Data Security

Ensuring security of data requires paying attention to physical security, network security and security of computer systems and files to prevent unauthorized access or unwanted changes to data, disclosure or destruction of data. Data security arrangements need to be proportionate to the nature of the data and the risks involved. Data security may be important to keep personal or sensitive information safer or to protect intellectual property rights or commercial interests. Attention to security is also needed when data are to be destroyed.

Data Security

Physical data security requires:

- controlling access to rooms and buildings where data, computers or media are held;
- logging the removal of, and access to, media or hardcopy material in store rooms;
- transporting sensitive data only under exceptional circumstances, even for repair purposes, for example, giving a failed hard drive containing sensitive data to a computer manufacturer may breach security.

Network security means:

- not storing confidential data such as those containing personal information on servers or computers connected to an external network, particularly servers that host internet services;
- firewall protection and security-related upgrades and patches to operating systems to avoid viruses and malicious codes.

Security of computer systems and files may include:

- locking computer systems with a password and installing a firewall system;
- protecting servers by power surge protection systems through line-interactive uninterruptible power supply (UPS) systems;
- implementing password protection of, and controlled access to, individual data files, for example, allocating 'no access', 'read only', 'read and write' or 'administrator-only' permissions;
- controlling access to restricted files or storage areas by encrypting them;
- imposing non-disclosure agreements for managers or users of confidential data;
- not sending personal or confidential data via email or other file transfer means without first encrypting them;
- destroying data in a consistent and robust manner when needed;
- remembering that file-sharing services such as Google Docs and Dropbox may not be suitable for certain types of information.

Storage and Security of Personal Data

It is important to be aware of the risks of storing personal data. Legally, data that contain personal information must be treated with more care than data that do not. This mandate is set out in the Data Protection Act 1998, which stipulates that personal data should only be accessible to authorized persons (The National Archives, 1998). We cover this in more detail in Chapter 7. In the UK, from mid-2008 financial penalties can be enforced for the wilful circulation of personal data without consent. Equally, there may be requirements placed upon researchers to retain data for a given specified certain period, such as for clinical trials data. An example of data retention in health research is given in the first case study in this chapter. Otherwise, there are few restrictions on the length of time funded research data must be kept, though the UK's Engineering and Physical Sciences Research Council (EPSRC) expects data to be maintained securely for at least 10 years (EPSRC, 2011).

Personal data may exist in digital and non-digital formats. Non-digital examples are paper-based patient records, signed consent forms, or interview cover sheets containing names, addresses and signatures. Regardless of format, personal information should be removed from data files and stored separately under more stringent security measures. Anonymous identification systems can help link the two sets of materials together if required, such as for re-contacting purposes.

The risks of identification of personal information are typically managed through the anonymization or aggregation of data and the regulation of access through a dedicated rights management framework. The UK Data Archive (2012) has produced useful guidance on handling sensitive microdata securely and the second case study below sets out how secure data are stored and handled at the UK Data Archive in order to make them available for reuse in research. Strategies for sharing personal and sensitive information for the purpose of making data available for reuse in research, are considered in detail in Chapter 7.

Strategies for storing confidential data or data containing personal information should be addressed when planning informed consent procedures for research. This ensures that the persons whom the personal data refer are informed and give their consent as to how the data are stored or transmitted.

| CASE STUDY | Data Retention in Health Research |

There is no overarching recommendation on the length of time research data should be kept, but some disciplines have specific requirements. Practice from the medical sciences has been adopted and accepted as good practice for some research.

The Medical Research Council (MRC) in the UK notes that retention time for research data depends on the type of study (MRC, 2012). They expect that all primary research data from studies be retained in their original form including samples, questionnaires, recordings and specimens, within the research establishment that generated them for a minimum of 10 years after completion of a study. This time is increased if consent for data collection was obtained in the study. Then a subset of the original records covering the study and consent procedures should be retained for 30 years after completion of the study. In the case of clinical or public health studies, records should be retained for 20 years after completion of the study to allow for review, re-appraisal or further research. Records from studies with historical importance,

(Continued)

(Continued)

studies using novel or controversial techniques or on-going studies should be retained longer than 20 years after completion of the study.

For most social science research there is no standard retention period for data, unless third party data have been obtained under a licence that requires data to be destroyed after use. Data retention practices need to be balanced against these data protection requirements, which expect personal information such as people's names, addresses and so on not to be held for longer than necessary. While this does not usually apply to most research data per se, it would apply to disclosive administrative data associated with a research project, such as fieldwork addresses. However, explicit permission can be gained to keep such data for a particular defined purpose, as in the case of longitudinal studies that need to keep track of their participants' addresses. Finally, academic institutions are increasingly requiring research data to be held for a minimal period of time to enable others to consult material supporting publications.

| CASE STUDY | Storing and Processing Secure Data at the UK Data Archive |

The UK Data Archive has stringent procedures in place for ingesting disclosive ('secure') data that is made available for research purposes under its secure access facilities.

Digital files for all secure data studies must be encrypted and stored in a directory marked 'RESTRICTED' on one of the designated drives located on the network storage device; where they must remain during all stages of processing. All digital processing files containing restricted survey data must also include the word 'RESTRICTED' in their filename, so they are easily identifiable as such. Associated physical media, printed reports and emails, and depositor licence agreements relating to all secure data studies are also labelled as 'RESTRICTED' and retained in a 'green folder', also marked as 'RESTRICTED'.

Secure data ingest work is confined to a dedicated office within the Archive building which must be locked at all times when not occupied by secure data processing staff. All processing work is carried out using designated workstations located in the office, which have appropriate security safeguards, including full disk encryption for computers and storage volumes, and authentication using secure personal passphrases. A five minute session lockout is also in place which requires password credentials to be re-entered.

Local workstations are used only as a terminal, but not for processing work. All data ingest work is carried out on a dedicated access-controlled processing server. Files being processed are stored on a secure remote server or storage device so that data are protected against unauthorized access during processing, and because these are outside the secure perimeter and *not* backed up by the university, as other network areas are. Copying or exporting restricted access files located on the secure servers and storage devices to the local workstation is not permitted.

Once processed, the secure studies are stored within their encrypted volumes in the dedicated directory. Before opening any restricted data files, processors must exit all non-essential applications on their local PC, particularly messaging applications such as Skype, but also non-work related websites. An audit trail spreadsheet is kept for recording the dates and responsible person for receipt of electronic files and any accompanying paperwork, their transfer between processing and storage areas, their disposal or deletion, and the various quality control checks that are carried out.

The secure processing office operates a 'clear desk' policy. When not in immediate active use, all green folders and any associated removable storage media must be stored and locked in the data processor's desk drawer during office hours. Associated removable storage media must be password or passphrase-protected. At the end of each day, all green folders and any associated removable storage media must be locked away in a filing cabinet or safe, whose keys are stored in a key holder whose combination is known only by secure processing staff.

Finally, secure processing work is undertaken in accordance with a 'clear screen' policy where all active sessions that involve secure data must be terminated when leaving the desk. 'Network places' must be closed when the session has been completed and encrypted storage volumes on the designated directory, secured by TrueCrypt, must be dismounted. Whenever a PC is left powered on but unattended, even though a five minute lockout is in place, the processor must manually lock the PC using Ctrl+Alt+Delete before leaving his or her desk.

Using email to transmit data, even internally within an organization provides vulnerabilities. First, emails and their attachments may persist on multiple email servers in the mail chain and thus be accessible to unknown people. While encryption can help to maintain security of data during email transmission, it should not be routinely used for data transfer or storage.

Encrypting Data

Encryption can be used for safely transferring or storing files, such as for backups or storage on mobile devices or for sending data files to others. Individual files can be encrypted, as well as entire storage devices or containers for multiple data files. Encryption software uses an algorithm to encode information; a key (password or passphrase) is needed to decrypt the information. Table 6.1 shows that the larger the key size, the more secure the encryption. Encryption can be used

Table 6.1   Relation between encryption key size and security

Key size	Time estimated to crack using a dedicated super computer	Related experience
8	0 milliseconds	Far, far less than the time needed to read this
56	1 second	Blip
64	5 minutes	Long enough to apologize for accidentally exposing data
128	150 trillion years	Longer than the history of the universe
256	Over a quadrillion years	A number greater than the number of atoms in the universe

for secure transmission and storage. It prevents unapproved access and it ensures that no changes can be made to a file. The practice of cryptography dates back thousands of years and has since evolved into elaborate systems, discussed in the case study on cryptography below.

CASE STUDY ⊣ **Background to Cryptography**

Prior to modern times, cryptography was concerned with preserving confidentiality in messages via conversion from a comprehensible form into an incomprehensible one and back again at the other end, rendering it unreadable by interceptors who did not have the key to decrypt that message. Spies, military planners and diplomats have all used encryption to keep their communications secret.

Transposition or substitution ciphers, such as replacing a letter with another, have a long history. One of the earliest recorded uses of cryptography is from Egypt using carved cipher text on stone (approx. 1900 BC). Another early method was stenography that involved hiding the existence of a message to keep it confidential. Herodotus was said to have concealed a message using a tattoo on a slave's shaved head under the regrown hair (Kahn, 1996). More modern examples of stenography include the use of invisible ink and digital watermarks to conceal information.

Many mechanical encryption/decryption devices were invented and patented early in the twentieth century, among them rotor machines like the famous Enigma machine invented by the German engineer, Scherbius at the end of the First World War. It was used commercially by the military and government from the early 1920s and by Nazi Germany during the Second World War (Singh, 1999). The Enigma machine combined mechanical and electrical subsystems: a keyboard, a set of rotating disks with pins for letters of the alphabet, arranged adjacently along a spindle, and stepping components to turn one or more of the rotors with each press of a key.

Innovations in cryptanalysis at Bletchley Park in the UK during WW2 led to the development of the world's first fully electronic, digital, programmable computer, named Colossus. This was used to decrypt ciphers generated by the German Lorenz SZ40/42 machine (Copeland, 2006) and paved the way for the encryption of data in binary format.

Software for Encryption

There are a number of software applications available for encrypting data. The UK Data Archive recommends the use of Pretty Good Privacy (PGP) standard technology. This is available as open source versions (GnuPG), or as commercial software (PGP). Encryption with such software requires the creation of a public and private key pair and a passphrase. The private PGP key and passphrase are used to digitally sign each encrypted file, and thus allow the recipient to validate the sender's identity. The recipient's public PGP key is installed by the sender in order to encrypt files so that only the authorized recipient can decrypt them. See the case study on the use of PGP.

Open-source Axcrypt software can be used to encrypt individual files. Software such as TrueCrypt or Safehouse Explorer can be used to create an encrypted storage area, or container, on portable devices or hard drives, or to encrypt an entire drive or disc. All files transferred to an encrypted container are held securely and can only be accessed via the key. Files can simply be copied to and from a TrueCrypt container and are automatically encrypted (in memory/RAM) when they are written or copied to the container and decrypted when being read or copied from an encrypted container. The same software can be used to encrypt an entire disk or device.

CASE STUDY | **Encrypting Data Files for Transfer to the UK Data Archive, Using the PGP Process**

Once only:

1. Install a PGP encryption software, such as GnuPG.
2. Create your own public/private key pair and passphrase.
3. Download the UK Data Archive Public Key and unzip it (UK Data Archive, 2013).
4. Import this Public Key into the PGP software.

Every time files need encrypting:

1. Select files for encryption.
2. Select the UK Data Archive Public Key.
3. Digitally sign the files to be encrypted using your private key and passphrase.
4. Encrypt selected files using the UK Data Archive Public Key.
5. Send files to the UK Data Archive by email or via file transfer protocol.

Backing up data

Making backups of files is an essential element of data management which ensures that original data files can be restored from backup copies, should they get damaged or go missing. Regular backups protect against accidental or malicious data loss due to:

- human error;
- hardware failure;
- software or media faults;
- virus infection or malicious hacking;
- power failure.

The form of backup procedure required for a project will depend on local circumstances, the perceived value of the data and the levels of risk of losing data you are prepared to take. Carrying out an informal risk analysis can provide a good indication of backup needs.

Your Risk Analysis for Planning a Backup Strategy for Your Research Data

Q. Is there any backup provision already in place?

Find out if your institution has an operational backup policy. Most universities have one for files held on a university network space. In most cases, their policies do not include your local drive; you must manually backup this drive if you use it for data storage. If you are not happy with the robustness of the solution you should carry out an independent backup of critical files.

Q. Which systems to back up?

You need a strategy for all systems where data are held, including portable computers and devices, non-network computers and home-based computers. If your institution does not provide any system backup, you may need to take full responsibility for all your own backups.

Q. How often should I back up my data?

Consider how often you make changes to your data, and which amount of changed data you are prepared to lose between backups. Consider backing up after each change to a data file or at regular intervals, such as daily or weekly.

Q. Where should I store my backups?

Depending on the form of backup and the risks associated with data loss, it is most convenient to keep backup files on a networked hard drive. For critical data, not available elsewhere, we would recommend that you also adopt offline storage on recordable CD/DVD, removable hard drive or magnetic tape. If you are backing up many small data files on a daily basis, copying them to a recordable CD probably suffices. If you are making backups of very large quantities of data from a networked hard drive, a removable hard drive or even magnetic tape is probably more convenient. Never rely on pen drives for backup media. Physical media should be safely stored in another location. Most manufacturers provide recommendations for the best storage conditions of physical media.

Q. How should I organize my backups?

If you are making your own backups on removable media, make sure they are well-labelled, indicating the content and date/time, and well-organized. Without some management, achieving the ultimate aim of restoring lost data may prove difficult.

Q. Are there any tools I can use to help with backing up?

It is good to use an automated backup process to back up frequently used and critical data files. Software such as Microsoft SyncToy and Mac TimeMachine are easy-to-use and can synchronize files across different locations.

Q. How about backing up personal data?

Where data contain personal information, care must be taken to create only the minimal number of copies needed, for example, a master file and one backup copy. Otherwise there could be a proliferation of data files containing personal information, which will be harder to securely destroy at the end of a project.

Q. Is there anything else to think about?

It is important that you verify and validate backup files regularly by fully restoring them to another location and comparing them with the original. Backup copies can be checked for completeness and integrity, for example by checking the file size, date and MD5 checksum value, explained in the checking data integrity box below.

Checking Data Integrity using MD5 Checksums

Checksums are not as complicated as they sound. They provide a simple way to compute the integrity of your data files and may also create an automatic list of your files. A checksum is like a fingerprint of a file and can be used to verify whether two files are identical.

Each time you run a checksum a number is created for each file. Even if one byte of data has been altered or corrupted that string will change. So, if the checksums before and after copying or backing up a data file match, then you can be sure that the data have not altered during this process.

An example of a free software tool for computing **MD5** checksums is MD5summer for windows (MD5summer, 2013). This software computes checksums according to the **MD5** checksum algorithm. No matter how big the source file is, it always has a short 128bit MD5 checksum value that can be easily stored and shared, and compared against the value for a non-identical file. For example, a checksum list copied onto a **USB** stick will allow you to detect problems early. If MD5summer finds any differences between the two checksums, then you should transfer your data onto another storage device immediately. The software is very easy to use.

| CASE STUDY | Data Backup and Storage |

A research team carrying out coral reef research collects field data using handheld Personal Digital Assistants (PDAs). Digital data are transmitted daily to the institution's network drive. All data files are identified by an individual version number and creation date. Version information, including version numbers and notes detailing differences between versions, were stored in a spreadsheet and also on a network drive. The institution's network drives

(Continued)

(Continued)

are fully backed up onto Ultrium LTO2 data tapes; incremental backups are made daily Monday to Thursday; and full server backups are made over Friday to Sunday. Tapes are securely stored in a separate building. Upon completion of the research the data were deposited in the institution's digital repository.

| CASE STUDY | Data Backup and Storage |

In February 2008 the British Library (BL) received the recorded output of the Survey of Anglo-Welsh Dialects (SAWD), carried out by University College, Swansea, between 1969 and 1995 (British Library, 2010). This survey recorded the English spoken in Wales by interviewing and audio-recording speakers on topics including the farm and farming, the house and housekeeping, nature, animals, social activities and the weather. The collection was deposited in the form of 503 digital audio files, which were accessioned as **WAV** files in the BL's Digital Library. Digital copies of all files are held at the Archive of Welsh English, alongside the original master recordings on 151 audio cassettes, from which the digital copies were created.

The BL's Digital Library is mirrored on four sites; Boston Spa, St Pancras, Aberystwyth and a 'dark' archive which is provided by a third party. Each of these servers has inbuilt integrity checks. The BL makes available access copies for users, in the form of **MP3** audio files, in the British Library Reading Rooms via the Soundserver system. A small set of audio extracts from the SAWD recordings are also available online on the BL's Accents and Dialects website, 'Sounds Familiar'.

Data Disposal

Deleting files and reformatting a hard drive will not entirely prevent the possible recovery of data that have previously been on that hard drive. Having a strategy for reliably erasing data files is a critical component of managing data securely and may be relevant at various stages in the datacycle.

During research, copies of data files which are no longer needed may be destroyed. It is often useful to keep 'working' files safely in order to back track in the research process. So do not destroy files thoughtlessly. At the conclusion of research, data files which are not required for preservation need to be disposed of securely.

Erasing Data

Hard Drives

For hard drives, which are magnetic storage devices, deleting files does not permanently erase a file from the physical drive; rather it only removes a reference to the file. It takes little effort to restore files deleted in this way and explains why data can be recovered from some damaged hard drives. Files need to be overwritten to ensure they are effectively deleted. Software is available for the secure erasing of files from hard disks, meeting recognized erasure standards. Example software is BC Wipe, Wipe File, DeleteOnClick and Eraser for Windows platforms. Mac users can use the standard 'secure empty trash' option; an alternative is Permanent Eraser software.

USB Flash Drives

Flash-based storage devices, such as memory sticks, are constructed differently to hard drives and techniques for securely erasing files on hard drives cannot be relied on to work for solid state disks as well, so physical destruction is advised as the only certain way to erase files.

The most reliable way to dispose of data is physical destruction. A risk-adverse approach for all drives is to encrypt devices before first use when installing operating software, and to physically destroy the drive using a secure destruction facility approved by your institution when data need to be disposed.

Paper and CDs/Optical Discs

Shredders certified to an appropriate security level should be used for destroying paper and CD/DVD discs. Examples of results of shredding of paper and CDs at various levels of shredding are shown in Figure 6.1, 6.2 and 6.3. Computer or external hard drives at the end of their life can be removed from their casings and disposed of securely through physical destruction.

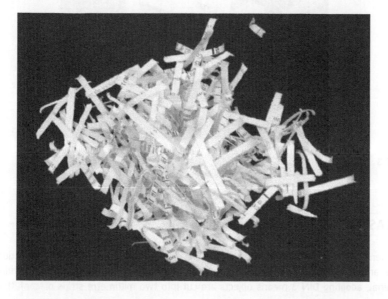

Figure 6.1   Paper shredded: cross cut 2 x 8 mm, for confidential or sensitive material

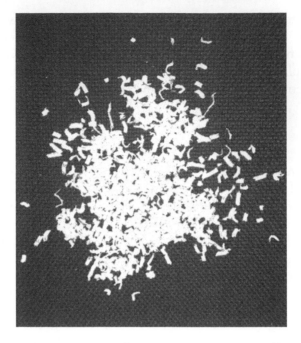

Figure 6.2 Paper shredded: cross cut confetti 1 x 5 mm, for top secret or classified material

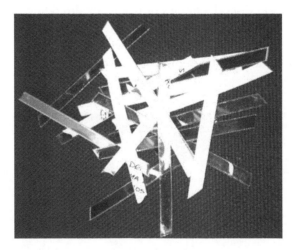

Figure 6.3 CDs shredded

| CASE STUDY | Data Destruction |

The German Institute for Standardization (DIN) has standardized levels of destruction for paper and discs that have been adopted by the shredding industry. For shredding confidential material, adopting DIN 3 means objects are cut into two millimetre strips or confetti- like cross-cut particles of 4 x 40 mm. The UK government requires a minimum standard of **DIN 4** for its material, which ensures cross-cut particles of at least 2 x 15 mm. The highest security level is known as **DIN 6**; this is used by the United States federal government for ultra-secure shredding of top secret or classified material, cross-cutting into 1 x 5 mm particles.

Exercise 6.1   Data security breaches

Read through the following real-life cases of data safety and security breaches. Think about what could have been done differently to prevent them from happening. What preventative measures could the researcher or team have taken?

Scenario 1. Unshredded and unanonymized printed data transcripts are found on the street in a clear plastic rubbish bag. It was too time-consuming to shred the large pile of documents with a basic office shredder so they were just thrown into the recycling bin.

Scenario 2. A senior lecturer stores personal and confidential data on the hard drive of her university computer. She is given a new computer by her department, while the old one is given to research students to use in their office. The students are able to access both her personal and research data.

Scenario 3. A researcher has a laptop stolen whilst away on a conference trip. Vital research data was kept on the hard drive and was not backed up anywhere else.

Scenario 4. A researcher sends a set of audio-cassettes for transcription in the post. The researcher writes the wrong address on the package and the tapes get lost in the post.

Scenario 5. Digital audio files are emailed to a transcriber who saves them to his computer desktop and also stores them in his email once received. The transcriber fails to remove the files from his email and from his computer once the transcription is completed and returned to the researcher. He later sells his computer on eBay.

Scenario 6. A researcher works in a shared office with four other researchers working on other projects. Whilst working on his project the researcher leaves paper copies of the signed consent forms loose on the desk. The other researchers have the opportunity to read through these confidential documents.

Scenario 7. A transcriber tells her friends and family about the 'interesting interview' that she is transcribing, giving details about the name and place of work of the interview participant.

Scenario 8. A fire at the university destroys a research office and all the paper copies of an important research collection that a researcher was preparing for archiving.

Scenario 9. Unanonymized data are inadvertently published on a project's website.

Scenario 10. A researcher encrypts his data folder, then forgets his password and can no longer access his data.

---| **Exercise 6.2   Data security breaches** |------------------------------

Which of the security breaches listed above for Exercise 6.1 might realistically pose a threat to your data?

---| **Exercise 6.3   Fun quiz** |------------------------------

1. The best place to store your current paper-based research data overnight or when leaving the office while you are actively using them on a daily basis is (choose one answer only):

    (a) on your desk

    (b) in an unlocked drawer

    (c) in a locked filing cabinet

    (d) in a high security bank vault

2. Backing up your data (choose all possible answers):

    (a) protects against data loss or corruption

    (b) preserves them forever

    (c) should be done regularly

    (d) is the sole responsibility of your institution

3. To guard against file storage media corruption, how frequently should you replace backup tapes? (choose one answer only)

    (a) every day

    (b) every month

    (c) every year

    (d) every 2–5 years

    (e) every 20 years

4. What should you do with paper-based data to ensure the longevity of the information? (choose all possible answers)

    (a) store them in a temperature/humidity-controlled environment

    (b) store them in direct sunlight

    (c) convert them to **PDF/A** format and store in a location fit for purpose

    (d) store them in your attic

5. How can you protect the security of research participants' personal information in a dataset? (choose all possible answers)

    (a) by anonymizing/reducing the precision of the data

    (b) by storing personal data such as names/addresses separately from the other data

    (c) by encrypting data files containing personal information

    (d) by requiring data users to sign the Official Secrets Act

6. Encrypting files on your mobile storage device ensures that your digital data are (choose one answer only):

    (a) open for anyone to see

    (b) protected and only those with the encryption key can view them

(c) completely deleted

(d) converted into a new format

7. What ways would be suitable for transferring transcribed interview records to a colleague? (choose all possible answers)

   (a) via an unencrypted email attachment

   (b) using Dropbox without encryption

   (c) using Dropbox with encryption

   (d) hand it in person to the recipient on a **USB** stick

8. How can you securely destroy data on a personal computer hard drive? (choose all possible answers)

   (a) delete files and reformat the hard drive

   (b) remove and destroy the hard drive

   (c) delete files and take the computer to the dump

   (d) overwrite files using secure deletion software

9. How can you securely destroy data on a **CD** or **DVD**? (choose one answer only)

   (a) put it through a **CD** shredder and throw the shreds away

   (b) break it in half and throw it away

   (c) put it in the plastic recycling bin

   (d) put it in the dishwasher on a hot cycle

   (e) overwrite files on the disc using proprietary software

   (f) cut it up into little pieces with nail scissors

Exercise 6.4   Checking data integrity with checksums

Try the following checksum exercise using the free software, MD5summer:

http://ukdataservice.ac.uk/manage-data/handbook.

Exercise 6.5   Encrypting data

Try the following encryption exercise that will create an encrypted storage space on your drive using the free software, SafeHouse Explorer:

http://ukdataservice.ac.uk/manage-data/handbook.

Answers to Exercise 6.1

Scenario 1. Unshredded and unanonymized printed data transcripts are found on the street in a clear plastic rubbish bag. It was too time-consuming to shred the large pile of documents with a basic office shredder so they were just thrown into the recycling bin.

(Continued)

(Continued)

Preventative measure: Ask your institution if there is an approved bulk shredding service available that can carry out the task instead of putting it out for recycling.

Scenario 2. A senior lecturer stores personal and confidential data on the hard drive of her university computer. She is given a new computer by her department, while the old one is given to research students to use in their office. The students are able to access both her personal and research data.

Preventative measure: Do not presume that IT services will clean or reformat the hard drive before passing on the computer. Always securely delete the data files stored on a hard drive when disposing of a computer. Only 'scrubbing' or physical destruction will sufficiently delete them from the machine.

Scenario 3. A researcher has a laptop stolen whilst away on a conference trip. Vital research data was kept on the hard drive and was not backed up anywhere else.

Preventative measure: Always keep a backup of data. When travelling you could remove all unnecessary data from the laptop and create a backup on an appropriate device and onto another hard-drive back at home/the office. Better still, you can encrypt devices such as laptops. Under the Data Protection Act you have a legal obligation to protect personal data relating to living people, for example, real names and addresses, so it should be stored securely, especially when travelling.

Scenario 4. A researcher sends a set of audio-cassettes for transcription in the post. The researcher writes the wrong address on the package and the tapes get lost in the post.

Preventative measure: Address packages carefully and send via a trackable courier service. Royal Mail offer special delivery services. Always make duplicate copies before sending.

Scenario 5. Digital audio files are emailed to a transcriber who saves them to his computer desktop and also stores them in his email once received. The transcriber fails to delete the files from his email and from his computer once the transcription is completed and returned to the researcher. He later sells his computer on eBay.

Preventative measure: Ask transcribers to sign an agreement to destroy their copies of the data once they have been returned and verify after transcription that this has indeed been done. It is best not to email files that you do not want to remain on other people's computer systems. You could encrypt the files before emailing them or send them via secure transmission.

Scenario 6. A researcher works in a shared office with four other researchers working on other projects. Whilst working on his project the researcher leaves paper copies of the signed consent forms loose on the desk. The other researchers have the opportunity to read through these confidential documents.

Preventative measure: Always keep confidential documentation and data in a locked filing cabinet. Don't keep the key in the lock; store the key in a secure place.

Scenario 7. A transcriber tells her friends and family about the 'interesting interview' that she is transcribing, giving details about the name and place of work of the interview participant.

Preventative measure: Ask transcribers to sign non-disclosure agreements, preventing them from divulging confidential information and remind them of the nature of information sent to them and their responsibility to keep that information confidential.

Scenario 8. A fire at the university destroys a research office and all the paper copies of an important research collection that a researcher was preparing for archiving.

Preventative measure: Always keep backup copies of important data in an offsite location. With important paper documents, these can be scanned and kept digitally.

Scenario 9. Unanonymized data are inadvertently published on a project's website.

Preventative measure: This is unacceptable. Unanonymized data must be kept safely and only accessed by those permitted to use it. Always double check that appropriate anonymization has been carried out before data are published.

Scenario 10. A researcher encrypts his data folder, then forgets his password and can no longer access his data.

Preventative measure: The researcher could also have kept a copy of the password but in a separate location to the data folder.

Discussion for Exercise 6.2

Unfortunately data safety and security breaches are not uncommon. All of the breaches discussed above are caused either by members of the research team or through unforeseen events such as fire. These non-malicious breaches are by far the most common, however all researchers should be aware that some breaches are caused through malice when someone who is determined to gain access to secure, confidential information uses unscrupulous or illegal means to obtain that data such as through hacking computers and stealing laptops.

Answers to Exercise 6.3

1. The best place to store your current paper-based research data overnight or when leaving the office, while you are actively using them on a daily basis is:

    (a) on your desk – Incorrect. This is not the ideal option if your data are important or unique, especially if you are in a shared office. It may be less problematic if you are in a single, lockable office and the only person with a key.

    (b) in an unlocked drawer – Incorrect. Again this is not the ideal option if you are in a shared office. It may be less problematic if you are in a single, lockable office and the only person with a key.

    (c) in a locked filing cabinet – Correct. This is the ideal solution to make sure that your data are kept safe, with minimal risk of losing them, especially if they contain personal information.

    (d) in a high security bank vault – Incorrect. Security needs to be at the optimal level, not the maximum level. This is inefficient, overly secure, and would be impossible to maintain.

(Continued)

(Continued)

2. Backing up your data:

    (a) protects against data loss or corruption – Correct. If your data files are deleted by mistake, become corrupted (unreadable) or the disk on which they are stored becomes unreadable, your files can be recovered from a backup.

    (b) preserves them forever – Incorrect, as backups can also be lost, or the medium on which they are kept can become damaged.

    (c) should be done regularly – Correct. This ensures your data are kept up-to-date and readable.

    (d) is the sole responsibility of your institution – Incorrect. Your institution may back up data on your networked drives but it is not the sole responsibility of the institution, you should also take responsibility for backing up your data, especially from laptops, portable devices or home computers.

3. To guard against file storage media corruption, how frequently should you replace backup tapes?

    (a) every day – Incorrect. This is overkill as tapes have a longer shelf-life than this.

    (b) every month – Incorrect. This is also unnecessary as tapes have a longer life than this, but if you are very cautious it would be acceptable.

    (c) every year – Incorrect. This is also unnecessary but, again, if you are cautious it would be acceptable.

    (d) every 2–5 years – Correct. This is the optimum time recommended to migrate files to new tapes; both optical (e.g. CDs) and magnetic (e.g. hard drives, tape) media are subject to degradation.

    (e) every 20 years – Incorrect. This is definitely not often enough; the risk is very high that after 20 years tapes are unreadable.

4. What should you do with paper-based data to ensure the longevity of the information?

    (a) store them in a temperature/humidity-controlled environment – Correct. This preserves paper longer. Moisture and warmth provide fuel for chemical reactions that cause paper deterioration, form ideal conditions for pest and mould infestations and cause physical damage to paper through swelling and shrinking.

    (b) store them in direct sunlight – Incorrect. Sunlight can cause print to fade rapidly and makes paper brittle.

    (c) convert them to PDF/A format and store in a location fit for purpose –Correct. PDF/A is a long-lasting digital preservation format.

    (d) store them in your attic – Incorrect. Unfortunately not! There may be some things kept safely in your attic, but research data are not one of them.

5. How can you protect the security of research participants' personal information in a dataset?

    (a) by anonymizing/reducing the precision of the data – Correct. This prevents identification of participants in data by masking disclosive information (See Chapter 7 for anonymization techniques).

    (b) by storing personal data such as names/addresses separately from the other data – Correct. Connections between administrative information and research data should be minimized and accessed via an ID number.

(c) by encrypting data containing personal information – Correct. Encryption offers controlled protection of data files; only people who know the encryption key can access the file.

(d) by requiring data users to sign the Official Secrets Act – Incorrect. This is really not necessary!

6. Encrypting files on your mobile storage device ensures that your digital data are:

(a) open for anyone to see – Incorrect. Encryption offers controlled protection of files; only people who know the encryption key can access the files.

(b) protected and only those with the encryption key can view them – Correct. Encryption offers controlled protection of files via a key or password.

(c) completely deleted – Incorrect. Encryption will not delete files.

(d) converted into a new format – Incorrect. Encryption offers controlled access to files but does not alter the format or integrity of files.

7. What ways would be suitable for transferring transcribed interview records to a colleague?

(a) via an unencrypted email attachment – Incorrect. This is not secure, especially if interviews contain personal information. Emails remain on public access servers and are not safe to store or transfer data.

(b) using Dropbox without encryption – Incorrect. This is not secure. Cloud storage is not as secure as may seem, as the stored files are held on servers in unspecified locations.

(c) using Dropbox with encryption – Correct. Encryption protects unauthorized access to files stored in this way.

(d) hand it in person to the recipient on a **USB** stick – Correct. This is fine, but make sure they look after it! Confirm that they have all the files you think you gave them.

8. How can you securely destroy data on a personal computer hard drive?

(a) delete files and reformat the hard drive – Incorrect. Data can still be retrieved by someone who knows how to do this, as deletion and reformatting only removes the links or pathway to where the files are kept on the hard drive.

(b) remove and destroy the hard drive – Correct. For secure destruction, hard drives should be physically destroyed and not just reformatted. Don't try stilettos, but a hammer might do nicely!

(c) delete files and take the computer to the dump – Incorrect. Data can still be retrieved by someone who knows how to do this.

(d) overwrite files using secure deletion software – Correct. Make sure you use approved software such as Government Standard software.

9. How can you securely destroy data on a **CD** or **DVD**?

(a) put it through a **CD** shredder and throw the shreds away – Correct. Once shredded there is no way anyone can piece together shredded plastic (and a small coating of aluminium)!

(b) break it in half and throw it away – Incorrect. Putting two pieces back together would not deter a determined data intruder.

(c) put it in the plastic recycling bin – Incorrect. And obviously **CDs** should be recycled with metals, not plastic!

(d) put it in the dishwasher on a hot cycle – Incorrect. The **CD** may survive this treatment. Try it out!

(e) overwrite files on the disc using proprietary software – Incorrect. This is certainly not failsafe, especially not for read-only discs.

(f) cut it up into little pieces with nail scissors – Correct. Well yes, failing access to a shredder.

References

Boston Computing Network (2013) *Data Loss Statistics*. Available at: http://www.bostoncomputing.net/consultation/databackup/statistics/.

British Library (2010) *Learning Sounds Familiar*, British Library. Available at:http://www.bl.uk/learning/langlit/sounds/credits/.

Burns, J. (2008) 'Atos could lose DWP contract after data loss', *Financial Times*, 3 November. Available at: http://www.ft.com/cms/s/0/6016afb0-a932-11dd-a19a-000077b07658.html#axzz2HfkTzv3G.

Copeland, B.J. (2006) *Colossus: The Secrets of Bletchley Park's Codebreaking Computers*. Oxford: Oxford University Press.

Curtis, P. (2005) 'Southampton fire expected to cost £50m', *The Guardian*, 31 October. Available at: www.guardian.co.uk/technology/2005/oct/31/news.research.

EPSRC (2011) *Data Policy Stipulations*, Engineering and Physical Sciences Research Council. Available at: http://www.dcc.ac.uk/resources/policy-and-legal/research-funding-policies/epsrc.

Finch, L. and Webster, J. (2008) *Caring for CDs and DVDs*. NPO Preservation Guidance, Preservation in Practice Series. Available at: www.bl.uk/blpac/pdf/cd.pdf.

Kahn, D. (1996) *The Codebreakers - The Story of Secret Writing*. New York: Scribner.

MD5summer (2013) *MD5summer*. Available at: www.md5summer.org/.

MRC (2012) *Archiving: Data and Tissues Tool Kit*, Medical Research Council. Available at: http://www.dt-toolkit.ac.uk/researchscenarios/archiving.cfm.

National Archives of Australia (2011) *Digital Preservation Policy*, National Archives of Australia. Available at: http://www.naa.gov.au/about-us/organisation/accountability/operations-and-preservation/digital-preservation-policy.aspx.

Singh, S. (1999) *The Code Book: The Science of Secrecy from Ancient Egypt to Quantum Cryptography*. London: Fourth Estate.

The National Archives (1998a) *The Data Protection Act 1998*, The National Archives. Available at: http://www.legislation.gov.uk/ukpga/1998/29/contents.

UK Data Archive (2011) *Preservation Policy*, UK Data Archive, University of Essex. Available at: http://www.data-archive.ac.uk/media/54776/ukda062-dps-preservationpolicy.pdf.

UK Data Archive (2012) *Microdata Handling and Security. Guide to Good Practice*, UK Data Archive, University of Essex. Available at: http://www.data-archive.ac.uk/media/132701/ukda171-ss-microdatahandling.pdf.

UK Data Archive (2013) *UK Data Archive Public Key*, UK Data Archive, University of Essex. Available at: http://www.data-archive.ac.uk/media/249917/ukdataarchive.zip.

Winnett, R. (2008) 'Home Office loses confidential data on all UK prisoners', *The Telegraph*, 21 August. Available at: www.telegraph.co.uk/news/uknews/law-and-order/2598204/Home-Office-loses-confidential-data-on-all-UK-prisoners.html.

SEVEN
Legal and Ethical Issues in Sharing Data

Collecting, using and sharing data in research with human subjects requires that ethical and legal obligations be respected. Most countries have laws that cover the use of data, but the scope of these laws varies widely. In addition to the legal requirements when working with human subjects, every researcher is expected to maintain high ethical standards. Every academic discipline has its own tailored guidelines produced by professional bodies and relevant funding organizations. Most institutions are also signed up to a code of conduct for researchers that ensures research integrity is maintained by its researchers (UK Research Integrity Office, 2009)

In this chapter we examine the main topics concerning legal and ethical matters that are most relevant to reusing and sharing data: confidentiality, informed consent, safe handling of data and strategies for sharing data. Following best practices and appropriate protocols, even sensitive and confidential research data can be shared legally and ethically.

The Legal Landscape

Most countries have legislation that covers the use of personal and organizational information and national data sources. In Europe, a cross-national approach has been taken, embodied in the European Union Data Directive, adopted in 1995. Member states were required to bring their national laws into compliance with that Directive. The UK adopted its Data Protection Act in 1998. In Germany, considered to have the strictest data protection regulation in the world, privacy is a constitutional right under the Volkszählungsurteil of 1983 and the Federal Data Protection Act, Bundesdatenschutzgesetz, formulates legal requirements to inform people of the purposes of collecting, processing or use of personal data and stipulates that consent must be given in written form. In other European countries, the nature of protection varies greatly, with countries like Norway following the EU Directive, even though they are not EU members, and others with very few, if any, protections in place.

In 2012, the European Parliament began discussing a proposed EU Data Protection Regulation to harmonize inconsistencies in implementation and enforcement of data protection legislation across the EU member states.

In the USA, there is no similar comprehensive legislation. Instead, there are sector-specific laws that define how any personal information may be used in separate areas such as medical and credit records, with much more reliance on self-regulation (Singer, 2013).

McAfee provides a comprehensive list of privacy and data protection legislation in countries around the world (McAfee, 2013).

UK: Data Protection Act 1998

Data protection regards the rights of an individual to know what data are being held by data controllers, how it is being used and to correct inaccuracies. The 1998 Data Protection Act (DPA) was formulated in response to individuals' concerns about the amount of personal information, and the accuracy of such information, being stored, processed and passed on by organizations or individuals (The National Archives, 1998a).

The **DPA** defines eight principles that deal with processing personal data relating to identifiable living people. All such data must be:

- processed fairly and lawfully;
- obtained and processed for a specified purpose;
- adequate, relevant and not excessive for the purpose;
- accurate;
- not kept longer than necessary;
- processed in accordance with the rights of data subjects, for example, the right to be informed about how data will be used, stored, processed, transferred, destroyed, and the right to access information and data held;
- kept secure;
- not transferred abroad without adequate protection.

An important point for researchers is that the Act provides some exemptions for personal data that is processed only for research, statistical, historical or other specific purposes among others. Furthermore, in the context of social research, the **DPA** applies only to personal or sensitive personal data, and not to all research data in general gathered from participants. Most importantly, the Act does not apply to anonymized data.

UK Data Protection Act 1998 Definitions

The **DPA** defines data, personal data, sensitive personal data, data controllers and data processors (Information Commissioner's Office, 2013a). If you are dealing with human subjects, it is important to understand each of these terms in relation to your research.

Data controller: a person or organization who either alone, or jointly, or in common with other persons, determines the purposes for which, and the manner in which any personal data are, or are to be, processed.

In research terms, this may be you as an individual or it may be your employer. While a data processor may be designated or out-sourced by the data controller, the data controller is always held responsible for compliance. Obligations apply throughout the period when you are processing personal data, as do the rights of individuals in respect of that personal data. In essence, you need to comply with the Act from the point at which you obtain the data until the time when the data has been destroyed, or fully anonymized.

Data processor: any person, other than an employee of the data controller, who processes the data on behalf of the data controller.

Personal data: records or other information that, on their own, or linked with other data or information in the possession of the data controller, can reveal the identity of an actual living person.

For example, if you de-identify individuals in a survey by allocating a numeric identifier to each person these data will technically remain personal if you (the data controller) have another file which links that numeric information to the real names or other personal information. Each record would be considered to contain personal information.

If you are able to process anonymized data instead of personal data for your research by destroying the linkage key between the identifiers and the personally identifying information, then you are likely to be exempt from the DPA entirely.

Sensitive personal data: personal data combined with information on a person's race, ethnic origin, political opinion, religious or similar beliefs, trade union membership, physical or mental health or condition, sexual life, committing or alleged committing of an offence, proceedings for an offence (alleged to have been) committed, disposal of such proceedings or the sentence of any court in such proceedings. The safest way to avoid worrying about sensitive personal data is to avoid collecting or holding information to do with these topics at all, unless your research actually requires it.

On the whole there are few examples of breaches of personal data in research, but like the cases of data loss highlighted in Chapter 6, there have been some accidental breaches of the UK's DPA. The Information Commissioner's Office has the power to issue penalties of up to £500,000 for serious breaches of the DPA (Information Commissioner's Office, 2013b).

| CASE STUDIES | Public Breaches Regarding Personal Data |

NHS Trust facing £375,000 fine over theft of patient data

Brighton and Sussex University Hospitals NHS Trust told Out-Law.com that hard drives containing patient data had been sold on the auction website by a contractor it employed to destroy them. A spokesperson for the Information Commissioner's

(Continued)

(Continued)

Office (ICO) said the watchdog had proposed fining the Trust £375,000 over the incident. The Trust has challenged the suggested penalty. (Pinsent Masons, 2012)

Police force fined £120,000 after theft of unencrypted memory stick

A police force has been fined £120,000 following the theft of a memory stick containing names of members of the public who gave statements in drug investigations. The unencrypted device with no password protection was stolen from an officer's home and had details of 1,075 people with links to serious crime investigations stored over an 11-year-period. (Press Association, 2012)

Troubled families tsar Louise Casey criticized over research: Report into dysfunctional households breached ethical standards, claims researcher

Using freedom of information requests, Nick Bailey, a lecturer in the University of Glasgow's School of Social and Political Sciences, claims that the head of the Troubled Families Unit, Louise Casey, did not 'seek or obtain ethical approval' from families interviewed in a much-heralded report published in July. Bailey also points out that while the names of the 16 families interviewed had been changed, the details on the number, age and gender of children had not, making it possible to identify them. (Ramesh, 2012)

As we mentioned earlier, the legislation on data protection in the USA is not as unified as in Europe but there is one sector with comprehensive legislation covering personal health information. The Health Insurance Portability and Accountability Act (HIPAA) Privacy Rule was passed in 1996 providing for both greater integration of health information and also privacy protection. The National Institutes of Health provides detailed guidance for researchers, explaining what is and is not covered by HIPAA requirements (National Institutes of Health, 2013).

UK: Other Key Legislation

In the UK, there is additional international and national legislation that may impact on the sharing of confidential data.

Human Rights Act 1998

Article 8 of the Human Rights Act 1998 enshrines the right to respect for one's private and family life, one's home and one's correspondence (The National Archives, 1998b). Researchers need to keep this in mind where it concerns using data that relate to human beings. Where data sharing is covered by, and complies with, the DPA then it is almost certain that it will also comply with HRA Article 8 (Ministry of Justice, 2011).

Statistics and Registration Services Act 2007

The Statistics and Registration Services Act 2007 is mainly concerned with the structure and function of the UK Statistics Authority and applies only to data designated as Official Statistics (The National Archives, 2007). Data access is an express statutory function of the Statistics Authority and the Act defines the legal gateways under which personal information can be disclosed. According to the Act, information identifies a particular person if the identity of that person is specified in the information, can be deduced from the information, or can be deduced from the information taken together with any other published information.

The Act allows disclosure of personal information to an 'Approved Researcher', that is, an individual to whom the Statistics Authority has granted access to personal information held for the purposes of statistical research. The criteria for access require the Statistics Authority to consider whether the individual is a fit and proper person, and the purpose for which access is requested. The Act also states that disclosure of personal information outside of the legal gateways is a criminal offence.

Although the Act does not apply to individual researchers managing confidential research data not designated as Official Statistics, such researchers might wish to adapt the Approved Researcher model for access to highly confidential data, as for example the UK Data Service has done for ESRC-funded data (UK Data Service, 2013a).

Environmental Information Regulations 2004

The Environmental Information Regulations 2004 give the public access rights to environmental information held by a public authority, including universities, in response to requests (The National Archives, 2004). This Regulation is similar to the Freedom of Information Act and both are discussed in more detail in Chapter 8 on rights. Freedom of access does not imply free access. There are circumstances under which requests may or must be refused, for example if the data contain personal information.

Protection of Freedoms Act 2012

This Act, passed in 2012 in the UK, provides for the destruction, retention, use and other regulation of certain evidential material, for example, imposing consent and other requirements in relation to processing of biometric information and surveillance data (The National Archives, 2012). This Act is unlikely to concern researchers.

Common Law to Protect Confidentiality
Duty of Confidentiality

In the UK there exists a duty of confidentiality that is based in common law, not in legislation. It applies only to information not already in the public domain. It applies when a provider supplies information, in confidence, to a recipient. If an explicit statement of agreement has been made on the extent of the confidentiality to be afforded to the provider of the information, for example, in a consent form, this may constitute a contract. This need not be in writing. Disclosure of information subject to such a confidentiality agreement would constitute a breach of the duty of confidentiality and possibly a breach of contract. A duty of confidentiality can also arise without an explicit statement, for example, when it has been supplied in circumstances in which the confidant might reasonably suppose it to be confidential.

The duty of confidentiality is not absolute and is not protected by legal privilege. Researchers may be required to give up research data in response to a court subpoena, or to the police as part of an on-going investigation.

Chatham House Rule

The world-renowned Chatham House Rule can be invoked at meetings to encourage openness and the sharing of information. Chatham House, home of the Royal Institute of International Affairs in the UK, is a think tank whose aims are independent analysis of and informed debate on critical global, regional and country-specific challenges. The Chatham House Rule is used to help facilitate free speech and confidentiality at meetings. The Rule states that:

> When a meeting, or part thereof, is held under the **Chatham House Rule**, participants are free to use the information received, but neither the identity nor the affiliation of the speaker(s), nor that of any other participant, may be revealed. (Chatham House, 2013)

For a researcher this means that when undertaking fieldwork, anything recorded or minuted under the Chatham House Rule needs to be flagged as such, with a clear record of where the Rule might apply to the recording or minutes of a meeting, so that the speaker's request is upheld. We would advocate that such information should not to be shared beyond the primary researcher, unless the original participant is consulted about its subsequent use.

Summary for Legal Section

The legal terrain for managing and sharing data can appear overwhelming, especially for researchers starting their first project. It is true that there are more laws and guidelines than in the recent past, and the landscape is constantly changing. In early 2013, there was growing tension between the USA and the EU regarding data protection (Singer, 2013) and even more troubling, the German MEP, Jan-Phillipp Albrecht proposed amendments to the EU data protection law that would require explicit consent for data reuse, dramatically curtailing all secondary research (Ustaran, 2013). Despite all the complexity and uncertainties for the future, a few key points are useful to remember:

- find out early what laws may apply to you;
- do not collect any personal or sensitive data not essential for your research;
- get advice from your research office.

Personal Data: Summary for Researchers

Before you embark on data collection, consider these things:

- *Do you really need to collect personal data?* Often information such as participants' names and addresses are collected for administrative purposes only and have no research value. Not collecting personal data in the first place may make it easier to manage and share your data. Alternatively if they do need to be collected, for example, for follow-up interviews, they should be stored separately from research data.
- *Inform your participants about use of personal data.* Inform research participants about how any personal data collected about them will be used, stored, processed, transferred and destroyed. Personal data can only be disclosed if explicit consent has been given to do so, although there may be exceptions for legal reasons.
- *Not all research data obtained from participants constitute personal data.* If data are anonymized, for example with key personal identifiers removed, then the Data Protection Act will not apply as they no longer constitute personal data.

Many organizations, including archives, have in-house procedures for staff on how to handle and store personal information while they are working on these sources. The case study below shows what procedures are in place for staff at the UK Data Archive.

| CASE STUDY | Handling Personal Information at the UK Data Archive |

At the UK Data Archive all staff sign a non-disclosure agreement, in view of the Archive's responsibility for ensuring that information assets within its care are only accessible to employees of the Archive and other authorized individuals. In particular, the Archive is responsible for ensuring the necessary level of protection for data that have been identified by their creators or by the Archive as being in some way disclosive, including containing personal data or personal information. The Agreement is designed to protect the Archive and the host university against any unauthorized release of the Archive's classified information assets outside of the Archive and the university. It is also one step in ensuring the compliance

(Continued)

(Continued)

of the Archive to ISO 27001, a code of practice for information security management (ISO 27001 Directory, 2013). Agreements include:

- marking or otherwise designating personal data or personal information (according to the Archive's Information Classification Policy) to show that it has been imparted in confidence, with staff taking all proper and reasonable measures to ensure that the confidentiality of such information is maintained;
- staff agreeing, at all times during their current contract of employment and thereafter in perpetuity, not to communicate or to divulge to third parties any personal data or personal information which they encounter during their work at the Archive;
- staff protecting Archive Information Assets in accordance with the provisions and principles of the Data Protection Act 1998 and its amendments.

Any incidents of unauthorized access to, processing of, or disclosing of the Archive Information Assets must be reported immediately to the Archive's Data Security Manager, and any breach of the Agreement may lead to disciplinary action being taken in accordance with any relevant disciplinary or breaches procedure.

Ethical Frameworks for Research

Ethical guidelines for research involving human subjects are published by professional bodies, host institutions and funding organizations. The six key principles for UK social science research ethics as defined by the Economic and Social Research Council (ESRC) are:

1. Research should be designed, reviewed and undertaken to ensure integrity, quality and transparency.
2. Research staff and participants must normally be informed fully about the purpose, methods and intended possible uses of the research, what their participation in the research entails and what risks, if any, are involved.
3. The confidentiality of information supplied by research participants and the anonymity of respondents must be respected.
4. Research participants must take part voluntarily, free from any coercion.
5. Harm to research participants and researchers must be avoided in all instances.
6. The independence of research must be clear, and any conflicts of interest or partiality must be explicit. (ESRC, 2012)

The principles of research ethics that have direct bearing on sharing or archiving confidential research data are informed consent, anonymity, and risks of future uses of data.

Informed Consent, Permissions and Data Handling
Core Principles of Consent

The Nuremberg Code 1947 and the Helsinki Declaration 1964 form the foundations for consent in research with human subjects (HHS, 2005; World Health

Organization, 2008). The resulting requirement is for valid consent, meaning consent that is competent, informed and voluntary.

Researchers are usually expected to obtain informed consent from people to participate in research and for use of the information collected. The situation is different across European countries with some countries asking for research projects to meet more stringent requirements than others, for example using signed consent forms. Here we address the UK situation where all proposals for research involving human subjects require ethics approval. In the USA, ethics approval and written consent is also mandatory.

Consent should take into account uses of data throughout the data lifecycle, from its creation to long-term preservation. At a minimum, consent forms should not preclude data sharing, such as by promising to destroy data unnecessarily.

When seeking consent to participate in research, researchers should provide participants with information about:

- the research and nature of their participation and withdrawal;
- how confidentiality will be maintained, e.g. by anonymizing data;
- options for varied consent conditions for participation, publication and data sharing;
- how research data will be stored and preserved in the long-term;
- how data may used for future research or teaching, including any restrictions on that use.

There are examples where consent for participation is more implicit, such as agreeing to have information shared by virtue of taking part in an activity or programme. For example, when applying for a store loyalty card one agrees that the store can use all the information collected for their own analytic and marketing purposes.

Reconciling Informed Consent with Unknown Future Uses

Data archiving raises questions specific to the requirement that consent be 'informed'. Once data are available to future researchers, the specific research projects or questions for which data may be used cannot be known in advance. However, participants can be informed about the possible ways in which their data will be used and by whom. Researchers can give examples to participants of how similar data have been reused and can inform them about possible options for limiting usage to the research community once data are archived with trusted repositories. Archives often impose terms and conditions of access to and for the use of data including: not breaching confidentiality; no further sharing of data with other people; and no use for commercial purposes. It is also possible to restrict access to particular groups of users.

There are some parallels with consent requirements for human tissue biobanks where future uses may be unknown, even though disclosure risks and potential for social benefits are likely to differ between medical and social research. The Council of Europe's *Convention on Human Rights and Biomedicine, concerning Biomedical Research* states that consent need not be specific, but it must be as specific as possible with regard to unforeseen uses (Kozlakidis, 2012). This approach, called broad, enduring or open consent, has produced high rates of participation (over 99%) in some instances, such as at the Wales Cancer Bank (2007).

Formats for Consent

Whether informed consent is obtained in writing through a detailed consent form, by means of an informative statement, or verbally, depends on the nature of the research, the kind of data gathered, the data format and how the data will be used.

For detailed interviews or research where personal, sensitive or confidential data are gathered:

- the use of written consent forms is recommended to assure compliance with the Data Protection Act and with ethical guidelines of professional bodies and funders;
- written consent typically includes an information sheet and consent form signed by the participant;
- verbal consent agreements can be recorded together with audio or video recorded data;
- different consent agreements for sharing may be necessary for different types of data, according to the likelihood of disclosing participants' identities; for example, less restrictive access conditions may be negotiated for anonymized transcripts with more restrictions placed on disclosive images.

For surveys, where personal identifiers such as people's names are not collected or not included in the digital data file can be easily removed from the data file, or where responses would only be used in aggregate form, written consent is often not gathered. Instead, the information sheet provided to participants would state that consent for the data being used for specified purposes is implied from participating in the survey, with a clause stating that an individual's responses would not be used in any way that would allow his/her identification. The information sheet should also detail the nature and scope of the study, the identity of the researcher(s) and what will happen to data collected, including any data sharing.

Practically, a consent form and information sheet should affirm the commitment to confidentiality where this is required. Broad but vague statements should be avoided and replaced with more specific explanations of how confidentiality will be maintained in future data analyses, such as by anonymizing records or controlling access. Sample consent forms and appropriate wording are available from various sources (Division of Health Research, 2013; ICPSR, 2013; National Research Ethics Service, 2012; UK Data Service, 2013b). While there is often a fear of risk of disclosure in research, this is typically more theoretical than practical. As we shall see later in this chapter, an appreciation of disclosure control techniques is useful in safeguarding data where confidentiality has been promised.

When to Seek Consent

As with all aspects of consent, the timing of when to seek it should balance the need for consent to be informed with careful consideration of when participants are best informed to make decisions. Consent needs, eventually, to address not only research participation, but also dissemination and sharing of data. However, these consent needs can be phased. Clearly, consent for research participation needs to be addressed first. At that time, it is also advisable to provide general information about possible dissemination channels and the intent to share. Completion of the consent process for dissemination and sharing of data that a participant contributes during the research can wait until the data have been collected. At this stage a participant is better positioned to be able to assess, retrospectively, any issues of confidentiality, prospects for how the data might be used, assignment of copyright, and so on.

Depending on the nature of the research, consent can either be a one-time, one-off occurrence or a more on-going process:

> *One-off consent* is simple, practical, and avoids possibly burdensome requests to participants for re-consent. Consent is gained early in the research process and covers all aspects of participation and data use. For research where no confidential or sensitive information is gathered, for example, some surveys, or where there will be only a single contact with the participant, this is usually sufficient and most practical. Criticism of this method is that it places too much emphasis on 'ticking boxes'. When research is more exploratory, or not all data uses, research outputs and methods are known in advance, or for many kinds of longitudinal research, a more process-oriented approach is usually preferred.

> *Process consent* is considered throughout the research cycle and assures active informed consent from participants. This is generally recommended, such as by the ESRC's Framework for Research Ethics (2012) and is especially important in a research design which involves more than one point of contact with a participant. Consent for various uses of data can be sought after their research contribution is complete. The risks of this approach include loss of contact with participants before all consent procedures have been completed and annoying participants with repeated consent requests.

A study in Finland by their national social science data archive found that participants were far more open to future uses of data by others than researchers often believe. The case study below sheds some light on our tendency, as researchers, to err on the side of 'over-protecting' participants in our research.

CASE STUDY	**Finnish Social Science Data Archive Retrospective Consent Study (Based on Kuula, 2011)**

Researchers collecting qualitative data often assume that research participants would not accept the idea of archiving their data. To check this assumption, staff from the Finnish Social Science Data Archive (FSD) asked a number of researchers to let them re-contact

(Continued)

(Continued)

their research participants. A joint letter to participants reminded them of the research project and informed them about the possibility of having their data archived, with their consent, for future reuse by other researchers. In follow-up phone interviews with participants, issues about the research, archiving and terms of future use of the data were fruitfully discussed.

For the re-contact project, four studies were chosen: three interview studies and one consisting of university students' written life stories. One interview dataset comprised discussions of equality and gender issues in working life, another concentrated on environmental conflicts, and the third focused on the life and experiences of women living in the Finnish countryside.

Notwithstanding the problem of locating research participants after a study has been completed, the team were able to find and re-contact 169 research participants, of whom 98% (165) agreed to archive their data; only four did not accept the idea of archiving. All datasets included unique and personal stories, and occasionally sensitive experiences about the issues at hand. The interviews with rural women had taken two to four hours and were very candid; participants had spoken widely about the joys and miseries of their personal lives. Despite initial concern that consent would not be granted for this dataset, every one of those women agreed to the idea of archiving the interviews for future research purposes.

The team learned that the main reason for participants giving consent for archiving was a desire to advance science; people had participated in the research because they had thought the subjects of the interviews were worth studying. Agreeing to share these data meant continuing to fulfil this wish. One research participant also noted that the original research results had not convinced him, and he warmly welcomed re-analysis by different researchers representing different disciplines. Others were slightly irritated by the re-contact because they already believed that any future and as yet unknown use of the data by researchers would not conflict in any way with their original decision to participate in the research.

The literature on informed consent is extensive, and an excellent overview is provided by Wiles et al. (2005). For those interested, debates about the best ways of handling consent for reusing qualitative data have been published (Bishop, 2009; Broom et al., 2009; Mauthner, 2012).

Anonymizing Data

Before data obtained from research with human subjects can be shared with other researchers or archived, they may need to be anonymized, or redacted, so that individuals, organizations or businesses cannot be identified. This could be for ethical reasons to protect people's identities in research, for legal reasons to avoid disclosure of personal data, or for commercial reasons. Personal data should never be disclosed from research information, unless a participant has given specific consent to do so, ideally in writing. In some forms of research, for example where oral histories are recorded or in some anthropological research, it is customary to publish and share the names of people studied, for which they have given their consent.

While anonymization processes aim to create 'safer' data, it is worth remembering that reusers of data via a trusted archive usually have the same legal and ethical obligations as primary users not to disclose confidential information. Procedures to anonymize data should always be considered alongside obtaining informed consent for data sharing or imposing access restrictions. Any strategy used should aim for a balance between removing or replacing disclosive information with retaining as much meaningful information as possible. Anonymizing research data can be time-consuming and therefore costly, but early planning helps reduce these costs.

Below are recommendations for anonymizing quantitative and qualitative data appropriately. Extensive detailed advice about anonymization procedures has also been published by the Information Commissioner's Office (2012).

Identifiers in Data

A person's identity can be disclosed from:

- *direct identifiers* such as names, addresses, postcode information, telephone numbers or pictures;
- *indirect identifiers* which, especially in combination with other publicly available information sources, could identify someone, such as information on workplace, occupation or exceptional values of characteristics like salary or age.

Direct identifiers are often collected as part of the research administration process but are usually not essential research information and can therefore easily be removed from the data.

Anonymizing Quantitative Data

Anonymization techniques for quantitative data may involve removing or aggregating variables or reducing the precision or detailed textual meaning of a variable. Special attention may be needed for relational data, where connections between variables in related datasets can disclose identities, and for georeferenced data, where identifying spatial references also have a geographical value.

For quantitative data, various anonymization techniques are recommended as follows:

- *Remove direct identifiers* from a dataset such as detailed personal information; such identifiers are often not necessary for secondary research.

Example: Remove respondents' names or replace with a code. Remove addresses, postcode information, institution and telephone numbers.

- *Aggregate or reduce the precision of a variable* such as the respondent's age and place of residence. As a general rule, report the lowest level of georeferencing that will not potentially breach respondent confidentiality. The exact scale depends on the type of data collected, but very detailed georeferences like full postcodes, wards or names of small towns or villages are likely to be problematic. Coded or categorical variables that may be potentially revealing can be aggregated into broader codes.

Example: Record the year of birth rather than the day, month and year; record postcode sectors (first 3 or 4 digits) rather than full postcodes; aggregate detailed 'unit group' standard occupational classification employment codes up to 'minor group' codes by removing the last digit.

- *Generalize the meaning of a detailed text variable* by replacing potentially disclosive free-text responses with more general text.

Example: Detailed areas of medical expertise could indirectly identify a doctor. The expertise variable could be replaced by more general text or be coded into generic responses such as 'one area of medical speciality' or 'two or more areas of medical speciality'.

- *Restrict the upper or lower ranges* of a continuous variable to hide outliers if the values for certain individuals are unusual or atypical within the wider group researched. In such circumstances the unusually large or small values might be collapsed into a single code, even if the other responses are kept as actual quantities, or one might code all responses.

Example: Annual salary could be top-coded to avoid identifying highly paid individuals. A top code of £100,000 or more could be applied, even if lower incomes are not coded into groups.

- *Anonymize relational data* where relationships between variables in related or linked datasets, or in combination with other publicly available outputs, may disclose identities.

Example: In confidential interviews on farms the names of farmers have been replaced with codes and other confidential information on the nature of the farm businesses and their locations have been disguised to anonymize the data. If related biodiversity data collected on the same farms, using the same farmer codes, contain detailed locations for biodiversity data alone, the farm location would no longer be confidential. Farmers could be identified by combining the two datasets. The link between farmer codes and biodiversity location data should be removed, for example by using separate codes for farmer interviews and for farm locations in published data.

- *Anonymize georeferenced data* by replacing point coordinates with non-disclosing geographical features or variables. Point data fixes the position of individuals, organizations or businesses studied, which could disclose their identity. Point coordinates may be replaced by larger, non-disclosing geographical areas such as polygon features (km² grid, postcode district, county), or linear features (random line, road, river). Point data can also be replaced by meaningful alternative variables that typify the geographical position and represent the reason why the locality was selected for the research, such as poverty index, population density, altitude and vegetation type. In this way, the value of data is maintained, whilst removing disclosing georeferences. A better option may be to keep detailed spatial references intact and to impose access controls on the data instead, as this would enable the data to be used in geospatial applications or for data linkage, under controlled circumstances.

This is, for example, the strategy used by the *Understanding Society* study – a longitudinal study carried out by the Institute for Social and Economic Research; the study's data are distributed via the UK Data Archive (University of Essex et al., 2013). Whilst the core dataset from this study, with the location of each household reduced to Government Office Region, is available under standard access conditions, the detailed location of each household surveyed, as British National Grid references at 1m resolution, are made available for research purposes via secure access. In this way, the study's data can, within this secure environment, be linked to a wide range of administrative and other survey data.

Statistical Disclosure Techniques

The use of confidential microdata for research requires giving researchers access to detailed disclosive data within a controlled environment. The controlled environment enables researchers to freely work with data but all statistical results and outputs are thoroughly checked for confidentiality. This is known as output-based statistical disclosure control (**SDC**), which contrasts with the more traditional input-based **SDC** where the dataset was anonymized, or redacted, before research access is given, in order to prevent disclosure risk (Ritchie, 2007). It basically means that checks are made to see whether particular individuals can be identified from the content of the output. **SDC** is not something that can be carried out automatically; it requires agreed understanding of the outputs being checked, the potential disclosure risks, and an agreed level of acceptable risk.

Ritchie identifies three methods of disclosure detection:

* primary disclosure: identifying information in table cells;
* secondary disclosure: identifying information by inference from totals or other sources;
* transforming data to make them non-disclosive. (Ritchie, 2007)

The method is judged as sufficient when a guarantee of confidentiality can be maintained, for example according to a pre-agreed standard. For the Office of National Statistics this is:

It would take a disproportionate amount of time, effort and expertise for an intruder to identify a statistical unit to others, or to reveal information about that unit not already in the public domain. (Office for National Statistics, 2004)

Threshold rules are usually set, for example cell counts in tables might be considered non-confidential if the frequency of units is at least five. Higher frequencies may be necessary if there is insufficient variation in the data or the data can be identified with a small number of statistical units. The following example shows how cell counts might be checked for confidentiality.

Primary Disclosure Example Based on Ritchie (2007)

Primary disclosure is the direct identification of an individual (or organization) from the data content of a table cell. In Table 7.1, which displays levels of turnover for companies in various industry groups, we can assess whether any of the cells are disclosive.

Table 7.1 Primary disclosure: outputs table

Industry	No. of companies	Total turnover	Turnover ←1,000	Turnover →1,000
101	2	2,000	1	1
102	1	100	1	0
103	6	5,000	6	0
Total	9	7,100	8	1

Source: Ritchie, 2007

In this table all the counts for companies in industry 102 are disclosive because the values for one company are visible. The counts for industry 101 are also disclosive because each company in industry 101, knowing its own turnover figure, can identify the figures for the other company. The counts for industry 103 are not disclosive, according to ONS rules (more than five, as described above), yet if five of the six companies in industry 103 got together they could identify the values for the other company. This is unlikely but it would be necessary to suppress the results.

The rules that govern access to disclosive data within a particular safe environment need to be fully understood by users. Best practice and training must always be part of this process. We discuss how archives operate this practice in the section on controlling access later in this chapter.

Anonymizing Qualitative Data

For the anonymization of qualitative material, such as transcribed interviews, textual or audio-visual data, pseudonyms or vaguer descriptors should be used to deal with any problematic identifying information. This is preferable to blanking out information as it helps to maintain data integrity. Consideration should be given to the level of anonymity required to meet the needs agreed during the informed consent process. Obtaining informed consent for data sharing or regulating access to data should also be considered together with anonymization.

Researchers should not presume the only way to maintain confidentiality is by keeping data hidden.

Pre-planning and agreeing with participants during the consent process what may and may not be recorded or transcribed can be a much more effective way of creating data that accurately represents the research process and the contribution of participants. For example, if an employer's name cannot be disclosed, it should be agreed in advance that it will not be mentioned during an interview. This is easier than spending time later removing it from a recording or transcript.

Often researchers presume that participants want their data destroyed or kept confidential and inaccessible. However, they might be quite willing to have their data shared with other researchers if appropriate pseudonyms and other protections are provided.

Anonymizing Text

Best practices for anonymizing text are to:

- not collect disclosive data unless this is necessary, for example, not ask for full names if they cannot be used;
- plan anonymization at the time of transcription or initial write up, except for longitudinal studies where relationships between materials may require special attention during editing;
- use pseudonyms or replacements that are consistent within the research team and throughout the project, for example, the same pseudonyms in publications or follow-up research;
- use 'search and replace' techniques carefully so that unintended changes are not made, and misspelled words are not missed;
- identify replacements in text clearly, for example with [brackets] or using XML (Extensible Mark-up Language) tags such as '<anonsec> section to be anonymized <anonsec>';
- retain unedited versions of data for use within the research team and for preservation;
- create an anonymization log of all replacements, aggregations or removals made, storing such a log separately from the anonymized data files; an example is shown in Table 7.2.

Table 7.2   Example anonymization log

Interview and page number	Original name	Changed to
Int1 p1	Age 27	Age range 20–30
Int1 p1	Spain	European country
Int1 p2	20th June	June
Int1 p2	Amy (real name)	Moira (pseudonym)
Int1 p3	Manchester	Northern metropolitan city or English provincial city
Int1 p4	Aunty Jean	aunt
Int2 p1	Francis	my friend
Int2 p8	Station Road primary school	a primary school
Int2 p10	Head Buyer, Produce, Sainsbury's	Senior Executive with leading supermarket chain
Int2 p11	North Colchester	North part of town

Table 7.2 shows how an interview transcript might be pseudonymized: real names of people are replaced with pseudonyms or with a label that typifies the person [Senior Executive with leading supermarket, aunt]; an exact geographical location may be replaced with a meaningful descriptive term that typifies the location [Northern metropolitan city, English provincial city, northern part of town].

Online Tools for Anonymizing Text

There is a range of tools available to partially automate some of the most straightforward processes of anonymizing text. ICPSR hosts a web-based tool called QualAnon which is simple to use, requiring the user to upload two files: the text and a name key that includes names to be changed with their replacement pseudonyms or codes. The tool returns the anonymized file along with a report (ICPSR, 2012). A similar tool is available from the Irish Qualitative Data Archive.

Anonymizing Audio-Visual Data

Anonymization of digital audio-visual data, such as editing of audio recordings or digital images, should be done sensitively. Bleeping out real names or place names is acceptable, but disguising voices by altering the pitch in a recording, or obscuring faces by pixellating sections of a video image significantly reduces the usefulness of data for research. These processes are also highly labour-intensive and expensive.

If confidentiality of audio-visual data is an issue, it is better to obtain the participant's consent to use and share the data in an unaltered form. Otherwise it is possible to impose access controls that are appropriate for those data files.

Regulating Access to Data

There are a growing number of options for sharing data, each with different strengths and weaknesses. We cover these options in detail in Chapter 11 on Publishing and Citing Research Data. If you are required to share your data, you will need to consider who would be able to access your data; what they are able to do with it; whether any specific use restrictions are required; and for how long you want the data to be available. Depending on how you answer these questions, different facilities for sharing and providing access to data will be appropriate.

If you decide you want some control over when to share your data, most data centres and institutional repositories will consider delaying publication for a limited period. An embargo of 18 months might be agreed to allow the primary investigators to publish findings. Longer periods of closure can be agreed if, for example, a special agreement was made between the researcher and participants.

Under certain circumstances, sensitive and confidential data can be safeguarded by regulating or restricting access to and use of data. Data centres and repositories have differing levels of capabilities in offering options for controlling access to data.

| CASE STUDY | Spectrum of Access at the UK Data Archive |

Most of the data collections held at the UK Data Archive are not in the public domain. Their use is restricted to specific purposes after user registration. Users agree an End User Licence which has contractual force in law, in which they agree to certain conditions, such as not to disseminate any identifying or confidential information on individuals, households or organizations; and not to use the data to attempt to obtain information relating specifically to an identifiable individual.

Thus users can use data for research purposes, but cannot publish or exploit them in a way that would disclose people's or organizations' identities. Controlling access to data should never be seen as the only way to protect confidentiality. As we saw earlier, a combination of obtaining appropriate informed consent and anonymizing data enable most data to be shared.

For confidential data, the Archive, in discussion with the data owner, may impose additional access controls:

- specific authorization needed from the data owner to access data;
- placing confidential data under embargo for a given period of time until confidentiality concerns are no longer pertinent;
- providing access to Approved Researchers only;
- providing secure access to data by enabling remote analysis of confidential data but excluding the ability to download or take data away.

Access controls should always be proportionate to the kind of data and the level of confidentiality involved and an assessment of the risks involved in the disclosure. Mixed levels of access control may be put in place for some data, combining standard access to non-confidential data with controlled access to confidential data.

In the USA, the National Opinions Research Centre (NORC) set up the first data enclave in 2008 providing a confidential, protected virtual environment within which authorized researchers could access sensitive microdata (Lane et al., 2008). Other countries have taken up this model of remote access to restricted social and economic data rather than relying on their existing procedures that require researchers to visit secure sites in person. In Europe a funded European Union project, *Data without Boundaries* (DwB), has been exploring supporting equal access to official microdata for the European Research Area, making use of these secure systems (DwB, 2011).

These secure access services allow researchers to analyse the data remotely from their institution, on a central secure server, with access to familiar statistical software and office tools, such as Stata, SPSS and Microsoft Office. No data travel over the network; the user's computer becomes a remote terminal, and outputs from the secure system are only released after statistical disclosure checks. Limited business and social survey data are available with detailed geographic information, such as postcode-level variables or grid-referenced versions. The provision of access to these restricted data is through a membership model, where approved members receive the training, support and advice necessary to manage and analyse the data in order to maximize research outputs while protecting respondents' privacy. Based on trust, a two-way commitment is upheld through user agreements and a shared Code of Practice (UK Data Service, 2013c).

Data Sharing and Formal Ethical Review

When undertaking research with human subjects the need for both data protection and data sharing may create a tension. In many cases, research data can be shared while upholding both the letter and spirit of data protection and the principles of research ethics. Being explicit about how data will be managed and shared should form part of the ethical review process. Research Ethics Committees (RECs), or in the USA, Institutions Review Boards (IRBs) should also support researchers' efforts to follow best practices of research integrity and data sharing.

RECs can help play a role in advising researchers and guiding them through the process of both gaining consent and looking after data ethically and legally. A **REC** may request that personal data collected during research should be destroyed after a certain time period to avoid possible disclosure. However, it is important to distinguish between personal data collected in research, and research data in general, as described earlier in this chapter under Data Protection Act definitions. Personal data should not be disclosed unless specific consent has been given and identifiable information can be excluded from data sharing. Thus, a **REC** should not ask researchers to destroy research data per se, but may ask for personal data, such as names and addresses, to be removed or destroyed.

A **REC** should also not object to any statement in a consent form that asks for wider sharing of research data. If research data contain sensitive or confidential information, then the sharing of such data should be considered carefully, but should not be dismissed as being impossible. Most **REC** members are informed and helpful, but in some cases, there can be information gaps. Researchers may need to inform **RECs** that most research data can be shared, that many funders require data to be shared, that anonymized data are exempt from the Data Protection Act, and that procedures are available to enable ethical sharing. Data centres and institutional repositories are available to support researchers on matters of data sharing during the ethical review process.

CASE STUDY	Working with IRBs in the USA (Based on Pienta and Marz, 2012)

ICPSR at the University of Michigan provides technical assistance and training to research investigators and their staff to prepare their data for archiving and to data users. There may be ethical approval required at both ends of the data lifecycle, when depositing and using data.

Under the federal regulations for human subjects research (45 CFR Part 46) use of publicly available datasets that are stripped of identifiers do not require Institutional Review Boards (IRB) review. Depositing de-identified data with ICPSR therefore typically involves less interaction with IRBs as many institutions know that ICPSR employs stringent disclosure risk procedures to protect the confidentiality of individuals when preparing data for release. However, researchers may need to contact their IRB to ask if additional steps are required by the IRB before depositing the data with ICPSR.

The National Addiction and HIV Data Archive Program (NAHDAP) is a 'topical archive' built upon ICPSR and is funded by the National Institute on Drug Abuse (NIDA). It offers web-based access to more than 300 studies on addiction and/or HIV. The NAHDAP offers a range of data release options ranging from public-use files, restricted-use files and delayed dissemination. NAHDAP requires its users to get IRB approval or exemption before accessing the restricted collections and defers to the user's own institutional guidance.

Summary

In summary, even sensitive and confidential research data can be shared ethically and legally, so long as certain criteria are met. Researchers should pay attention, from the beginning of research, to three important aspects, which can be considered jointly:

- when gaining informed consent, include provision for data sharing;
- where needed, protect people's identities by anonymizing data;
- consider controlling access to data if necessary.

These measures also form part of good research practice even if data sharing is not envisioned.

Exercise 7.1 Consent and data sharing

Here we present two examples of consent forms taken from real-life collections held at the UK Data Service, together with background information about each study. Read through each consent form and related background information for each study and then answer these questions.

- What are your initial impressions of each of the consent forms and information sheets?
- How effective do you think the consent forms are?
- Is there anything that is missing from the example forms or anything that you feel is unnecessary?
- Compare these consent forms to any consent forms that you have created for your own project. Would you change anything on your own consent forms?

It is good to be critical of each form, as all have their pluses and minuses.

1. Consent forms for qualitative interview and diary study

Health and Social Consequences of the Foot and Mouth Disease Epidemic in North Cumbria, 2001–2003 (Mort, 2006)

Background to the study: The 2001 foot and mouth disease outbreak had an enormous effect on the economic, social and political life of rural areas in the UK. This research project, which was funded by the Department of Health, produced evidence about the human health and social consequences of the epidemic.

The study recruited a standing panel of 54 local people from the worst affected area (North Cumbria). This panel wrote weekly diaries over a period of 18 months describing how their lives had been affected by the crisis and the process of recovery they observed around them. The panel was recruited to reflect a broad range of occupations including: farmers and their families; workers in related agricultural occupations; those in small businesses including tourism, hotel trades and rural business; health professionals; veterinary practitioners; voluntary organizations; and residents living near disposal sites.

The panel members produced 3,200 weekly diaries of great intensity and diversity over the 18-month period. The data were supplemented by in-depth interviews with each respondent, focus group discussions, and 16 other interviews with stakeholders.

The Institute for Health Research Lancaster University

CONSENT FORM

Name _____

Address _____

_____

_____

_____

I consent to participating in the health and social consequences of the 2001 foot and mouth outbreak project, which involves:

- Completing a weekly diary for a period of 18 months

- Competing a questionnaire about my quality of life (3 times during the study)

- Individual and group interviews about my life experiences, my work and my health.

I understand that:

1. Everything that I tell you will be held in the strictest confidence. Some of the information that I give you may be used in reports and articles, but my identity will remain anonymous (my name will not be given).

2. I am free to withdraw from the project at any time.

Signature _____ Date _____

Figure 7.1   Initial consent form: Foot and Mouth Study

Source: Mort et al., 2006

The research team gained consent from participants for primary participation in the project, but did not initially consider consent for sharing or archiving their data. When the project was finished they wanted to archive their data, so returned to the panel to gain retrospective consent to archive the data and make them available to other researchers. They sought expert advice from copyright law specialists to help draft terms of agreement, which would give participants a series of options about how their written diaries, transcribed interviews, and audio-recorded interviews would be archived.

Archiving Deposit or Consent Form
(Diary – Economic and Social Data Service, UK Data Archive)

Terms of Agreement

Below are sets of statements that give you the depositor, a series of options in terms of how you wish your diary, copy of your diary, or portion of your diary, to be archived. For each numbered statement, **please delete the part that is not applicable**. Please note that 'diary' refers to 'anonymised diary' (you are not named).

By signing below:

1.1   I agree to deposit **the whole/a portion** of my diary (or copy of my diary) with Economic and Social Data Service, UK Data Archive.

1.2   I agree that **my diary/ or the agreed portion** of my diary will be available from .... to researchers and the public for scholarly and educational purposes.

By giving my permission I also:

2.   **I do/do not agree** that the Economic and Social Data Service, UK Data Archive may use this diary/portion of the diary, including making a copy or copies of it or a part or parts of it, in any form or medium, and may authorize others to do so, without any further approval on my part.

3.   **I do/do not agree** that a part or parts of the whole diary/portion of the diary may be published from .... as long as I am not identified.

4.   I hereby assign ownership of the **diary/copy of the diary/portion of the diary** to Economic and Social Data Service, UK Data Archive. I understand that I nevertheless retain copyright, subject to the rights which I have granted Economic and Social Data Service, UK Data Archive to make copies and publish and to grant permissions to others to do so.

Signature of depositer ....   Date..............

Name of depositer (print) ....

Witnessed By ....[name, print]

Signature of Witness ....

Figure 7.2   Retrospective consent form for diaries: Foot and Mouth Study

Source: Mort et al., 2006

The resulting data collection comprised a large body of sensitive and confidential information which was archived with minimal need for anonymization. These data are now available to other researchers.

Consent forms: The study used three consent forms for initial consent and retrospective consent as shown in Figures 7.1, 7.2 and 7.3.

Archieving Deposit or Consent Form
(Audio material – Economic and Social Data Service, UK Data Archive)

Terms of Agreement

Below are sets of statements that give you the depositor, a series of options in terms of how you wish your audio material, or extract of your audio material, to be archived. For each numbered statement, **please delete the part that is not applicable**. Please note that 'audio material' refers to 'anonymised' audio material (you are not named).

By signing below:

1.1   I agree to deposit **the whole/extracts of my audio material** with Economic and Social Data Service, UK Data Archive.

1.2   I agree that **my audio material/or the agreed extracts of my audio material will be available from** .... to researchers and the public for scholarly and educational purposes.

By giving my permission I also:

2.   **I do/do not agree** that the Economic and Social Data Service, UK Data Archive may use this **audio material/the agreed extracts of my audio material**, including making a copy or copies of it or a part or parts of it, in any form or medium, and may authorise others to do so, without any further approval on my part.

3.   **I do/do not agree** that a part or parts of the **audio material/the agreed extracts of the audio material** may be **published from** .... as long as I am not identified.

4.   I hereby assign ownership of the **audio material/the agreed extracts of the audio material** to Economic and Social Data Service, UK Data Archive. I understand that I nevertheless retain copyright, subject to the rights which I have granted Economic and Social Data Service, UK Data Archive to make copies and publish and to grant permissions to others to do so.

Signature of depositer ....   Date..............

Name of depositer (print) ....

Witnessed By ....….......... [name, print]

Signature of Witness ....….......

Figure 7.3   Retrospective consent form for audio material: Foot and Mouth Study

Source: Mort et al., 2006

2. Consent form for focus group study

Understanding People's Attitudes Toward Current Events: The Qualitative Election Study of Britain (QES Britain) (Winters, 2007)

Background to the study: The aim of the Qualitative Election Study of Britain (QES Britain) was to record and analyse the views and concerns of British citizens in their own words before and after the 2010 General Election. The goal was to generate rich qualitative data that could be used to provide insights into the opinions of citizens on politicians, party leaders, political issues and perceptions of civic duty, political alienation, and campaigns both before and after the general election, and to facilitate analysis of the language used and meanings conveyed when participants articulated their assessments. Through qualitative analysis this project investigated the sources of people's normative values, made explicit the tacit assumptions participants used to reach their judgements, and identified new research themes. The research collected focus groups and interviews.

Consent forms: This study used an information sheet and a consent form, as shown in Figures 7.4 and 7.5.

The British Academy and Brikbeck College are committed to ethically conducted social research. We ask you to consider the following points **before** agreeing to participate.

- Your contribution to the research will take the form of a focus group participant. This will be digitally video recorded and transcribed.

- **Your name and any information which may directly or indirectly identify you will be altered to protect your anonymity.**

- Any recordings of the discussion will be kept securely, and only authorised to other researchers on the condition they preserve your anonymity.

- The transcriptions (*excluding* names and other identifying details) will be retained by the researcher and analysed as part of the study. They will also be deposited with the UK Data Archive which has strict regulations about accessing data for research and protecting participant confidentiality.

If you would like to discuss any aspect of the study, or the details of this form, please contact **Dr. Kristi Winters**.

Phone:

E-mail:

Web page:

Focus group details:

Date:

Time:

Location:

Other research in the media:

Drs. Rosie Campbell and Kristi Winters (2007) 'The myth of the homogonous voter.' **Thinking Aloud** Podcast available at: www.bbk.ac.uk/ polsoc/research/ rcampbellvoting/

Understanding people's attitudes toward current events

A study funded by the British Academy

Seeking participants for focus group discussions about current events

£25 participation compensation

Research conducted by Dr.Kristi Winters *Birkbeck College, University of London British Academy Postdoctoral Fellow* email

---

(Continued)

Figure 7.4 (Continued)

Common Questions:

Q: What is this research about?

Local elections, an up-coming general election, economic worries, climate change, the future of public services, personal and national security...

At the start of the 21st century, Britain faces many challenges. The aim of this research is to talk to people about current events and issues and learn more about what people think about the challenges facing Britain.

What do I have to do?

Just talk and give your views.

The focus groups will consist of 5 to 10 other people and will be led by a moderator. You will first be asked to fill out a brief questionnaire. In order to get a good cross-section of the public not everyone who applies will be invited to participate in the focus groups, however you might be invited to participate in a one-on-one interview instead.

There will another focus group after the next general election which will review many of these topics again. If you are invited to the first focus group you may participate in the post-election focus group, and will again be eligible for £25 in participant compensation.

The focus group will take place at a location convenient for you. It will be recorded with a digital video recorder and transcribed.

The transcripts will be analysed to better understand the views of Britons today.

I also understand your time is valuable, and to help offset the costs you might occur travelling to and from the focus groups I am offering £25 compensation to all participants.

How long will it take?

The focus group will last about 90 minutes. The first 5 minutes will be devoted to reviewing and signing a consent form which lists your rights as a participant and to answer any other questions you might have before we begin. You may also request a copy of the consent form in advance of our meeting.

Participants will also be required to fill out a questionnaire after the focus group session.

What happens to the video files and written transcripts?

You will be assigned a participant ID number so your contact details will never be kept with the video or transcript files.

All files will be kept in a password-protected file on a password-protected computer. Files **will not** be sent by email, only on password-protected data sticks and by registered post.

Transcribers will be required to sign documentation binding them legally to protecting your anonymity. During the course of transcription all <u>direct identifiers</u> (names, addresses, employment, streets, etc.) and <u>indirect identifiers</u> (workplace, organisation) will be <u>removed</u> or <u>changed</u>.

Any other researchers who use the data must comply with strict regulations about accessing

data for research and protecting participant confidentiality.

The findings of this research will be written up and published. They may also be used for teaching and research training. The published works may include quotations from your discussions, but **individuals will never be named**. To aid in the use of your words in published works I request that you assign copyright to the researcher.

Can I change my mind about participation?

Your contribution is immensely valuable. However, if you wish to withdraw at any time I will respect your decision immediately.

How do I find out about publications which come out of this study?

Participants who would like to be notified of publications which come out of this research should identify how they would like to be notified on the participation consent form.

How do I find out more or become a participant in this study?

Just contact Dr. Kristi Winters by email or by phone with any questions.

Figure 7.4 Information Sheet for the Qualitative Election Study of Britain

Source: Winters (2007)

Understanding people's attitudes toward current events. Dr. Kristi Winters (Birkbeck College, University of London) Funded by the British Academy

o   I have read and understood the project information brochure **Understanding people's attitudes toward current events.**

o   I agree to take part in the project. Taking part in the project will include being interviewed and recorded (video).

o   I understand that my taking part is voluntary; I can withdraw from participating at any time and I will not be asked any questions about why I no longer want to take part. The focus group discussions I have participated in until my withdrawal may still be used.

o   I agree for the data I provided to be archived at the UK Data Archive and I understand that other researchers will have access to this data only if they agree to preserve my anonymity and confidentiality terms as specified in this form.

o   I understand that my words may be quoted in publications, reports, web pages, and other research outputs **but my name or other identifying details** will not be used.

o   I hereby assign the copyright of my contribution to Dr. Kristi Winters, so that my words may be quoted in publications, reports, web pages, and other research outputs.

o   I would / would not (delete as appropriate) like to be notified of any publications which are produced from this research. I would like to be notified of this by email / text / phone call (delete as appropriate) and have provided the relevant contact information to Dr. Winters.

o   I understand my personal details such as phone number and address will not be revealed to anyone except Dr. Kristi Winters or her assistants.

o   I confirm that I have freely agreed to participate in this qualitative research project conducted by Dr. Kristi Winters. I have been briefed on what this involves and I agree to the use of the findings as described above. I understand that the material is protected by a code of professional ethics.

_____   _____   _____

Name of Participant   Signature   Date

Figure 7.5   Consent Form for the Qualitative Election Study of Britain

Source: Winters (2007)

Exercise 7.2   Anonymization of qualitative data

In this exercise on anonymization we will be using the same Foot and Mouth study (Mort, 2006) used in the first consent Exercise 7.1. Re-read the Background to the study again first.

We present one interview transcript based on an interview with a Department for Environment, Food and Rural Affairs (Defra) field officer. He was interviewed about his experiences, during the Foot and Mouth crisis, as a Defra field officer and as part of an affected farming family. The interviewee consented to his transcript being made available for research and educational purposes, as long as he would not be identified.

Read through the interview transcript extract shown in Figure 7.6 and consider what anonymization would be needed before archiving this transcript for future sharing. Although this is taken from a real interview, all identifying information in the extract is fictitious.

**Health and Social Consequences of the Foot and Mouth Disease Epidemic
in North Cumbria, 2001–2003 (SN 5407)**

M. Mort, Lancaster University. Institute for Health Research

Note: all identifying info contained in this transcript is fictional

Interview with Lucas Roberts, DEFRA field officer

Date of Interview: 21/02/02
Date of birth: 2 May 1965
Gender: Male
Occupation: Frontline worker
Location: Plumpton, North Cumbria

Lucas was living at home with his parents, "but I'm hoping to move out soon" so we met at his parents' small neat house. We sat in a very comfortable sitting room with an open fire and Lucas made me coffee and offered shortbread. Although at first Lucas seemed a little nervous, quick to speak and very watchful he seemed to relax as we spoke and to forget about the tape.

I will just start by asking you to tell me a little bit about yourself and your background.

Well it is an agricultural background. I grew up on the farm where my brother is now. After I left school I did work on the farm but went to college and did exams, did land use recreation, sort of countryside/environmental management course. So I obviously left agriculture, did the course and came back [to the farm] at weekends. During vacations, worked on the farm until I got my first placement in Suffolk. Went away in my early twenties, so wasn't a teenager and did that and then I took the Diploma, then took my studies further and did a degree in rural resources management in Bedfordshire and after that I worked on a community forestry project, actually based within a natural forest. I did that for 4 years and came back near the end of '95.

I think with countryside management, I think personally it's quite difficult to get in to, and as a job it's quite competitive. It's whether I kept my options a bit too broad or indeed simply gone into this like general management, I just wanted to stay connected with the environment. I did bits and pieces with CumbrExt which is now Milbro Ltd as has been privatised a few years. I had several contracts over the years with them off and on. Also did work for environmental consultancy agency, went to Germany, Slovakia, did various projects on a freelance self employed basis, and in between that I have a good friend who has a market garden business so I work there sometimes [laughs]. Do bits and pieces and obviously when he's gone on holiday, so I suppose I class myself as self employed. It's all continous but it's very sort of like bits and pieces really. I did one office job as a research assistant, though it wasn't quite as [PAUSE] with a traffic consultancy looking at local transport links and their problems. I found it quite difficult being office based and stuck behind a computer all the time, and sort of like used to being outdoors. Up until the out-break I had been working for Milbro Ltd doing some surveying work, and that finished there in February. I had the job in the market garden and then obviously it [foot and mouth] all flared up and we thought well it will be nipped in the bud. The case in the abattoir in Essex and then I think it went to Devon. And then it was traced [pause], it didn't reach Cumbria until March 3rd., I think, over a week later anyway, and even then [EMPHASIS], it obviously didn't seem quite serious but still thought they would eventually get on top of it., There seemed to a starting a sort of triangle. There was the one at Longtown aunction mart and there was an earlier one near Maryport. It did appear to sort of close in and erm…[pause]

Can I just take you right back to your parents. Is it a mixed farm?

It's a diary farm, we did do like a little bit of beef cattle, sort of stores, but no it's a diary farm.

And there is you and your brother?

Well it is my brother's now [the farm], I just help out.

When you were growing up?

I forgot, I've got another brother, there is three of us. He worked on the farm for a year after he left school then he went to work on another farm and now he's a plasterer and a builder. So he left the farm as well, so it was only my eldest brother. What he did, he did 'A' levels and worked at a neighbour's farm for a year and then did a course at Newton Rigg and then stayed at the farm ever since.

So your parents.? You probably weren't old enough to remember the 67 out-break?

No I don't remember it all. In fact I wasn't really aware of it until they were making comparisons with this last one.

And have they [parents] said anything about the 67 out-break?

No, well it didn't really affect Cumbria, it got to Westmoreland, it just got there but Cumbria wasn't affected and they certainly weren't affected but I remember my parents didn't really speak about it. My Dad's in his seventies now and he doesn't really talk about it now, he sort of feels he's retired now and he just accepts that.

Figure 7.6   Interview transcript with Defra field officer

Source: Mort, 2006

Exercise 7.3   Anonymization of survey data

Polish and Lithuanian Workers: Opportunities and Challenges for Trade Unions, 2004–2006
(Anderson and Trades Union Congress, 2009)

Background to the study: This research project, conducted jointly by the Centre on Migration, Policy and Society (COMPAS) at the University of Oxford, and the Trades Union Congress (TUC), surveyed Polish and Lithuanian nationals working in the UK who had requested TUC leaflets on employment rights and the role of trades unions. The survey explored the kinds of difficulties experienced by Polish and Lithuanian workers in the UK labour market, and their potential for joining trades unions. More specifically, it addressed:

- Who is a member of or wants to join a trades union and why?
- What are the obstacles to joining a trades union?
- Where are prospective union members working?
- What are the kinds of difficulties that Polish and Lithuanian workers in the UK face in their employment relations and conditions?

Explore the study's survey report and questionnaire for Study Number 6284, available as study documentation at: http://discover.ukdataservice.ac.uk/catalogue/?sn=6284.

Now look at the partial data file table in Figure 7.7 which shows the data for only 10 respondents. Identifying information in this table is fictitious to be able to demonstrate this example. How might the data tables be anonymized before archiving?

Polish and Lithuanian Workers: Opportunities and Challenges for Trade Unions, 2004-2006 (SN 6284), by B Anderson, University of Oxford.
NOTE: all identifying info contained in this sample file is fictional

code	qutype	lang	c_age2	gender	engepea2	engread2	mthswkuk	mthswkho	mthswkot	monwtot	retotmhw	yrswokuk	yrswkhom	yrswkoth	yrswtot	app4reg2	dateapr2	mylasten	ylasten
106p	4	3	33	2	3	3	8	16	0	26	3	0	0	0	0	1	23-Mar-2005	1-Jan-2005	2,005
	4	3	32	1	2	2	18	120	0	138	5	0	0	0	0	1	1-Aug-2004	1-Feb-2004	2,004
129p	4	3	31	1	2	2	0	0	0	0	0	0	0	0	0	1	21-Apr-2005	1-Mar-2005	2,005
15p	4	3	31	2	3	3	12	12	0	24	3	0	0	0	0	1	11-Sep-2004	1-Sep-2004	2,004
196p	4	3	29	1	2	1	12	36	0	48	3	0	0	0	0	1	1-Oct-2005	1-Oct-2004	2,004
202p	4	3	27	1	2	2	7	42	0	49	3	0	0	0	0	1	1-May-2005	1-Feb-2005	2,005
214p	4	3	27	1	3	3	0	60	0	60	3	0	5	0	5	1	1-Apr-2005	0-Jan-1900	888
433p	4	3	23	1	2	2	12	0	12	24	3	0	0	0	0	1	21-Sep-2004	1-Jun-2004	2,004
491l	4	2	22	1	2	2	0	180	0	180	5	0	0	0	0	1	1-Oct-2005	1-Aug-2005	2,005
111p	4	3		2	2	2	12	24	0	36	3	0	0	0	0	1	2-Jun-2004	1-Jun-2004	2,004

migproc0	othmigp0	jobukfi2	myjbukfi	yrjbukfi	currwk	empag	wktown	wkcounty	typebus	numwowp1	natwowp1	propna	numwobu1	natwobu2
5		9-Feb-2005	1-Feb-2005	2,005	1	2	Gerrards Cross	Buckinghamshire	pizzeria	8	5	0.6250	80	40
5		0-Jan-1900	1-May-2004	2,004	1	0	Paisili	Lambs	chicken factory	20	11	0.5500	100	25
5		17-Mar-2005	1-Mar-2005	2,005	1	1	Trowbridge	Wiltshire	factory of packages for car parts	30	3	0.1000	40	888
5		4-Nov-2004	1-Nov-2004	2,004	1	2	Peterborough	Cambridgeshire	fruit factory	40	12	0.3000	50	12
5		0-Jan-1900	1-Oct-2004	2,004	1	2	Tunbridge Wells	Kent	restaurant, supermarket	20	4	0.2000	888	888
5		0-Jan-1900	1-Feb-2005	2,005	1	2	Cromarty	Ross Shire	scrap metal	20	5	0.2500	20	5
1		0-Jan-1900	1-Apr-2005	2,005	1	1	Leominster	Hereford	food factory	120	11	0.0917	200	11
5		11-May-2004	1-May-2004	2,004	1	2	Huntingdon	Cambridgeshire	food factory	300	200	0.6667	300	200
5		0-Jan-1900	1-Aug-2005	2,005	1	2	London	London	security	3	3	1.0000	40	25
7	through acquaintances	2-Jun-2004	1-Jun-2004	2,004	1	1	Cambridge	Cambs	kitchen in barracks	30	10	0.3333	777	777

(Continued)

Figure 7.7   (Continued)

w11	w12	w13	w14				w16		w15	w17	w18	w19		w20a	w20b	w21	
empcont2	nijob	whyni	whyniot	payhr	paywk	paymth	jobhrs	jobhrsgroup	jobtitle	overtime	bankacc	howpay	payoth	busemp	agemp	foundacc	accoth
2	2	3		0.00	0.00	1,046.00	70.00	4	topping pizzas	4	2	1		1	0	2	
1	1	999		0.00	234.00	0.00	50.00	4	bookings and sending goods to the shops	1	1	3		1	0	1	
2	1	999		5.50	0.00	0.00	40.00	3	welding, gluing, packing	1	1	3		2	2	4	
1	1	999		5.35	0.00	0.00	54.00	4	packing	1	1	3		1	1	3	
1	1	999		4.85	0.00	0.00	60.00	4	pizza chef (caffe uno) and cleaning operative (Tesco -- £6/h)	1	1	3		2	0	1	
2	1	999		4.85	0.00	0.00	50.00	4	almost everything	2	1	3		2	0	3	
1	1	999		0.00	0.00	1,916.16	42.00	3	Arbor Contract Engineers Ltd- machine engineer	3	1	3		0	1	1	
1	1	999		5.80	0.00	0.00	45.00	3	line runner	2	1	3		0	1	4	
1	1	999		6.00	0.00	0.00	50.00	4	security officer	1	1	3		1	1	3	
1	1	999		5.25	0.00	886.63	37.00	3	kitchen porter; sometimes waitress	1	1	3		1	1	2	

w22	w23					
livecond	PROBWK	prob1	prob2	prob3	prob4	prob5
5	1	no work schedule	racism from the manager's side	mobbing	spreading fear	lack of contract or P60
3	1	overtime not paid. bank holidays not paid, no holiday pay, no sick pay	worse treatment			
2	2					
3	2					
4	2					
1	2					
2	2					
1	1	agency took £50 and documents for registration at HO, but they didn't send the money so I couldn't get registered, so I had to fight to get the money back from agency	when I gave the HO registration documents to the factory's office, they disappeared and then reappeared only when I said that I would call the police			
2	1	doesn't pay all the salary -- pay several hours to several days less	deduct for travel from agency to the workplace and back -- £3,5 per day (			
4	1	farm -- constantly made mistakes when calculating salary; held passport	frequent mistakes with calculations of payment, we don't understand whether we get paid for overtime or not	payslip is difficult to read	don't inform about our rights and benefits; hide such information	

Figure 7.7   Partial survey data files from Trades Union study of Polish and Lithuanian Workers

Source: Corti et al., 2011

Answers to Exercise 7.1

1. Consent forms for qualitative interview and diary study

The retrospective consent forms are well-thought through giving the participants the opportunity to decide whether they wanted their interviews and diaries archived and thus sharable or not. Researchers often worry that participants will be reluctant to share their data, but in this case retrospective consent was quite successful. A large dataset of sensitive, confidential information was archived with minimal anonymization.

The drawbacks of using many different forms and options for consent within a small-scale project are that additional paperwork puts a greater burden on respondents who have to complete them and on the research team who have to administer them; and there is a danger of making the final collection difficult to access as a whole if its various elements have different consent agreements.

The second and third consent forms offer multiple choice text answers. On the diary consent form, respondents are given the option to select a date for their data to become available. While this offers greater freedom for participants to record their wishes, too many permutations of consent will be hard to manage when providing access to data. We recommend setting an agreed date as to when the data should be accessible.

The first consent form is less formal in its approach. The second and third forms are more formal and read more like legal documents, which may be off-putting. The researchers later went back to respondents to gain retrospective consent, by which time the political and legal situation surrounding this foot and mouth outbreak had changed; there was more public awareness and sensitivity to the issue. The team sought expert advice from a copyright specialist to help draft terms of agreement for these forms. Some projects may benefit from a more rigorously designed form. Others may require a more informal agreement.

The second and third forms also state that the participant can assign ownership to the archive. Most data centres and repositories will not wish to assert ownership of research data so instead this could be phrased 'I hereby license use of the diary….'.

2. Consent form for focus group study

A few points arise from the otherwise excellent information sheet and consent form.

The consent form is a simple one and does not offer the option to agree to some particular statements and not to others. However it does set out very clearly what is expected by taking part, and that data will be shared. Separate consent statements could have been obtained for being interviewed and being videoed, allowing the participants to opt out of the videoing if necessary.

As this study required follow-up of participants after the election, the question of what happens to data from earlier interviews if a participant withdraws can be difficult. This researcher's strategy was to gain full consent for participation and archiving prior to the fieldwork. She also reserved the right to keep any prior contributions, and respondents were only allowed to withdraw from future contributions.

Copyright is explicitly mentioned to enable citation of participants' words in resulting publications and outputs.

Compare this form with that of the UK Data Archive's model consent form shown in Figure 7.8.

Consent Form for [name of project]		
Please tick the appropriate boxes	**Yes**	**No**
Taking Part		
I have read and understood the project information sheet dated DD/MM/YYYY.	☐	☐
I have been given the opportunity to ask questions about the project.	☐	☐
I agree to take part in the project. Taking part in the project will include being interviewed and recorded (audio or video).[1]	☐	☐
I understand that my taking part is voluntary, I can withdraw from the study at any time and I do not have to give any reasons for why I no longer want to take part	☐	☐
Use of the information I provide for this project only I understand my personal details such as phone number and address will not be revealed to people outside the project.	☐	☐
I Understand that my words may be quoted in publications, reports, web pages, and other research outputs.	☐	☐
Please choose **one** *of the following two options:*		
I would like my real name used in the above	☐	
I would **not** like my real name to be used in the above.	☐	
Use of the information I provide beyond this project I agree for the data I provide to be archieved at the UK Data Archive.[2]		
I understand that other genuine researchers will have access to this data only if they agree to preserve the confidentiality of the information as requested in this form.	☐	☐
I understand that other genuine researchers may use my words in publications, reports, web pages, and other research outputs, only if they agree to preserve the confidentiality of the information as requested in this form.		

(Continued)

So we can use the information you provide legally
I agree to assign the copyright I hold in any materials related to this project
to [name of researcher].   ☐   ☐

Name of participant   [printed]   Signature   Date

Name of participant   [printed]   Signature   Date

Project contact details for further information: Names, phone, email addresses, etc.

Notes:

    1.   Other forms of participation can be listed.
    2.   More detail can be provided here so that decisions can be made seperately about
        audio, video, transcripts, etc.

Figure 7.8   UK Data Service Model Consent Form

Source: UK Data Service, 2013b

Answer to Exercise 7.2

The terms that were anonymized in this interview are shown in Figure 7.9.

**Health and Social Consequences of the Foot and Mouth Disease
Epidemic in North Cumbria, 2001-2003 (SN 5407)**
M. Mort, Lancaster University. Institute for Health Research

NOTE: all identifying info contained in this transcript is fictional

Date of Interview: 21/02/02

Interview with Lucas Roberts, DEFRA field officer ----------------------------- ⟨ Comment [v1]: Replace: Ken ⟩
Date of birth: 2 May 1965 --- ⟨ Comment [v2]: Delete ⟩

Gender: Male

Occupation: Frontline worker
Location: Plumpton, North Cumbria --------------------------------------- ⟨ Comment [v3]: Delete ⟩

Lucas was living at home with his parents, "but I'm hoping to move out ---- ⟨ Comment [v4]: Replace: Ken ⟩
soon" so we met at his parents' small neat house. We sat in a very
comfortable sitting room with an open fire and Lucas made me coffee ------- ⟨ Comment [v5]: Replace: Ken ⟩
and offered shortbread. Although at first Lucas seemed a little nervous, ... ⟨ Comment [v6]: Replace: Ken ⟩
quick to speech and very watchful he seemed to relax as we spoke and
to forget about the tape.

I will just start by asking you to tell me a little bit about yourself and your
background.

Well it is an agricultural background. I grew up on the farm where my brother
is now. After I left school I did work on the farm but went to college and did
exams, did land use recreation, sort of countryside/ environmental
management course. So I obviously left agriculture, did the course and came
back [to the farm] at weekends. During vacations, worked on the farm until I
got my first placement in Suffolk. Went away in my early twenties, so wasn't a
teenager and did that and then I took the Diploma, then took my studies
further and did a degree in rural resources management in Bedfordshire and
after that worked I on a community forestry project, actually based within a
natural forest. I did that for 4 years and came back near the end of '95.

I think with countryside management, I think personally it's quite difficult to get
in to, and as a job it's quite competitive. It's whether I kept my options a bit too

broad or indeed simply gone into this like general management, I just wanted to stay connected with the environment. I did bits and pieces with CumbrExt which is now Milbro Ltd as has been privatised a few years. I had several contracts over the years with them off and on. Also did work for environmental consultancy agency, went to Germany, Slovakia, did various projects on a freelance self employed basis, and in between that I have a good friend who has a market garden business so I work there sometimes [laughs]. Do bits and pieces and obviously when he's gone on holiday, so I suppose I class myself as self employed. It's all continuous but it's very sort of like bits and pieces really. I did one office job as a research assistant, though it wasn't quite as [PAUSE]   with a traffic consultancy looking at local transport links and their problems. I found it quite being difficult being office based and stuck behind a computer all the time, and sort of like used to being outdoors. Up until the out-break I had been working for Milbro Ltd doing some surveying work, and that finished there in February. I had the job in the market garden and then obviously it [foot and mouth] all flared up and we though well it will be nipped in the bud. The case in the abattoir in Essex and then I think it went to Devon. And then it was traced back to Heddon-on-the-Wall. There were several cases where I think [pause], it didn't reach Cumbria until March 3rd. I think, over a week later anyway, and even then [EMPHASIS], it obviously didn't seem quite serious but still thought they would eventually get on top of it., There seemed to a starting a sort of triangle. There was the one at Longtown auction mart and there was an earlier one near Maryport. It did appear to sort of close in and erm...[pause]

Can I just take you right back to your parents. Is it a mixed farm?

It's a dairy farm, we did do like a little bit of beef cattle, sort of stores, but no it's a dairy farm.

And there is you and your brother?

Well it is my brother's now [the farm], I just help out.

When you were growing up?

I forgot, I've got another brother, there is three of us. He worked on the farm for a year after he left school then he went to work on another farm and now he's a plasterer and a builder. So he left the farm as well, so it was only my eldest brother. What he did, he did 'A' levels and worked at a neighbour's farm for a year and then did a course at Newton Rigg and then stayed at the farm ever since.

So your parents   .? You probably weren't old enough to remember the 67 out-break?

No I don't remember it all. In fact I wasn't really aware of it until they were making comparisons with this last one.

And have they [parents] said anything about the 67 out-break?

No, well it didn't really affect Cumbria, it got to Westmoreland, it just got there but Cumbria wasn't affected and they certainly weren't affected but I remember my parents didn't really speak about it. My Dad's in his seventies now and he doesn't really talk about it now, he sort of feels he's retired now and he just accepts that.

Figure 7.9   Annotated interview transcript with Defra field officer

Source: Corti et al., 2011

Possibly fewer words have been anonymized than you might have chosen yourself. Pseudonyms were used for names of interviewees and relatives, village, company names, and dates of birth was generalized. For the majority of interviews and diaries in this collection only minimal anonymizing was required. This is due to a well-thought-through informed consent process whereby consent was asked for various data uses, including data archiving.

Answer to Exercise 7.3

While the survey questionnaire needed to collect identifying information to help code occupations and industry sectors, the disclosiveness of the data was not considered as it was entered directly into the data table, which was then further offered for sharing. While it is helpful to collect detailed information in order to code effectively, the information should have been numerically coded before sharing to prevent the risk of disclosure.

- typebus: replace the rich description with standard industrial classification code (SIC)
- pademp: replace the textual description with standard organizational classification (SOC)

For some date variables more detailed information was gathered during the survey and submitted to the data table than was asked for in the form: this detail had to be removed later:

- dateapr2 and mylasten: the questionnaire asks for date and month only, yet a full date DD/MM/YYYY was noted in the data file; day and month were later removed;

Detailed place names were anonymized:

- wktown and wkcounty: replace the actual place with workplace region, such as Government Office Region.

In free text questions, some disclosive information was noted; this could have been avoided by coding or anonymizing answers before preparing the data for sharing:

- prob1 and prob2: identifying companies like Seraco, Big Talk Contract Ltd, Tottenham, Fowlers and Parmak should all be removed.

References

Anderson, B. and Trades Union Congress (2009) *Polish and Lithuanian Workers: Opportunities and Challenges for Trade Unions, 2004–2006* [computer file], Colchester, Essex: UK Data Archive [distributor], September. SN: 6284. Available at: http://dx.doi.org/10.5255/UKDA-SN-6284-1.

Bishop, L. (2009) 'Ethical sharing and re-use of qualitative data', *Australian Journal of Social Issues*, 44(3): 255–72. Available at: http://www.data-archive.ac.uk/media/249157/ajsi44bishop.pdf.

Broom, A., Cheshire, L. and Emmison, M. (2009) 'Qualitative researchers' understandings of their practice and the implications for data archiving and sharing', *Sociology*, 43: 1163–80, DOI: 10.1177/0038038509345704.

Chatham House (2013) *Chatham House Rule*, Chatham House. Available at: http://www.chathamhouse.org/about-us/chathamhouserule.

Corti, L., Van den Eynden, V., Bishop, L. and Morgan, B. (2011) *Managing and Sharing Data: Training Resources*, UK Data Archive, University of Essex. 82–1.

Division of Health Research (2013) *Sample Consent Forms and Information Sheets, Social Science Research Ethics*. Available at: http://www.lancs.ac.uk/researchethics/1-4-samples.html.

DwB (2011) *Data without Boundaries (DwB)*, Data without Boundaries. Available at: http://www.dwbproject.org/.

ESRC (2012) *Framework for Research Ethics*, Economic and Social Research Council. Available at: http://www.esrc.ac.uk/_images/Framework-for-Research-Ethics_tcm8-4586.pdf.

HHS (2005) *The Nuremberg Code*, USA Department of Health and Human Services. Available at: http://www.hhs.gov/ohrp/archive/nurcode.html.

ICPSR (2012) *QualiAnon Tool. DSDR Qualitative Data Anonymizer. Data Sharing for Demographic Research*, ICPSR. Available at: https://www.icpsr.umich.edu//icpsrweb/DSDR/tools/anonymize.jsp.

ICPSR (2013) *Confidentiality Language for Informed Consent Agreements*, ICPSR, University of Michigan. Available at: http://www.icpsr.umich.edu/icpsrweb/content/datamanagement/confidentiality/conf-language.html.

Information Commissioner's Office (2012) *Anonymisation Code of Practice*, Information Commissioner's Office. Available at: http://www.ico.gov.uk/for_organisations/data_protection/topic_guides/anonymisation.aspx.

Information Commissioner's Office (2013a) *Key Definitions of the Data Protection Act*, Information Commissioner's Office. Available at: http://www.ico.gov.uk/for_organisations/data_protection/the_guide/key_definitions.aspx.

Information Commissioner's Office (2013b) *Monetary Penalty Notices*, Information Commissioner's Office. Available at: http://www.ico.gov.uk/enforcement/fines.aspx.

ISO 27001 Directory (2013) *An Introduction to ISO 2700*, ISO 27001 Directory. Available at: http://www.27000.org/iso-27001.htm.

Kozlakidis, Z. (2012) 'Human tissue biobanks: The balance between consent and the common good', *Research Ethics*, 8: 13–23.

Kuula, A. (2011) 'Methodological and ethical dilemmas of archiving qualitative data', *IASSIST Quarterly*: 34(3–4) and 35(1–2): 12–17.

Lane, J., Heus, P. and Mulcahy, T. (2008) 'Data access in a cyber world: Making use of cyberinfrastructure', *Transactions on Data Privacy*, 1(1): 2–16. Available at: http://www.tdp.cat/issues/tdp.a002a08.pdf.

Mauthner, N. (2012) 'Accounting for our part of the entangled webs we weave: Ethical and moral issues in digital data sharing', in T. Miller et al. (eds), *Ethics in Qualitative Research*, 2nd edn. London: Sage. pp. 157–75.

McAfee (2013) *International Privacy and Data Protection Laws*, McAfee. Available at: http://www.mcafee.com/us/regulations/international.aspx.

Ministry of Justice (2011) *Public Sector Data Sharing: Guidance on the Law, Annex H in Data Sharing Protocol*. Ministry of Justice. Available at: http://www.justice.gov.uk/downloads/information-access-rights/data-sharing/annex-h-data-sharing.pdf.

Mort, M. (2006) *Health and Social Consequences of the Foot and Mouth Disease Epidemic in North Cumbria, 2001–2003* [computer file]. Colchester, Essex: UK Data Archive [distributor], November. SN: 5407. Available at: http://dx.doi.org/10.5255/UKDA-SN-5407-1.

National Institutes of Health (2013) *HIPAA Privacy Rule*, National Institutes of Health. Available at: http://privacyruleandresearch.nih.gov/pr_03.asp.

National Research Ethics Service (2012) *Consent Guidance and Forms*, NHS Health Research Authority. Available at: http://www.nres.nhs.uk/applications/guidance/consent-guidance-and-forms/.

Office for National Statistics (2004) *Protocol on Data Access and Confidentiality. National Statistics Code of Practice*, Office for National Statistics. Available at: http://www.ons.gov.uk/ons/guide-method/the-national-statistics-standard/code-of-practice/protocols/data-access-and-confidentiality.pdf.

Pienta, A. and Marz, K. (2012) *The National Addiction and HIV Data Archive Program: Navigating Your IRB to Share Research Data*, presentation at ICPSR. Available at: http://www.icpsr.umich.edu/icpsrweb/ICPSR/support/announcements/2012/11/video-slides-available-from-webcast-on.

Pinsent Masons (2012) 'NHS Trust facing £375,000 fine over theft of patient data', *Out-law.com*, 12 January. Available at: http://www.out-law.com/en/articles/2012/january-/nhs-trust-facing-375000-fine-over-theft-of-patient-data/.

Press Association (2012) 'Police force fined £120,000 after theft of unencrypted memory stick', *The Guardian*, 16 Oct. Available at: http://www.theguardian.com/uk/2012/oct/16/police-force-fine-theft-memory-stick.

Ramesh, R. (2012) 'Troubled families tsar Louise Casey criticized over research', *The Guardian*, 24 Oct. Available at: http://www.guardian.co.uk/society/2012/oct/24/families-tsar-louise-casey-criticised?newsfeed=true.

Ritchie, F. (2007) *Statistical Detection and Disclosure Control in A Research Environment*, mimeo, Office for National Statistics. Available at: http://doku.iab.de/fdz/events/2007/Ritchie.pdf.

Singer, N. (2013) 'Data protection laws, an ocean apart', *The New York Times*, 2 Feb. Available at: http://www.nytimes.com/2013/02/03/technology/consumer-data-protection-laws-an-ocean-apart.html?_r=0.

The National Archives (1998a) *The Data Protection Act 1998*, The National Archives. Available at: http://www.legislation.gov.uk/ukpga/1998/29/contents.

The National Archives (1998b) *Human Rights Act 1998*, The National Archives. Available at: http://www.legislation.gov.uk/ukpga/1998/42/contents.

The National Archives (2004) *The Environmental Information Regulations 2004*, The National Archives. Available at: http://www.legislation.gov.uk/uksi/2004/3391/contents/made.

The National Archives (2007) *Statistics and Registration Service Act 2007*, The National Archives. Available at: http://www.legislation.gov.uk/ukpga/2007/18/contents.

The National Archives (2012) *Protection of Freedoms Act 2012*, The National Archives. Available at: http://www.legislation.gov.uk/ukpga/2012/9/contents/enacted.

UK Data Service (2013a) *Join Us: Secure Access*, UK Data Service, University of Essex. Available at: http://ukdataservice.ac.uk/get-data/secure-access/join-us.aspx.

UK Data Service (2013b) *Examples of Consent Forms*, UK Data Service, University of Essex. Available at: http://ukdataservice.ac.uk/manage-data/consent-and-ethics.aspx.

UK Data Service (2013c) *Code of Practice. Secure Data Service Members*, UK Data Service, University of Essex. Available at: http://ukdataservice.ac.uk/manage-data/legal-ethical/consent-data-sharing/consent-forms.aspx.

UK Research Integrity Office (2009) *Research Code of Practice*, UK Research Integrity Office. Available at: http://www.ukrio.org/what-we-do/code-of-practice-for-research/.

University of Essex, Institute for Social and Economic Research and NatCen Social Research (2013) *Understanding Society: Waves 1–2, 2009–2011* [computer file], 4th edn. Colchester, Essex: UK Data Archive [distributor], January 2013. SN: 6614. Available at: http://dx.doi.org/10.5255/UKDA-SN-6614-4.

Ustaran, E. (2013) 'Editorial: "Killing the internet"', *Data Protection Law and Policy*, 10(1). Available at: http://www.e-comlaw.com/data-protection-law-and-policy/article_template.asp?Contents=Yes&from=dplp&ID=1055.

Wales Cancer Bank (2007) *Annual Report 2006–2007*, Wales Cancer Bank. Available at: http://www.walescancerbank.com/documents/WCBAnnualReport_2007.pdf.

Wiles, R., Heath, S., Crow, G. and Charles, V. (2005) 'Informed consent in social research: A literature review', *NCRM Methods Review Papers*, NCRM/001. Available at: http://eprints.ncrm.ac.uk/85/.

Winters, K. (2007) *Qualitative Election Study of Britain, 2010* [computer file]. Colchester, Essex: UK Data Archive [distributor], February. SN: 6861. Available at: http://dx.doi.org/10.5255/UKDA-SN-6861-2.

World Health Organization (2008) *Declaration of Helsinki*, World Health Organization. Available at: http://www.who.int/bulletin/archives/79%284%29373.pdf.

EIGHT
Rights Relating to Research Data

Many kinds of data created as part of a research project are subject to the same rights as literary or artistic work. These might include texts, maps or audio-visual recordings, or information that is arranged in a database structure. Such items acquire rights like copyright or more general Intellectual Property (IP) rights when they are created. This gives the rights owner control over the exploitation of their work, such as the right to copy and adapt the work, the right to rent or lend it, the right to communicate it to the public and the right to licence and distribute (JISC Legal, 2011). Rights need to be taken into account when creating, using and sharing data.

In general these rights should not cause problems relating to the sharing and reuse of research data. When problems do arise, they can be due to misuse of data obtained under a licence or from public requests to obtain data. While the area of IP rights can be legally complex, it is nonetheless helpful to understand the conditions under which you can use, share and publish original research data, or data derived from third-party sources, within the boundaries of IP rights and copyright.

Intellectual Property Rights

Intellectual Property (IP) rights refer in general to intellectual works created by individuals or organizations for which exclusive rights are recognized. Examples include literary, musical, artistic or dramatic works, designs and discoveries, and can be in the form of a manuscript, an invention, software, a business or brand name or logo. Common types of IP rights include copyright, patents, trademarks and designs. Some rights require registration, for example patent rights, whereas other rights such as copyright accrue automatically when the work is created (Intellectual Property Office, 2013). The exclusive rights granted cover the right to publish to various markets, license the manufacture and distribution of products, and protect against unauthorized or unlawful copying.

In most research institutions, such as universities, the institution owns **IP** rights arising from research undertaken by employees in the course of their employment. A research funder may also wish to exert some claim over rights, although, in most cases, **IP** rights are attributed to the researcher unless an output becomes commercially viable. If a university research project has commercial collaborators there may be joint **IP** rights in the research outputs, which are best handled via consortium agreements or legal contracts.

The important point to note is that researchers should clarify ownership of, and rights relating to, research data sources; both data created and third-party data being used, before embarking upon research. This in turn will help determine how those data can be published and accessed in the future.

The two most relevant types of rights as far as research data are concerned are copyright and database rights.

Copyright and Exemptions Under Fair Dealing

Copyright is an intellectual property right assigned automatically to the creator. It prevents unauthorized copying and publishing of an original work. Copyright cannot be taken away without consent and cannot be abused without the possibility of legal action ensuing. The creator is automatically the first copyright owner, unless there is a contract that assigns copyright differently or there is written transfer of copyright signed by the copyright owner.

Under the UK Copyright, Designs and Patents Act 1988 (The National Archives, 1998) copyright applies to:

- original literary, dramatic, musical or artistic works;
- sound recordings, films, broadcasts or cable programmes;
- the typographical arrangement of publications.

Most research outputs, including spreadsheets, publications, textual files, reports and computer programs, fall under literary work and are therefore protected by copyright. Facts, however, cannot be copyrighted. For copyright to apply, the work must be original and fixed in a material form, for example, written or recorded. There is no copyright in ideas as such or in unrecorded speech. The duration of copyright depends on the type of work, as set out in a simplified way in Table 8.1.

Normally copyright clearance needs to be obtained from the rights holder before data can be reproduced. Fortunately, under the 'fair dealing' exemption, which exists in many countries, data can be copied in part for non-commercial teaching or research purposes, private study, criticism or review and news reporting without infringing copyright. This applies to literary, dramatic, musical or artistic work. An acknowledgement should give credit to the data source used, the data distributor and the copyright holder.

Limits on the amount of a work that may be copied under fair dealing, to 'a reasonable proportion', only apply to copies made by or on behalf of a librarian,

Table 8.1 Duration of copyright under the UK Copyright Act

Type of work	Copyright duration
Literary and artistic works	70 years from the end of the year of the death of creator
Sound recordings	50 years from the end of the year in which they are made, or published, or played or communicated to the public
Typographical arrangements	25 years from date of publication
Crown Copyright	50 years from date of publication or 125 years from date of creation
Database right	15 years from date of creation or publication
Unpublished work	work unpublished on 1 August 1989, or created between 1 August 1989 and 31 December 2005, remains in copyright until 31 December 2039, no matter how long ago it was created or when its author died

Source: UK Copyright Service, 2009

not copies made by a researcher or student (Copyright Licensing Agency, 2013). Therefore, using research data solely for research purposes should not infringe any rights under the concept of fair dealing where legitimate users may copy sections of material for non-commercial, teaching or research purposes. The fair dealing principle also exists in other countries such as Canada and Australia.

In the USA, copyright exceptions are formulated as 'fair use', a defence permitting limited use of copyrighted material without the need for permission from a rights holder, for example for commentary, criticism, news reporting, research, teaching, library archiving and scholarship (USA Copyright Office, 2013). Despite some similarities it is not synonymous with fair dealing, as there is no rigid set of defences.

While details of copyright law vary between countries, the Berne Convention for the Protection of Literary and Artistic Works lays down a common framework and agreement between nations in respect to intellectual property rights (copyright and moral rights) (UK Copyright Service, 2013). The convention, originally accepted as far back as 1886, is administered by the World Intellectual Property Organization (WIPO). The balance of interest enshrined in the Berne Convention is in practice applied to the advantage of rights-holders rather than of researchers and students.

In Europe the EU Copyright Directive (2001) was developed to harmonize copyright legislation and exceptions and implement the WIPO copyright treaty across members, with member states applying the directive into national legislation. However, at present there is no harmonization of copyright exceptions or limitations for education, research and libraries across the national legislations implemented in the EU. A survey of the laws of four EU countries showed that copyright law differs between the UK and the continental countries. In the UK, the threshold for copyright protection was relatively low and it was easier to allow for collections of factual data to be protected by copyright, as the principal criteria for copyright to apply is effort. In the continental countries, the threshold was found to be much higher as both originality and creativity are required for copyright to apply (CIER, 2011).

Examples of the Kinds of Works Covered by Copyright in the UK (Charlesworth, 2012)

- Literary works: original and fixed works such as fiction and non-fiction books, journals, newspapers, magazines, letters, email, webpages, etc.; the spoken word falls within this category if recorded in writing or otherwise.
- Artistic works: graphic works, photographs, sculptures, collages, maps, charts and plans.
- Sound recordings: every type of sound recording on any type of medium from which sounds can be reproduced.
- Films: any medium from which a moving image may be reproduced.
- Broadcasts: any transmission capable of lawfully being received by members of the public.

Database Rights

Rights in databases are treated differently. If information is structured in a database, the structure acquires a database right alongside the copyright in the content of the database. According to the UK's Copyright and Rights in Databases Regulations 1997 a database is a collection of independent works arranged in a systematic or methodical way (The National Archives, 1997). Database right protects and rewards the creation and arrangement of a database. A database may be protected by both copyright and database right. For database right to apply, the database must be the result of substantial intellectual investment in obtaining, verifying or presenting the content in an original manner. Simply entering facts into a spreadsheet would not count as substantial effort, but translating or synthesizing and coding information from multiple sources probably would. The author's time, skill and labour would need to be directed to the selection and arrangement of the database, over and above gathering the information. The database right is an automatic right and protects databases against the unauthorized extraction and reuse of the contents.

While most database rights are protected for 15 years from the date of creation or publication, for some complex databases the structure itself can be categorized as a literary work, even if its contents are of a visual nature, and therefore attract 70 years' copyright similar to other literary material. The European Union Database Directive offers protection in some European countries for the contents of a database in the same way as in the UK (Europa, 1996).

If a researcher uses parts of data from a database, as well as the structure in which those data are held, to create another dataset, they should obtain explicit copyright and database right clearance before they publish these data.

Useful Facts About Intellectual Rights Ownership and Transfer

- The author or creator of a work automatically owns copyright as soon as the original work is fixed in a material form (written or recorded).
- There is no copyright in ideas or unrecorded speech.
- Copyright subsists in the typescript of a book before it is published.
- If a work has multiple creators, the copyright will by default be owned by all creators.
- For work created during employment, legally the copyright owner is the employer, subject to 'any agreement to the contrary'; in practice many academic institutions assign copyright in research materials and publications to the researchers; researchers should check how their institution assigns copyright.
- For research undertaken by a PhD student, that student is the copyright owner of data and outputs created, and not the institution since a student is not an employee of an institution.
- For collaborative research or derived data, copyright is held by all the investigators or institutions involved.
- For data collected via interviews that are recorded and/or transcribed, the researcher holds the copyright of recordings and transcripts but each speaker is an author of his or her recorded words in the interview (Padfield, 2010).
- If a researcher wishes to publish large extracts from an interview, it is advisable to obtain a transfer of copyright from interviewees, using a signed form.
- Those wishing to reproduce or publish data must obtain copyright clearance from the rights holder, but the data can be analysed or used for research without permission.
- Data can be reproduced for non-commercial purposes without infringing copyright under the fair dealing exemption, providing that the data source used, data distributor and the copyright holder are acknowledged.
- Copyright can be transferred by the copyright owner, but only in writing, by means of a transfer document called an assignment.
- Ownership of copyright can be sold and bequeathed and is unrelated to the ownership of an object; the transmission of copyright does not affect its duration.
- A database may be protected by copyright in the content and database right in the structure.
- In the UK a creator of a work can also hold moral rights under the Copyright, Designs and Patents Act 1988, which gives the creator the right to be identified as the author or creator of a work; this right must be asserted by the author in writing and typically lasts the same length of time as copyright.
- Publication rights are equivalent to copyright and reward the creative effort used when editing another research work, for example transcribing and publishing a database based on an unpublished historical source that has fallen out of copyright.

More information on copyright in academia is provided by JISC Legal (2011), the British Academy and the Publishers Association (2008) and Korn et al. (2007).

Freedom of Information Legislation:
Your Responsibilities

There exist rights for people to request access to recorded information held by public sector organizations. This can include research data held by universities or research institutions. Many countries have some form of Freedom of Information legislation, which is designed to ensure accountability and good governance in public authorities. In 2003 the European Union issued a directive for the Reuse of Public Sector Information (European Union, 2003). In turn this directive has been implemented by member states in their national legislation. In the USA, the Freedom of Information (**FOI**) Act was passed as early as 1966 by Lydon B. Johnson; this only applies to federal agencies (USA Department of Justice, 2013).

In the UK, the Freedom of Information (**FOI**) Act was established to increase transparency in the public sector and has been in force for over 10 years (The National Archives, 2000). The Act requires every public authority to have a publication scheme, approved by the Information Commissioner's Office (ICO), and to publish information covered by the scheme. The scheme should set out the organization's commitment to make defined classes of information routinely available, such as policies and procedures, minutes of meetings, annual reports and financial information (ICO, 2013). Research data can be requested under the **FOI** Act and legally supplied to anyone, but copyright and **IP** rights to such data remain with the original researcher.

While there is a general presumption in favour of release, certain exceptions exist to the Act in the UK, such as:

- Personal data about living individuals cannot be requested, unless it is about you.
- Information that is accessible by other means, for example via a website.
- Information intended for future publication.
- Information that is subject to a confidentiality agreement, such as in a signed consent form or sensitive data held under restricted access by a data archive.
- Information whose release would prejudice legitimate commercial interests.
- In Scotland, information that is part of a finite research programme for which there is a publication schedule and clear intent to publish; the UK government plans to implement this same exemption (Matthews, 2012).
- If the public interest in withholding the information is greater than the public interest in disclosing.

Data cannot be withheld forever, and if they are requested and not released there should be a presumption that they may be requested again, and steps should be taken to ensure that the data are not destroyed in the meantime.

There have recently been several high profile cases where access to research data held by universities in the UK has been requested under the FoI Act.

Requests to Access Research Data Under the UK FOI Act

'University told to hand over tree ring data'

Queen's University in Belfast has been told by the Information Commissioner to hand over 40 years of research data on tree rings, used for climate research. ... This is the latest development in an on-going process that has seen 'climate skeptics' attempting to obtain raw data and documentation on methodologies from researchers, especially those working to understand the climate of the past. (BBC, 2010)

'Scientists broke the law by hiding climate change data: But legal loophole means they won't be prosecuted'

Scientists at the heart of the 'Climategate' email scandal broke the law when they refused to give raw data to the public, the privacy watchdog has ruled. The Information Commissioner's office said University of East Anglia researchers breached the Freedom of Information Act when handling requests from climate change sceptics (Derbyshire, 2010).

'Philip Morris: Tobacco firm using FOI laws to access secret academic data'

Philip Morris International has tried to force the University of Stirling to hand over secret data into teenage smoking and cigarette packaging gathered over more than a decade. ... In June the commissioner's office said the university's reason for refusing to hand over the information, because the request was considered 'vexatious', was not a correct reason and ordered it to issue another response. The university has since refused the request because it believes it will cost too much money to process (Hough, 2011).

In the end this request was dropped by Philip Morris because of public relations damage, not because the request would be legally unfounded.

Overall, it is better for researchers to consider planned releases of their research data, for example, via a data management plan, rather than be faced with unanticipated FOI requests. Following the cases cited in this chapter, and the concerns that the Act could allow research that has not been through the peer-review process to be interpreted incorrectly by members of the public or by journalists, in early 2013, the British government agreed to introduce an exemption to the FOI to prevent the premature disclosure of research data (Matthews, 2012).

JISC developed a useful questions and answers resource for researchers on how to deal with and respond to FOI requests for research data (Charlesworth and Rusbridge, 2010). In general, a first course of action would be to contact your local institutional FoI practitioner.

On the other hand, researchers can also use FOI as a method of data collection to access essential information and materials for their own research (Bourke et al., 2012).

Environmental Information Regulations 2004

Like the FOI Act, the Environmental Information Regulations (EIR) legislation gives the public access rights to environmental information held by a public authority, including universities, in response to requests, in this case for 'environmental' information (The National Archives, 2004). Freedom of access does not imply free access. There are circumstances under which requests may or must be refused, for example if the data contain personal information.

For the purposes of this legislation, environmental information constitutes:

- The state of the elements of the environment: air and atmosphere, water, soil, land, landscape, natural sites, biological diversity and its components, genetically modified organisms, and the interaction among these elements.
- Factors such as substances, energy, noise, radiation, waste, emissions, discharges and other releases into the environment, affecting or likely to affect the elements of the environment.
- Measures such as policies, legislation, plans, programmes, environmental agreements, and activities affecting or likely to affect the elements and factors as well as measures or activities designed to protect those elements.
- Reports on the implementation of environmental legislation.
- Cost-benefit and other economic analyses and assumptions used within the framework of the measures and activities.
- The state of human health and safety, including the contamination of the food chain, conditions of human life, cultural sites and built structures inasmuch as they are or may be affected by the state of the elements of the environment.

Sharing Data and Licensing

If a researcher wishes to share research data by publishing or disseminating them, all the rights holders need to be identified and the necessary copyright permissions be granted for data to be shared. Researchers may not have the right to share data, for example if data were obtained under a licence with specific conditions of use attached. The data publisher, be it a data centre, archive or repository, usually does not expect to have rights in the data collections it distributes or provides access to. Rather, a researcher or data creator will retain the copyright in their data and give the centre a non-exclusive licence to redistribute the data. All copyright holders with some claim over the data collection need to agree to the terms of deposit. Without this licence agreement in place, a data centre or institutional repository cannot legally provide access to the data. A data centre's policy typically sets out terms and conditions of data use, such as how data should be acknowledged and cited when they are used, the need for maintaining confidentiality about participants' information in data, and whether or not commercial use is permitted.

Assigning copyright correctly is particularly important where data collections have been created from a variety of sources, for example when data have been bought or lent by other researchers. No obvious third party organization exists to negotiate rights on behalf of researchers, unlike the Performing Rights Society, which administers rights relating to the public performance and broadcast of musical works. In most cases the researcher will need to contact the rights holder, or the rights holder's estate, and come to an agreement whereby the terms and conditions of reproduction can be laid down in an agreement or licence. There may be financial implications.

Copyright extends beyond the life of a data owner whether this is a person or a company. It is wise to make provision for rights to be transferred explicitly to a known third party in the event of a death of an owner or the dissolution of a company. This will prevent 'orphan' works in the future.

When considering sharing your data, you need to consider how you want your data to be reused by other researchers or students. You can specify this by licensing the data to match the intended uses. While any type of licence can be drawn up by a legal representative to meet specific criteria, various types of licences for sharing data have been developed. Data archives have had redistribution licenses in place for many years such as those used by the UK Data Service (UK Data Service, 2013). Other licenses at the more open end of the sharing spectrum include Creative Commons, Open Data Commons and Open Government Licence. Ball (2012) has developed guidance for licensing data collections.

Creative Commons Licences

Creative Commons (CC) licences were designed for generic digital content such as text, images and film. They allow creators to easily communicate the rights they wish to keep and the rights they wish to waive in order for other people to make reuse of their intellectual property (Creative Commons, 2013). Most Creative Commons licences have an 'Attribution' condition, which means that the creator is given due credit when a work is copied, distributed, displayed or performed. Additional conditions that can be selected are: 'Non-Commercial', which means that the work cannot be used for commercial purposes; 'Share Alike' which means that any derived works must be released under the same licence as the original work; and 'No Derivatives' which means that altering, transforming or building upon the work is forbidden. As a result, six different Creative Commons licences that specify attribution exist, as shown in Figure 8.1.

Creative Commons also offers a CCO licence to release work into the public domain, with no rights reserved. CCO requires no attribution and there are no conditions on use, publishing or redistribution. This is not recommended for sharing substantive research data.

(Continued)

(Continued)

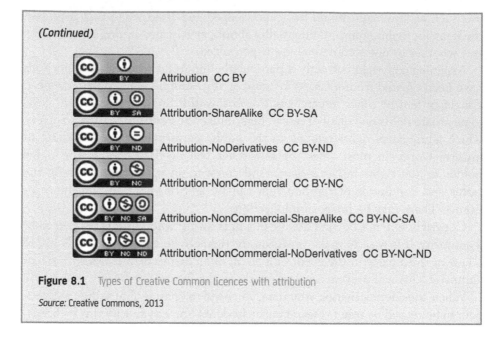

Figure 8.1 Types of Creative Common licences with attribution

Source: Creative Commons, 2013

For some data collections Creative Commons licences are appropriate, but they are not recommended for databases. Open Data Commons licences may be more suitable as they take database rights into consideration, considering both the entity relationship model for the database and its content. The Open Data Commons Open Database License (ODbL) specifies that the database can be copied, distributed, adapted and have works produced for it, with full attribution and a promise to 'share alike' any adapted version in an open manner (Open Data Commons, 2013).

Exercise 8.1   Copyright scenarios and solutions

This exercise presents a number of plausible scenarios that a researcher might face when collecting or working with data. Find a solution for each scenario suggesting what the rights implications are and how best to deal with them.

Scenario 1   Interviews with company directors

A researcher has interviewed company directors about their careers and produced audio recordings and near verbatim transcripts herself. The researcher analyses this material and offers it to a data archive. The researcher did not get signed copyright transfers for the interviewees' words. What are the rights issues surrounding this offer of data?

Scenario 2   Transcription from a printed work into a spreadsheet

A researcher has copied a series of statistical information from a printed work into a spreadsheet. The transcription is a direct copy with minimal alterations. The book is still in copyright. What are the rights issues surrounding this research?

Scenario 3   Data in the public domain

A researcher studies how health issues around obesity are reported in the media in the last 10 years. Freely available newspaper websites and library sources are used to obtain articles on this topic. Articles or excerpts are copied into a database and coded according to various criteria for content analysis. Can the researcher use such public data without breaching copyright? Can the database be archived and shared with other researchers?

Scenario 4   Archived data

A researcher uses International Social Survey Programme (ISSP) data obtained from ZACAT/GESIS – Leibniz Institute for the Social Sciences in Germany. These data are freely available to registered users. The researcher incorporates some of the ISSP data within a database containing his own research data. Can this database be placed on the researcher's website?

Scenario 5   Media database

A researcher has collated articles about the British Prime Minister from *The Guardian* newspaper over the past ten years, using the LexisNexis database to source articles. They are then transcribed by the researcher into a database so that content analysis can be applied. The researcher offers a copy of the database with the original transcribed text to a data centre. Can these transcribed data be offered for sharing?

Scenario 6   Data obtained from a data centre

A researcher has used the National Diet and Nutrition Survey (NDNS) data, obtained via the UK Data Archive. NDNS data are Crown Copyright. The researcher has processed the NDNS data (filtered, integrated and aggregated data across variables, while maintaining individual records) and used the processed data to model food chain risks. The researcher would like to archive the processed data that were used as input data for the modelling, as well as the modelling code, at the UK Data Archive. What issues might arise?

Scenario 7   Survey questions

A researcher wishes to reuse a set of questions from an existing survey questionnaire, to compare results between the newly proposed survey and the original.

Scenario 8   Third party and licensed data

Researchers at the Stockholm Environmental Institute (SEI) have created an integrated spatial database, Social and Environmental Conditions in Rural Areas (SECRA). This contains a wide range of socio-economic and environmental characteristics for all rural Census 2001 Super Output Areas (SOAs) for England. Multiple third party data sources were used, some gained under licence, such as Census 2001 data, Land Cover Map data and data from the Land Registry, Environment Agency, Automobile Association, Royal Mail and British Trust for Ornithology. Derived data were calculated and mapped onto SOAs. The researchers would like to distribute the database for wider use.

Answers to Exercise 8.1

Scenario 1   Interviews with company directors

Solution: In this case the company directors hold the copyright in their words, while the researcher holds the copyright over the transcribed interviews.

Quoting large extracts of the data, either in publications, or by archiving the transcripts, would breach the copyright of the interviewees in their words. While many interviewees may not be concerned over such copyright, in this case where company directors have shared information about their careers, they may want to exert copyright over this content, for example, they may wish to write their memoirs at a later stage.

If the researcher wants to publish large extracts of data, or archive transcripts, it is best to ask for transfer of copyright of the interview content from interviewees.

Scenario 2   Transcription from a printed work into a spreadsheet

Solution: Technically, the researcher should have cleared copyright before transcription. If the work is for personal use only, this can be disregarded as fair dealing. If the newly constructed dataset is to be archived and disseminated, copyright clearance must be gained from the copyright holder.

Scenario 3   Data in the public domain

Solution: Even though the articles obtained are in the public domain, they are still under copyright. Whilst such information can be used for personal research purposes (fair dealing), the articles cannot be archived, unless permission is obtained from the newspapers; otherwise this would breach copyright.

Scenario 4   Archived data

Solution: Although the ISSP data are available for free to all researchers, this does not mean that the data can be published on a website and made available to others. The data can be incorporated into a database and used for personal analysis. Before this dataset is placed on a website, permission must be sought from the data owner.

Scenario 5   Media database

Solution: Researchers cannot share either of these data sources as they do not have copyright in the original material. A data centre cannot accept these data as to do so would be a breach of copyright. The rights holders, in this case *The Guardian* and LexisNexis, would need to provide consent for archiving.

Scenario 6   Data obtained from a data centre

Solution: There is joint copyright over the processed data, shared between the researcher and the Crown, the latter holding copyright over the NDNS data. The researcher must declare this joint copyright for the modelling data and requires no further permission from the Crown.

The End User Licence, which the researcher signed when obtaining the **NDNS** data from the UK Data Archive, specifically states: 'offer for deposit any new data collections derived from the data supplied or created by the combination of the data supplied with other data'. Thus the UK Data Archive can archive the processed data with a joint copyright declaration; another data centre or repository might not be able to do this.

Scenario 7   Survey questions

Solution: It should be assumed that all survey questions and instruments are copyright protected, with copyright residing with the organization(s) that commissioned, designed or conducted the survey.

Our advice, therefore, is to contact the copyright holder(s) directly for permission to reproduce questionnaire text for any new use. In our experience the copyright holder will almost always grant that permission. Some questionnaires contain measurement scales, batteries of questions or classifications. These particular instruments are copyrighted to the institution or company that produced them and they must not be reproduced without permission. In many cases, the copyright statement relating to these instruments is printed on the relevant page of the questionnaire.

Scenario 8   Third party and licensed data

Solution: While the database contains no original third party data, only derived data, there is still joint copyright shared between the SEI and the various copyright holders of the third party data. The researchers have sought permission from all data owners to distribute the data and the copyright of all third party data is declared in the documentation. The database can therefore be distributed.

References

Ball, A. (2012) *How to License Research Data*, DCC How-to Guides, Digital Curation Centre, University of Edinburgh. Available at: http://www.dcc.ac.uk/resources/how-guides.

BBC News (2010) 'University told to hand over tree ring data', *BBC News Online*, 19 April. Available at: http://news.bbc.co.uk/1/hi/northern_ireland/8623417.stm.

Bourke, G., Worthy, B. and Hazell, R. (2012) *Making Freedom of Information Requests: A Guide for Academic Researchers*, UCL Constitution Unit, University College London. Available at: http://www.ucl.ac.uk/constitution-unit/research/foi/foi-universities/academics-guide-to-foi.pdf.

British Academy and the Publishers Association (2008) *Joint Guidelines on Copyright and Academic Research*, British Academy and the Publishers Association. Available at: http://www.publishers.org.uk/images/stories/AboutPA/Joint_Guidelines_on_Copyright_and_Academic_Research.pdf.

Charlesworth, A. (2012) *Intellectual Property Rights for Digital Preservation*, DPC Technology Watch Report 12–02, Digital Preservation Coalition. Available at: http://dx.doi.org/10.7207/twr12–02.

Charlesworth, A. and Rusbridge, C. (2010) *Freedom of Information and Research Data: Questions and Answers*, JISC. Available at: http://www.jisc.ac.uk/publications/programmerelated/2010/foiresearchdata.aspx.

CIER (2011) *The Legal Status of Research Data in the Knowledge Exchange Partner Countries*, Centre for Intellectual Property Law (CIER), Utrecht University. Available at: http://knowledge-exchange.info/Files/Filer/downloads/Primary%20Research%20 Data/Legal%20Status%20Research%20Data/KE-CIER_Report_legal_status_of_ research_data_Final.pdf.

Copyright Licensing Agency (2013) Available at: http://www.cla.co.uk/.

Creative Commons (2013) *About the Licenses*, Creative Commons. Available at: http:// creativecommons.org/licences.

Derbyshire, D. (2010) 'Scientists broke the law by hiding climate change data: But legal loophole means they won't be prosecuted', *Mail Online*, 28 January. Available at: http://www.dailymail.co.uk/news/article-1246661/New-scandal-Climate-Gate- scientists-accused-hiding-data-global-warming-sceptics.html#axzz2KXjDIc00.

Europa (1996) *Access to European Law*, Europa. Available at: http://eur-lex.europa.eu/ LexUriServ/LexUriServ.do?uri=CELEX:31996L0009:EN:NOT.

European Union (2003) *Re-use of Public Sector Information Directive 2003/98/EC, OJEU, L345/90*, Europa. Available at: http://ec.europa.eu/information_society/policy/psi/ docs/pdfs/directive/psi_directive_en.pdf.

Hough, A. (2011) 'Philip Morris: Tobacco firm using FoI laws to access secret academic data', *The Telegraph*, 1 September. Available at: http://www.telegraph.co.uk/health/ healthnews/8734295/Philip-Morris-tobacco-firm-using-FOI-laws-to-access-secret- academic-data.html.

ICO (2013) *What Information do we Need to Publish?*, Information Commissioners Office. Available at: http://www.ico.org.uk/for_organisations/freedom_of_ information/guide/publication_scheme.

Intellectual Property Office (2013) *Types of Intellectual Property*, Intellectual Property Office. Available at: http://www.ipo.gov.uk/types.htm.

JISC Legal (2011) *Copyright and Intellectual Property Law*, JISC Legal Information Service. Available at: http://www.jisclegal.ac.uk/LegalAreas/CopyrightIPR.aspx.

Korn, N., Oppenheim, C. and Duncan, C. (2007) *IPR and Licensing Issues in Derived Data*, JISC. Available at: http://www.jisc.ac.uk/media/documents/projects/ iprinderiveddatareport.pdf.

Matthews, D. (2012) 'Research data win exemption from FoI Act', *Times Higher Education*, 6 December. Available at: http://www.timeshighereducation.co.uk/422049. article.

Open Data Commons (2013) *Open Data Commons Open Database License (ODbL)*, Open Data Commons. Available at: http://opendatacommons.org/licenses/odbl/.

Padfield, T. (2010) *Copyright for Records Managers and Archivists*, 4th edn. London: Facet Publishing.

The National Archives (1997) *The Copyright and Rights in Databases Regulations 1997*, The National Archives. Available at: http://www.legislation.gov.uk/uksi/1997/3032/ contents/made.

The National Archives (1998) *Copyright, Designs and Patents Act 1988 (c. 48)*, The National Archives. Available at: http://www.legislation.gov.uk/ukpga/1988/48/ contents.

The National Archives (2000) *Freedom of Information Act 2000*, The National Archives. Available at: http://www.legislation.gov.uk/ukpga/2000/36/contents.

The National Archives (2004) *The Environmental Information Regulations 2004*, The National Archives. Available at: http://www.legislation.gov.uk/uksi/2004/3391/ contents/made.

UK Copyright Service (2009) *Copyright Duration*, Fact sheet P-01, UK Copyright
  Service. Available at: http://www.copyrightservice.co.uk/copyright/p01_uk_copyright_
  law#duration.
UK Copyright Service (2013) *International Copyright Law: The Berne Convention*, UK
  Copyright Service. Available at: http://www.copyrightservice.co.uk/copyright/p08_
  berne_convention.
UK Data Service (2013) *Help with the Licence Agreement*, UK Data Service. Available at:
  http://ukdataservice.ac.uk/deposit-data/support/regular-depositors/licence.aspx.
USA Copyright Office (2013) *Copyright*, USA Copyright Office. Available at: http://
  www.copyright.gov/.
USA Department of Justice (2013) *Freedom of Information Act Resources*, USA
  Department of Justice. Available at: http://www.justice.gov/oip/foia-resources.html.

NINE
Collaborative Research: Data Management Strategies for Research Teams and Research Managers

Large-scale and collaborative research is becoming increasingly common, with a move away from smaller-scale research within single universities, other than postgraduate research projects. Many collaborative projects are multi-institutional, even cross-national, and interdisciplinary, which brings additional data management challenges for providing shared storage, access and transfer of research data across various partners or institutions.

In large-scale projects and research centres, the coordination and streamlining of data management becomes an important task. A 2011 survey about data sharing practices amongst 1,329 researchers reported that overall organizations did not provide sufficient technical support, funding or training to their researchers for data management in either the short or longer term (Tenopir et al., 2011). However, project and centre managers can support researchers through a coordinated data management framework comprising policies, shared best practices, tools, infrastructure and training. This can include providing a virtual research environment or shared research space to share research data and documents; providing guidance, templates and pointers to key policies relating to data management; and keeping track of created and acquired data to plan and implement data management measures throughout the research process. Such a framework could apply equally at the level of a research organization or a university.

Standard Procedures, Protocols and Policies

Research centres and large collaborative projects benefit from dedicated organized central research coordination. This can provide important input into planning and implementing data management and sharing. A centralized approach to data management provides both economies of scale and a lasting framework for shared best practices.

Obvious benefits of centralized data management include:

- researchers can share good practice and data management experiences with each other, thereby building capacity, collective knowledge and resources for the centre; new researchers can immediately implement good data practices from this shared expertise;
- a uniform approach to data management by creating standard data policies and procedures, for example, for file-naming or IP rights;
- keeping track of projects and owners of data over time, especially when researchers come and go;
- storing and backing up data in a central location;
- making researchers and staff aware of duties, responsibilities, funder and legal requirements relating to research data, with easy access to relevant information;
- ensuring that data management is costed into funding proposals.

Setting up shared procedures and references at a centralized level is helpful to encourage a positive culture of data management and sharing data, and is discussed in more detail in the section below on using a resources library. At the same time, researchers themselves take the ultimate responsibility for managing their research data. However, consideration needs to be given to whether researchers and support staff have the necessary skills for all aspects of data management, or whether training may need to be provided.

Regarding infrastructure, a centre or project can consider where research data will be held, both in the short- and long-term. Institutional server space is the obvious solution for the short-term; for long-term storage dedicated data repositories can be considered. For cross-institutional research a collaborative research space may need to be provided, described in the section later in this chapter.

Setting up a coordinated framework for data management can be helped by building a resources library, a place where documents and tools to keep track of research data being created can sit.

Using a Data Management Resources Library

A research hub can centralize all relevant data management and sharing planning resources for researchers and staff in a single location on an intranet site, website, wiki, shared network drive or within a virtual research environment. Such a resources library can contain relevant data policy and guidance documents, templates, tools and exemplars developed by the centre, as well as external policy and guidance resources or links to key documents. Resources can either be developed by the centre, or good practices used by particular researchers or projects can be used as exemplars for others, so good practices can be shared.

A resources library might contain two types of resources: local ones specific to the project; and others that are external, or relate to higher level policy and procedures.

Locally Created Documents

These may include:

- a centre-wide data inventory;
- a local statement or policy on data sharing;
- exemplar data management plans;
- local information on acts and regulations relating to data;
- a statement on copyright of research data and outputs;
- a statement of institutional IT data management and existing backup procedures;
- security policy for data storage, file-sharing and transmission procedures;
- standard data format recommendations;
- statement on retention and destruction of data, as it relates to particular kinds of data;
- quality control standards for data collection and data entry;
- digitization and transcription guidance;
- file-naming and version control guidance;
- a data inventory for individual projects, including roles and responsibilities (see Table 9.1);
- template consent forms and information sheets which take data sharing into account;
- example ethical review forms;
- data anonymization guidelines;
- confidentiality agreements for data handlers.

External Resources

These may cover:

- country-specific research funder data policies;
- research ethics guidance of professional bodies;
- codes of practice or professional standards relevant to research data;
- Acts and Regulations on country-specific data protection, freedom of information, and other legal information requirements;
- discipline-specific guidance on managing and sharing data;
- procedures for handling data, for example, governmental guidelines.

Roles and Responsibilities in a Team

In Chapter 3, we discussed how data management roles and responsibilities need to be agreed early on in a research project. For collaborative research across sites, this is vital, as is communication and reporting along the way.

It is useful to set out a spreadsheet of roles and responsibilities, with real names attached, and a clear understanding of what is involved and required of each individual. Particular attention may need to be paid to: deciding who has access to which data; ensuring standard protocols for data collection, entry and processing are used; and planning how data may need to be harmonized into a central database or file structure.

CASE STUDY	**Roles and Responsibilities in a Research Team, SomnIA: Sleep in Ageing**

SomnIA: Sleep in Ageing was a project coordinated by the University of Surrey as part of the UK's cross-council research council programme on New Dynamics of Ageing (SomnIA, 2010). This multidisciplinary project with research teams based at four UK universities, created a wide range of data from specialized actigraphy and light sensor measurements, self-completion surveys, randomized control clinical trials and qualitative interviews.

The project employed a research officer with dedicated data management responsibilities. Besides undertaking research on the project, the research officer coordinated the management of research data created by each work package via SharePoint Workspace 2010. This allowed controlled permission-levels of access to data and documentation and provided encryption and automated version control.

The officer was also responsible for operating a daily backup of all data and documentation to an off-site server. Individual researchers themselves were responsible for other data management tasks.

Keeping Track of Data

A research centre or large project benefits from maintaining a research data inventory to keep track of all data and related documentation and outputs that are being created or acquired by the various researchers. The inventory can record information such as:

- what the data mean;
- how they were created;
- where they were obtained;
- who owns them;
- who has access, use and editing rights;
- who is responsible for managing them;
- storage and backup strategies;
- data quality control procedures;
- different versions of files;
- how they will or can be shared.

At the same time an inventory can be used as a tool to plan data management measures when research starts and to keep track of their implementation during the research cycle via a regular update strategy. Data management can be reviewed annually, or alongside research review such as during project progress meetings.

An inventory can also facilitate data sharing as it contains essential information to enable future reuse and to make data archiving as straightforward as possible.

The UK Data Archive developed a template for a data collection inventory, designed to meet the requirements for data management of the ESRC research data policy and specifically for research centres to coordinate data archive submissions (UK Data Service, 2011). The columns for recording information are shown in Table 9.1. The grid could be maintained as a spreadsheet or as a database tool.

Table 9.1   Basic fields used for an inventory of data collections for a research centre

Field
Funding source (e.g. grant, centre budget, other)
Programme or initiative name
Project title
Principle investigator first name
Principle investigator surname
Other data contacts
Project start date dd-mm-yyyy
Project end date dd-mm-yyyy
New datasets created Y/N
Number of datasets created
Data type (qualitative, quantitative, mixed methods, model)
Data deposit to UK Data Service Y/N
Other data sharing plans
Data sharing constraints

Source: UK Data Service, 2011

Collaborative Environments and File-Sharing

Collaborative research brings with it the need for the sharing of information, documents and data, in a controlled, organized and managed way, often across various organizations or institutions. This can be challenging. Requirements of researchers for a collaborative environment typically are:

- storing and sharing information, documents and data files;
- organizing documents and files in folders and working spaces;
- user account management to control who can access which information;
- version management of documents and files;
- discussion via a forum or wiki.

Available options for setting up a collaborative research environment are:

- an institutional or departmental drive where access can be provided to external researchers, for example, through remote access via virtual private network (**VPN**) techniques;
- a secure file transfer protocol (**FTP**) server;
- a Virtual Research Environment (**VRE**) or portal environment, such as Sakai, My Experiment or MS Sharepoint;
- a content management system such as Drupal;
- cloud-based file-sharing areas such as Dropbox, Google Docs, Google Drive, iCloud or Microsoft SkyDrive (adapted from the earlier Microsoft Office Groove and Windows Live Folders);
- a data repository such as DSpace, Fedora, Eprints, CKAN or cloud-based figshare.

All of these options have their advantages and disadvantages. For an institutional drive, secure ftp server or content management system, one institution takes responsibility for setting up the area or system, controlling and enabling access, organizing storage and backup. Remote external access is granted to researchers at other institutions. Institutions may be reluctant to allow external people to access their server area via institutional credentials.

A content management system can be fully customized, yet may require significant technical input to set up and also requires on-going maintenance. The commercial product MS SharePoint is used in many universities, with varying degrees of satisfaction. It can enable external access and collaboration, the use of document libraries, team sites, workflow management processes, and version control capability. The open source Sakai platform has been used by projects of the UK's JISC virtual research environment programme and can be obtained under an educational community licence (Sakai, 2011). It has an established support network and features announcement facilities, dropbox for private file-sharing, an email archive, a resources library, communications functions, scheduling tools and control of permissions and access.

Cloud-based solutions tend to be easy to set up and use, be very convenient and versatile for mobile researchers, and have low maintenance and low cost if not much storage space is required. Users can easily create workspaces, and allow controlled access to folders and files by inviting members. Private, shared or public workspaces can be set up. File changes are tracked, using versioning, and sent to all members, with copies of the workspace synchronized via the network in a peer-to-peer manner. Google Drive has efficient document co-authoring tools.

Disadvantages of cloud-based systems are: storage size limitations, unless additional space is purchased; possible security concerns over where data files are held in a global network of data centres; and uncertainty over how permanent and robust longer-term storage is. Leading authorities on information security risk advise that cloud data storage should be avoided for high-risk institutional information, such as files that contain private or sensitive information, information that is covered by federal regulations or that has a very high intellectual property value to the institution (Borgmann et al., 2012; Higher Education Information Security Council, 2013). As there may be potential violation of data protection legislation for files containing personal data, such data should not be transferred to other countries without ensuring adequate protection. Chapter 7 deals with data protection in some detail. While file encryption can be used to safeguard data files to a certain degree, it would still not meet the requirements of data protection legislation. It is advised to always keep a backup version of data files offline.

Open source repository software like Fedora and DSpace are in development by some institutions but require significant set-up and maintenance costs, and progress is often limited to local bespoke instances. A repository is more suitable for storage of consolidated data after research projects end, rather than for active use during research.

To find the best solution for a particular research project that has collaborative workspace requirements it is worth discussing your needs first with your local institutional IT services.

For file transmission, several universities have developed dropbox-like services which they host themselves. For example the UK Data Service recommends data deposits from researchers to be submitted via the University of Essex ZendTo service. Data files containing sensitive or personal information should be encrypted before submission (University of Essex, 2012).

Secure Cloud-Based Collaborative Research Environments

In the UK, Janet Brokerage (Janet, 2013) provides a framework and support hub for securing cloud services for academia. This might include assessment of service security through a rigorous audit process. An alternative is to operate an internally hosted cloud service such as open source ownCloud, where you retain ownership and control of data. The UK Orbital Project (2012), part of JISC's Managing Research Data programme, reviewed the ownCloud service, and concluded that it could be ideal for a research environment.

The UK Biomedical Research Infrastructure Software Service kit (BRISSkit) is an open source cloud-enabled research platform for biomedical research informatics, using Janet Brokerage. It was developed by the University of Leicester and the Leicester Cardiovascular Biomedical Research Unit (BRU) based at the Glenfield Hospital in the University Hospitals Leicester NHS Trust. BRISSkit includes two data warehouses; one within the hospital and one maintained by the university. Patient data in the hospital warehouse is anonymized and pushed to the university warehouse, where they are available to university researchers hosted on a cloud infrastructure.

BRISSkit provides a range of interfaces for the creation or receipt of research data from interviews, surveys, biospecimen inventories, genomic data and registries of clinical trial participants. A range of potential sources for clinical data can also be added.

BRISSkit facilitates data transformation in two key ways, firstly in the anonymization of clinical data and secondly in the combining of data from disparate services for use in research (Tedds, 2012).

Exercise 9.1 Keeping track of data using collaborative tools and resources

Consider a research project that you have been involved in and create the following:

1. A data inventory for the project to log and keep track of types of data being collected. Set up an MS Excel spreadsheet and complete a row for the project and data that has been created.
2. A list of any protocols or templates that would be useful for ensuring good data practices for the research.
3. Concrete ideas about how you might put these systems into practice within a large research group or centre. What expertise might you need to bring in to help set it up? What kind of staffing might you need to make this work in a research centre environment or large collaborative project?

Exercise 9.2 Fun quiz

1. Using a dropbox area to store my research data is (choose all possible answers):

    (a) a good way to back up my data daily

    (b) the safest solution as my dropbox area is password protected

(c) OK for data that contain no confidential information and are regularly backed up elsewhere

(d) an easy way to be able to always access the most recent version of my data, whether in the office, in the field or at home

(e) a good way to publish a dataset that supports an open access article I have published

(f) ideal to make sure my files are always in the most recent software version.

2. As a PhD student working within a research organization, it is the organization's responsibility to (choose all possible answers):

(a) provide me with 100 GB of free storage space for my research data

(b) point me to relevant data governance procedures that apply to my research

(c) arrange daily backups of the files I keep on my personal laptop

(d) set up a secure storage area for sensitive data I am collecting

(e) share with me good examples of consent forms that colleague researchers have used.

3. For a collaborative research project between a UK university and a Ugandan university, comparing informal family support systems for young mothers in Uganda and amongst Ugandan immigrants in the UK, through interviews and questionnaires, which options are there for research data (interview transcripts, fieldwork notes, database of numerical coded questionnaire responses) to be easily shared for joint analysis between researchers based at the two involved institutions? (choose all possible answers)

(a) place all data files in a shared dropbox area

(b) send data files back and forth as email attachments

(c) securely transfer all data to both sites, using secure **FTP** arranged by one of the universities, and keep them on secured servers

(d) use the UK university's SharePoint instance to set up a **VRE** for the project that all parties involved can access

(e) researchers carry data on **USB** sticks each time someone travels back and forth between the two countries

(f) send encrypted anonymized data files back and forth as email attachments.

Answers to Exercise 9.1

1. Compare your data inventory with the UK Data Service list of data inventory fields set out in Table. 9.1.
2. Compare your list of protocols and templates with these example data management resources:

Locally created documents:

- Statement on copyright of research data and outputs.
- Institutional IT data management and central backup procedures.
- Statement on retention and destruction of data.
- File-naming conventions and version control system.
- Roles and responsibility spreadsheet for individual projects.
- Exemplar ethical review forms, consent forms and information sheets for data sharing.
- Guidance on anonymization for qualitative data.
- Transcription guidance for teams and external suppliers.

(Continued)

(Continued)

3. Keeping a data inventory up to date when principle investigators and research grant holders are coming and going can be challenging. However, a simple spreadsheet that keeps track of all new projects starting and all projects finishing is a good start. The director and administrator in a centre will usually have access to this information. It is advisable for one person to be responsible for this spreadsheet, rather than multiple people entering information. Having all the information about research data held within a department or centre in one single place can really help with data governance and data sharing mandates.

The templates and protocols can be sourced from various places: the centre's standard operating procedures if they exist; the centre's host institution who will have in place rules on research integrity and data governance; relevant funding bodies; and data archives, such as the UK Data Service or ICPSR in the USA, that provide reusable templates and procedures for the coherent collection of data and subsequent sharing.

Setting up a data management working group that can meet at regular intervals to discuss relevant topics, to plan a good data management strategy and to compile relevant resources can be very useful. It may be that such a group is only needed for a fixed time period until a strategy and procedures are established at the centre.

Answers to Exercise 9.2

1. Using a dropbox area to store my research data is:

   (a) a good way to back up my data daily – Incorrect. It is not a good idea to rely on a dropbox area for backups of your data. Backups are best made on offline media.

   (b) the safest solution as my dropbox area is password protected – Incorrect. Whilst a password offers protection, encryption and encrypted storage areas would offer more protection. Everything depends on what level of security you need for your data.

   (c) OK for data that contain no confidential information and are regularly backed up elsewhere – Correct. Dropbox is convenient for accessing certain kinds of information.

   (d) an easy way to be able to always access the most recent version of my data, whether in the office, in the field or at home – Correct. It offers a very easy and flexible way to handle active data files, as long as you are aware of its limitations.

   (e) a good way to publish a dataset that supports an open access article I have published – Incorrect. Data repositories are a better solution for publishing a dataset. It is not only about making a dataset accessible, but also about how you can maintain and preserve that dataset in an unaltered form, and how you can ensure the long-term accessibility of that dataset.

   (f) ideal to make sure my files are always in the most recent software version – Incorrect. Dropbox makes no changes to the software version of your files.

2. As a PhD student working within a research organization, it is the organization's responsibility to:

   (a) provide me with 100 GB of free storage space for my research data – Incorrect. You may get an amount of storage space if it is needed for your research, but it is certainly not a standard requirement.

   (b) point me to relevant data governance procedures that apply to my research – Correct. The organization needs to make sure you are informed about any relevant procedures.

   (c) arrange daily backups of the files I keep on my personal laptop – Incorrect. The organization typically is responsible for backing up their servers that would be available to you (still check it out!), but not for your personal devices, even if you use these for your research.

(d) set up a secure storage area for sensitive data I am collecting – Correct. They are responsible for ensuring that you can properly look after your data and fulfil any data protection or other legal requirements to protect and safeguard data.

(e) share with me good examples of consent forms that colleague researchers have used – Correct. Although not an essential requirement, we'd still like to think this forms part of the support an organization provides for you.

3. For a collaborative research project between a UK university and a Ugandan university, comparing informal family support systems for young mothers in Uganda and amongst Ugandan immigrants in the UK, through interviews and questionnaires, which options are there for research data (interview transcripts, fieldwork notes, database of numerical coded questionnaire responses) to be easily shared for joint analysis between researchers based at the two involved institutions?

(a) place all data files in a shared dropbox area – Incorrect. This would not be a sufficiently secure solution for the kinds of data being collected and would contravene data protection legislation if interviews or questionnaires contain personal information.

(b) send data files back and forth as email attachments – Incorrect. Definitely not secure enough, as email traffic remains on many servers in between.

(c) securely transfer all data to both sites, using secure FTP arranged by one of the universities, and keep them on secured servers – Correct. Still, check out which data protection measures need to be put in place under the legislation of both countries; it may be that data files need to be anonymized before they are transferred to the other country. Also make sure that the location where files are stored locally is sufficiently secure and consider how you will keep track of changes made to data files at either site.

(d) use the UK university's SharePoint instance to set up a VRE for the project that all parties involved can access – Correct. This also helps you keep track of versions, as all files are held in a single location accessible to both parties.

(e) researchers carry data on USB sticks each time someone travels back and forth between the two countries – Incorrect. This is inefficient, when secure and encrypted transfers are fairly easily set up.

(f) send encrypted data files back and forth as email attachments – Correct. Still, check out which data protection measures need to be put in place under the legislation of both countries. It may be that data files need to be anonymized before they are transferred to the other country. Also make sure that the location where files are stored locally is sufficiently secure and consider how you will keep track of changes made to data files at either site.

References

Borgmann, M., Hahn, T., Herfert, M., Kunz, T., Richter, M. und Viebeg, U. (2012) *On the Security of Cloud Storage Services*, Fraunhofer Institute for Secure Information Technology, Darmstadt. Available at: http://www.sit.fraunhofer.de/content/dam/sit/en/studies/Cloud-Storage-Security_a4.pdf.

Higher Education Information Security Council (2013) *Information Security Guide: Effective Practices and Solutions for Higher Education*, Higher Education Information Security Council. Available at: https://wiki.internet2.edu/confluence/display/itsg2/Home.

Janet (2013) *Janet Brokerage*. Available at: https://www.ja.net/products-services/.

Orbital Project (2012) *ownCloud: An Academic Dropbox?*, University of Lincoln. Available at: http://orbital.blogs.lincoln.ac.uk/2012/08/06/owncloud-an-academic-dropbox/.

Sakai (2011) *Sakai Project* Available at: http://www.sakaiproject.org/.

SomnIA (2010) *SomnIA Project: Sleep in Ageing*, University of Surrey. Available at: http://www.somnia.surrey.ac.uk/.

Tedds, J. (2012) *BRISSkit: Biomedical Research Infrastructure Software Service Kit*, University of Leicester. Available at: https://www.brisskit.le.ac.uk/.

Tenopir C., Allard S., Douglass K., Aydinoglu A.U., Wu L., Read, E., Manoff, M. and Frame, M. (2011). 'Data sharing by scientists: Practices and perceptions', *PlosOne*, 6(6): e21101. DOI:10.1371/journal.pone.0021101. Available at: http://www.plosone.org/article/info:doi/10.1371/journal.pone.0021101.

UK Data Service (2011) *Data Collection Inventory*, UK Data Service, University of Essex. Available at: http://ukdataservice.ac.uk/manage-data/collaboration.aspx.

University of Essex (2012) *ZendTo Service*, University of Essex. Available at: https://zendto.essex.ac.uk/about.php.

TEN
Making Use of Other People's Research Data: Opportunities and Limitations

Research data are collected across a range of social science disciplines using a variety of research approaches and methods. Social surveys and interviewing projects represent the most common methods, but primary data can also be gathered from fieldwork observation, diaries, self-completion questionnaires and other activities. Administrative and routine business data collected in the course of government activities further represent a rich source of statistical information.

Many researchers have some quantity of unpublished data, and a significant proportion of such data may well be under-exploited, not having been fully analysed or used in publications. As we saw in Chapter 1, there are good reasons for making already analysed research data available for further scrutiny and replication, and to provide transparency and accountability for scientific activities. Beyond the informal practices of sharing data with colleagues or collaborators, there is a growing volume of primary research data finding its way into data archives and repositories.

These resources represent a rich and unique stock of material that can be reanalysed, reworked, used for new analyses, and compared or combined with contemporary data. In time, archived data become historically important research materials. Using existing data also enables research where the required data may be expensive, difficult or impossible to collect, for example in the case of global administrative data, large scale surveys or historic data.

It is difficult to place a lifespan on the usefulness of data, as future research uses can never be anticipated. In the experience of national data archives, richer, more detailed and more representative collections offer wider opportunities for data exploitation; for example collections that are in-depth, national in breadth, time series or longitudinal in duration.

In 2005 in the USA, the National Research Council (2005) noted that secondary analysis reduces respondent burden; can enable data linkage and the creation of new datasets; informs policy disputes about the interpretation of analyses; provides transparency within research as other analysts can interrogate the data sources used; and enables methodologists to learn from each other. Secondary analysts are also well placed to make comparisons of competing data sources and evaluate their respective strengths or weaknesses.

Alongside academic research use, an increasing number of lecturers are using archived data sources to teach both quantitative and qualitative research methods, preferring to introduce real-life data sources into their instruction, and thus paving the way for best practices in secondary data analysis.

The provision of flexible online access to data resources via data centres can help develop and support evidence-based research within the social sciences.

In this chapter we present opportunities and challenges for reusing data collected by someone else, demonstrate how data have been used for both scholarly and educational purposes, and provide examples of how to gain access to data.

Opportunities for Reusing Other People's Data

In the 1970s and 1980s a number of authors published key methods books on the practices of secondary analysis, on which later books have built (Hyman, 1972; Hakim, 1982; Marsh, 1982; Dale et al., 1988). Hyman defines secondary analysis of surveys to mean, 'the extraction of knowledge on other topics other than those that were the focus of the original survey'. Dale et al.'s text offers very practical guidance on how to approach the reworking of large-scale government survey data from questioning and evaluating the opportunities and limitations of the source, to interpretation of analytic results. More recent volumes have built on these first texts, providing more up-to-date examples of analysis software and data sources (Dex, 1991; Singer and Willett, 2003; Elliot and Marsh, 2008). While the underlying methods of secondary analysis of social survey data remain fairly constant, there is a less mature, but growing, culture of reusing qualitative data. In this chapter we present some of the opportunities for reusing numeric and non-numeric data sources.

Collecting high quality, reliable, representative data is expensive and technically demanding. One example is Labour Force Surveys which are statistical surveys conducted in a number of countries designed to capture information about the labour market. All European Union countries are required to conduct a Labour Force Survey on an annual basis. In the UK, the Labour Force Survey (LFS) is a quarterly sample survey of households living at private addresses in the United Kingdom. Over 100,000 household members aged 16 years and over are interviewed each quarter. Dating back to 1992, its purpose is to provide official measures of employment and unemployment using international definitions of employment, unemployment and economic inactivity. It also captures a wide range of related topics such as occupation, training, hours of work and personal characteristics (Office for National Statistics, 2013). In the USA, the Current Population Survey (CPS) is conducted every month by the Bureau of Census and analysed by the Bureau of Labor Statistics (Bureau of Labor Statistics, 2013). Like the LFS, it interviews those over the age of 16 in approximately 60,000 households. The survey provides a comprehensive body of data on the labour force, employment and unemployment dating back to 1994.

These surveys provide both microdata (data records at the individual, household or organization level) and aggregate data (summary statistics such as counts reported in tables in government publications or websites). Such major survey series provide accurate population estimates about labour market activity and offer great opportunities for time series analysis, offering the chance to explore changing employment patterns from the 1990s to the present day. Labour force survey microdata are typically made available via their their host national data archives, such as UK Data Archive and ICPSR in the USA, allowing the data to be readily consulted for research use.

Secondary analysis can be undertaken on longitudinal data sources, where data are collected from the same individuals over a period of time. The research potential of a longitudinal dataset, be it a cohort study or a panel survey, increases as the study matures. These surveys are even more costly to conduct and offer great potential for powerful re-analysis of changes in individuals' circumstances over time and life-course patterns (Ruspini, 2002).

A growing number of acclaimed longitudinal and panel studies make data available for reuse: the USA Panel Study of Income Dynamics started in 1968, the German Socioeconomic Panel began in 1984 and the British Household Panel Study started in 1991 (DIW, 2013; ISER, 2013; ISR, 2013). There also exist well-established birth cohort studies and studies relating to particular cohorts, such as youth and those in later life. Famous UK birth cohorts whose data are available for reuse are: the 1958 National Child Development Study; the 1970 British Birth Cohort Study and the 2000 Millennium Cohort Study (CLS, 2013). The largest cohort study in Africa is the Birth to Twenty Study following over 3,000 children born in 1990 (Birth to 20 Study, 2012). The largest cohort study of women is the USA-based Nurses' Health Study, started in 1976, which tracks over 120,000 nurses (Nurses' Health Study, 2012). Other major cohorts include the 68-year Grant Study of Adult Development of white male Harvard graduates from the 1940s and the UK Whitehall Studies using two cohorts to follow over 18,000 and 10,000 civil servants (Vaillant, 2012; Whitehall Study, 2012).

Rich comparative global data are also collected by governments and non-governmental organizations. Socio-economic time series data for a range of countries over a substantial time period are available to researchers. In the area of labour statistics the International Labour Organization (ILO) website provides access to many international databases. The World Bank, International Monetary Fund and United Nations provide access to data on topics covering national accounts, industrial production, employment, trade, demography, human development and other indicators of national performance and development (UK Data Service, 2013a).

Linking multiple sources of data can add power to the analytic potential of individual sources. Microdata from surveys can be linked to other microdata files directly through common identifiers or indirectly via probabilistic linkage.

Common identifiers need to be coded in exactly the same way in both datasets. The internet also enables open, usually aggregate, data sources to be published through web interfaces and linked. Increasingly anyone can gain access via the internet to updated 'data feeds' which are drawn from a vast number of public data sources and updated in real-time, such as weather reports or current stock market share prices. Data.gov in the USA provides thousands of datasets and a range of data tools to help analyse them (Data.gov, 2013). NYC Open Data is a collection of hundreds of New York City public datasets that have been made available by city agencies and organizations in an effort to improve the accessibility, transparency and accountability of the city's government. Some of the most popular data from these sources include parking facilities, federal stimulus expenditures and electric consumption by zip code (The City of New York, 2013). An example of a published linked dataset is DBPedia which enables linking of structured information in Wikipedia entries to each other and beyond to other data sources (DBPedia, 2013).

Cross-disciplinary data sources can be linked, as is illustrated by Huby's (2010) *Social and Environmental Inequalities in Rural England* project. To investigate social and environmental inequalities and injustice in rural England and inform policy, a dataset of socio-economic and environmental characteristics was compiled into a geodatabase, at the level of census Super Output Areas (**SOAs**). Numerous existing data sources were used to calculate key characteristics for each **SOA**, some of which are: census data, National Travel Survey, land cover map, Countryside Stewardship, Environmental Stewardship and Environmentally Sensitive Area schemes data, Land Registry house prices data, Centre for Sustainable Energy and Road Traffic Accident data.

Other than these large-scale numeric data sources, specialist research units and academics also create and make available a variety of data types. These range from smaller topic-based surveys like election studies and social attitudes surveys to qualitative interviewing projects, oral histories and psychology experiments. Mixed methods studies, for example, undertaken through interdisciplinary projects, have become popular over the past few years and the increasing availability of these datasets, at least in the UK, reflects this trend.

In qualitative research, the types of data collected vary with the aims of the study and the nature of the sample. Samples are usually small, but can rise to hundreds of participants. Data might include in-depth interviews, semi-structured interviews, focus groups, field notes and research diaries, observational data, diaries, records of meetings, open-ended survey questions or related ephemera. The richness of qualitative data is rarely fully exploited leaving untapped treasures that offer fascinating and otherwise inaccessible accounts of the past and present for researchers and students to explore.

The scope and format of data may determine their potential for reuse. But as with many archived resources, sometimes the most exciting discoveries arise from re-examining material that hitherto has not been thought worthy of researchers' attention. We identify six ways in which archived data, both quantitative and qualitative, can be used (Corti and Thompson, 2004):

Providing Description and Historical Context

The possibilities for using data descriptively are extensive; pictures of contemporary and historical attitudes and behaviour of individuals, groups and organizations, or societies can be gleaned. Indeed, data created now will in time become potential historical resources. Historical records and surveys from the 1960s are available to reanalyse providing evidence from that period. Oral testimony complements official, public and press sources, and such evidence can also be used to document individual lives from a biographical perspective.

From the 1960s into the 1970s, sociology was an exceptionally popular subject with students, and was given more national research resources than at any time before. This enabled social researchers to carry out surveys and in-depth investigations of a significant scale, leaving behind large collections of rich descriptive material.

Comparative Research, Restudy or Follow-Up

Data can be compared with other data sources or be used to provide comparisons with other contexts, for example, over other periods of time or across other social groups and cultures. In Britain the original returns of the population census were kept as public records and have proved an invaluable basis for consultation and comparative study over time. Well-known early classic restudies include Rowntree's (1901) repeated surveys of poverty in York and Hubert Llewellyn Smith's (1930–35) repeat of Charles Booth's (1891–1902) poverty survey in London. Sidney and Beatrice Webb (1920 [1894]), on completing their pioneering study of British trade unionism, archived their field notes from their national sample of interviews, which still feature today as the principal source of information on trade unionism in the late nineteenth century. Comparison brings greater power to answer research questions, for example when data can be combined with data beyond its original sample or geographical limitations.

Survey time series and comparative international macrodata provide excellent opportunities for comparative research. In the USA, Glen Elder's *Children of the Great Depression* (1974), is based on both new fieldwork and a reorganization of the earlier interviews and participant observation of California cohorts interviewed on a regular basis since the 1920s. These data are archived at Harvard University. Felstead and Green (2012) used several datasets and surveys spanning a time period from 1986 to 2007 to analyse changing patterns in the quality of employment and the skills used in work in the UK.

Secondary Analysis

Re-analysing data allows both for re-interpretations and for new questions to be asked of older data. Also, new methods can be employed which may not have been possible at the time of the original data analysis. Typically, the richer and more detailed the original research material, the more potential there is for further exploitation. There are many good examples of reuse of survey data for a range of purposes, particularly where the survey topics are broad and individual level information is detailed. Examples include the many published analyses of the long-running large-scale government survey series like the General Social Survey (NORC, 2013).

Secondary analysis can help make more use of data about sensitive topics or collected from hard to reach populations by extracting the maximum value from those studies that are able to negotiate access for future researchers (Fielding and Fielding, 2000).

Replication or Validation of Published Work

While reanalysis, in the way described above, does not usually involve attempts to validate or undermine researchers' previous analyses, verification of results is a more recent area of interest following from examples of fraudulent research, such as those highlighted in Chapter 11. Archived data can be scrutinized with scientific rigour to support or challenge a set of findings or to appraise the method. Dale et al. (1988) cite a classic case where McKee and Vihjalmson (1987) reanalysed data on clinical depression in women from Brown and Harris's (1978) classic UK study on the social origins of depression. Their results sparked an international debate on the validity of a statistical approach used and its subsequent interpretation.

Hammersley (1997) discusses the benefits and weaknesses of using replication to check findings, arguing that true scientific replication is not possible, as studies generally do not cover identical social phenomena. Restudies suffer from differences in time, the researchers' subjective perspectives and loss of fieldwork context. Well-documented datasets can help the new investigator to reconstruct the evidence by re-tracing the original analytic steps. The practice of opening data for inspection is becoming increasingly important in the natural sciences, as it encourages greater transparency in research. Examples of master classes on replication in the field of econometrics and sociology have been run, for example by the Social Science Research Methods Centre (2012) at the University of Cambridge.

Research Design and Methodological Advancement

Consulting descriptions of the research methods used in an original investigation can help in the design of a new study or the development of a methodology or research tool. Examples include: sampling methods, data collection and field-work strategies, and interview protocols. Tried and tested harmonized survey questions can be reused when designing local surveys to ensure direct comparability with the results of major household surveys. For example, a well-established UK question to measure longer-term ill-health is: 'Do you have any physical or mental health conditions or illnesses lasting or expected to last for 12 months or more? Yes or No' (Office for National Statistics, 2012).

While a discussion of methodology is usually published in research findings in many social science journal articles, details offered can be brief and sanitized. Books based on a study may offer more detail on methods and tools used. Researchers' own fieldwork diaries or analytic notes can offer much insight into the history and development of the research and can help inform new thinking. Peter Townsend's in-depth investigation into the nature and status of older people's institutions in post-war Britain, *The Last Refuge* (1962), was considered a pioneering piece of research when it was published in 1957. It attracted much publicity for its focus on an important and neglected area of policy, and also for its rigorous methodology and policy recommendations. The meticulously preserved fieldwork descriptions of old people's institutions and accompanying interviews, provide an insight into the production of the final polished policy reports, exposing how the researcher approached the study and the methods he used.

As discussed in Chapter 4, capturing the methodological perspectives and context within which studies are undertaken, across all stages, provides added value for a secondary user who may be unfamiliar with the raw data.

Teaching and Learning

The use of real-life data in teaching in the social sciences adds interest and relevance to courses. Data can be chosen to be of particular relevance to the subject being taught and thus can bring both substantive and methodological topics alive. Students can learn many fundamental aspects of research methods, and the theoretical and methodological strategies that helped to create chosen data outputs, while also gaining first-hand experience of critically re-analysing and comparing data from well-known sources. Having real data to hand can free students from having to collect their own data, so they can instead focus on the vital skills that sit either side of that process; formulating research questions and analysing data (Smith, 2008; Haynes, 2010). Efforts to improve statistical literacy have produced some creative data-oriented resources to help students confront secondary data (McInnes, 2012; ICPSR, 2013a). Examples of using data in teaching and learning in the UK are discussed by Corti and Bishop (2005), Smith (2008) and Bishop (2012).

| CASE STUDY | Instructional Materials for Reusing Data, ICPSR |

ICPSR's Data-driven Learning Guides are intended to enhance teaching of core concepts in the social sciences and make use of topics drawn from concepts that are included in introductory

(Continued)

(Continued)

level social science textbooks. The guide *Age and Attitudes about the Rights of Homosexuals* investigates trends in attitudes regarding the rights of homosexuals in the United States from the early 1990s to 2007 (ICPSR, 2009). The guide suggests research questions that could be explored using a particular dataset, in this case the longitudinal Houston Area Survey, 1982–2007 (Klineberg, 2011). The guide selects a small number of variables to explore and prompts the reader to work through recoding some of these to be able to answer questions of interest, such as:

- why younger people seem to be more supportive of the rights of homosexuals;
- why the general population seem more supportive of some rights of homosexuals while being less supportive of other rights;
- what the similarities and dissimilarities are between the gay rights movements, the women's movements, and the civil rights movements;
- what the relationship is between education and support for same-sex marriage.

The reader can work through all exercises via their web browser through the Survey Documentation and Analysis (SDA) online data analysis system. An interpretation guide takes the reader though analytical issues relevant to the data, such as inference and weighting, and provides a summary of key findings.

Limitations of Using Other Researchers' Data

Reuse of any dataset collected by a third party can be a complex undertaking, but once the methods and challenges are understood, the researcher can embrace making use of existing sources. There are different and perhaps more challenging intellectual, epistemological and practical problems for the user to consider when reusing qualitative data compared to quantitative data. Building on existing literature, we identify real and perceived limitations to reusing data and propose ways of overcoming these (Dale et al., 1998; Corti and Thompson, 2004; Hammersley, 2010).

Lack of Availability of Suitable Data

While thousands of data collections in data archives are available for consultation across the world, it can be difficult to find them without prior knowledge. Inability to locate relevant sources makes it more likely that researchers will turn to primary data collection for their research. In the past, discovering key collections in institutions' and museums' special collections has been difficult with limited finding aids and non-federated online catalogues. However, efforts to join up catalogues of archival holdings have been forthcoming, creating some excellent portals where the user can search for and locate older historical materials, digitized or otherwise. We showcase methods and hubs for finding data in the last part of this chapter.

Fit of Secondary Analysis to Your Own Research Questions

Even if archived data that look potentially useful can be located, it may be that data will not meet your exact needs. This can be for statistical reasons, for example if the sample size of a survey is too small to conduct robust analysis on a particular subpopulation like a region, age or ethnic group; or if specific and necessary questions have not been included in a module of a survey.

To assess the fit to your research questions, data sources must be evaluated by exploring available documentation such as technical reports, sample design and question selection, and any other information about research design. It may also be necessary to view the data files themselves, which will rely on whether or not access to the data is straightforward and without too many barriers.

Time to Use Unfamiliar Data

Reusing data requires time to get fully acquainted with research materials created by someone else. This can be seen as a barrier to exploring data that you have not collected yourself. Social historians have been more forthcoming in revisiting data sources because of their willingness to embrace the slow and rigorous, but commonly accepted, practice of document analysis and the need to evaluate methodically the very sources they are revisiting. It can be time-consuming for new users to locate suitable data sources and to check variables and codes or read interview transcripts to see whether they can answer the research questions. Time needs to be built in to any secondary analysis project. Once you are familiar with a particular data series or collection it becomes easier to use those same data again. The internet is enabling faster and more efficient discovery of digital data sources that may help reduce the burden on researchers.

Unfamiliarity with the Appropriate Methods of Secondary Analysis

In fields such as econometrics, policy analysis and epidemiology, secondary analysis is taken for granted. However, this is still not the case in other social science disciplines. Lack of statistical literacy and fears about the complexity of modelling microdata can push trainee and early career researchers to the softer end of cross-tabulating survey analysis. Strong statistical skills are becoming sought after in the workplace and there are many excellent courses on introductory statistical methods and techniques for analysing survey data. The methods literature is rich in guidance on secondary analysis of numeric data but less so for secondary analysis of qualitative data.

Reuse of qualitative materials requires the new investigator to first evaluate the evidence, examine its provenance, and assess the veracity of the sources. Such research practices are, on the whole, fairly unfamiliar even to trained sociologists. Historians' research practices can teach us how to confront primary sources that we did not create, as discussed further in the next section. Slowly scholars are beginning to incorporate social historical methods into mainstream sociology as seen in work by Crow and Edwards (2012) and Kynaston (2005). There are also challenges of sampling from large quantities of qualitative data that have become available for reuse (Savage, 2010; Gillies and Edwards, 2012). As more researchers undertake and publish on reusing qualitative data, and methods courses start covering such approaches, we envisage the practice to increase.

Lack of 'Rich-Enough' Documentation

As we saw in detail in Chapter 4, unless data are thoroughly documented, understanding the context of data can be troublesome. Surveys should have technical reports, instruments used and data dictionaries available alongside data. Qualitative data benefit from having accompanying information on study methodology, tools used in the field and any other relevant contextual information.

In Chapter 4 we presented the challenges of providing context for qualitative data, in particular the loss of original fieldwork experiences. While some researchers argue that data cannot ever be appropriately reused when secondary users lack the context of the original project, others claim that this privilege does not prevent reusers from deriving new interpretations from those data (Moore, 2007; Hammersley 2010; Irwin et al., 2012). The debates have helped to shed light on how researchers can best approach using existing data and the caveats that need to be considered when examining them.

Historians routinely have to deal with lack of immediate rich context for information sources they use. Part of their analytical task is to establish the provenance and veracity of their sources by undertaking related investigation about the event, period, place and so on. As social scientists learn how to use such historical methods and understand better how to describe their data to facilitate later reuse, so argument about lack of documentation may decrease.

Concerns about Ethical Reuse of Data

The constraints of informed consent or unintended statistical disclosure may be seen as an obstacle to reusing data. There are ethical questions about informed consent for unknown future uses of data and about the changed relationships with participants when data are shared (Bishop, 2009; Mauthner, 2012). Informed consent is an ethical and legal requirement of the research process, certainly in the UK and USA, and archived data should always conform to ethical and legal guidelines with respect to the preservation of anonymity when this has been guaranteed to participants or requested by them. As we saw in Chapter 7, for data to be ethically reused, consent for future reuse must be thought through at the time of the original research proposal planning and writing. Primary researchers can then ensure that consent for future research uses is asked from participants, or that data are suitably anonymized to safeguard participants' anonymity. All data archives have user agreements in place that require users to conform to legally binding undertakings, such as not to disclose identities and not to pass data on to third parties. Users of more disclosive data, such as those held in safe rooms, will have been through rigorous training in how to avoid malicious or accidental disclosure (see Chapter 7).

Case Studies of Reuse of Quantitative Data

Presented here are two selected examples of research based on reuse of archived cross-sectional survey data, with the findings published as journal articles. These case studies are drawn from the UK Data Service's library of case studies of using archived data (UK Data Service, 2013a).

CASE STUDY	Do Parenting Programmes Reduce Conduct Disorder and its Costs to Society? (Bonin et al., 2011)

Research question: Conduct disorders, the most common psychiatric conditions amongst children, is where a child's behaviour violates either the basic rights of others or is outside age-appropriate norms. The disorder develops into adulthood anti-social personality disorder in approximately 50% of cases, and it is estimated that 5% with the most severe behaviour problems in childhood are responsible for more than 20% of all crimes committed. Researchers from the London School of Economics, King's College London and the Centre for Mental Health used archived survey data to investigate the potential costs of, and savings from, parenting programmes designed to reduce persistent conduct disorder.

Data used: This research used the UK's 2006 Offending, Crime and Justice Survey to measure the prevalence of crime and drug use in England and Wales, especially amongst young people (Home Office, 2008). The survey was held annually as a self-reported survey of offending between 2003 and 2006. For 2006 the survey included more than 5,300 interviews with people aged 10 to 25.

Methods used: This research used a decision-analytic model, populated with data from the best available research findings that compared two scenarios over 25 years: a five-year-old with clinical conduct disorder receives an evidence-based parenting programme; and a five-year-old with clinical conduct disorder does not receive the programme. A cost-savings analysis was conducted by comparing costs associated with persistent conduct disorder in both scenarios, considering both the public sector costs, such as health and criminal justice services, and costs to society, such as the wider costs of crime.

Data from the Offending Crime and Justice Survey were used to obtain an estimate of the number and types of crimes committed by 10- to 25-year-olds. Home Office estimates of the cost per crime were used to calculate the average cost of crime per person with

(Continued)

(Continued)

conduct disorder, assuming that 5% of children were subsequently responsible for over 20% of crimes.

Brief findings: The research strongly suggested that, given the assumptions used in the model, evidence-based parenting programmes do reduce the chance that conduct disorder would persist into adulthood. It shows that consequently there is a cost saving effect within five to eight years under base case conditions. Most of the savings were associated with reductions in offending.

CASE STUDY	Does Premature Birth Affect a Child's Long-Term Health or Development? (Boyle et al., 2012)

Research question: Thanks to advances in modern medicine, the chance of babies surviving if they are born prematurely is high. However, there is a concern that children surviving such early births will suffer from ill-health and developmental effects. This research investigated whether a premature birth has these negative consequences on child development.

Data used: This research used data from the first (2001–03), second (2003–05) and third (2006) surveys of the Millennium Cohort Study (MCS) as well as a special dataset featuring birth registration and maternity hospital episode data (Centre for Longitudinal Studies, 2010a, 2010b, 2010c). The MCS is a longitudinal survey of a cohort of around 19,000 children born across the UK between September 2000 and January 2002. Topics covered include family socio-economic background, the circumstances of pregnancy and birth, child health, child behaviour, childcare and parenting style.

Method used: Data on gestational age were determined from the maternal report included in the first survey of the MCS and the data in the hospital records dataset. Groups of children born in one of four pre-term gestational ages – early term (37–38 weeks); late pre-term (34–36 weeks); moderately pre-term (32–33 weeks); very pre-term (32 weeks or less) – were compared with those children born at full-term (39–41 weeks). Logistic regression was conducted on each of the gestational age groups listed above. The analysis took into account the clustered study design of the survey.

Brief findings: The researchers discovered that the higher the prematurity, the greater risk of these ill effects. However the differences between each group were small. Those children born late or moderately pre-term were the most likely to have a higher disease burden at ages 3 and 5. Compared with full-term births those born in late pre-term or early term also had poorer health and educational outcomes at ages 3 and 5.

Case Studies of Reuse of Qualitative Data

Here we present two selected examples of research based on reuse of archived qualitative data collections, again drawn from the UK Data Service's library of case studies of using archived data, with the findings published as books.

CASE STUDY	*The Secret Battle: Emotional Survival in the Great War* (Roper, 2009)

Research question: As part of his research into the Great War, Roper used psychoanalysis to help explore the emotional survival of men fighting in the war, as well as a way to understanding their lives and personal relationships. Using archived data he aimed to investigate how young soldiers survived trench warfare on the Western Front by drawing on the emotional and practical support of their families.

Data used: Roper exhaustively researched over 80 collections of wartime correspondence, together with 40 published and unpublished memoirs of the war. One of Roper's key sources was Paul Thompson's collection of 450 life story interviews conducted for Family Life and Work Experience before 1918, undertaken in the 1970s, and better known as The Edwardians study (Thompson, 1975; Thompson and Lummis, 2009). Participants interviewed in the project were born between 1870 and 1906, thereby creating a unique record of their lives and times from childhood through to old age. The open-ended interviews were guided by a schedule and covered a range of themes.

Methods used: The material gave insight into the experiences of men from working and lower-middle-class families, who constituted the mainstay among rank-and-file soldiers, thus balancing the middle-class emphasis of the more widely published written memoirs. Roper searched the textual collection with key words such as: servant; death; First World War; veteran; and wound.

Brief findings: In his book, Roper writes about the importance of connections for the young men at war; connections with their families at home, despite being separated by the gulfs of distance and experience; connections across time, linking soldiers' wartime experiences with both their late Victorian and Edwardian upbringings; their post-war experiences; the disconnections between people who experienced war differently; and ultimately the reconnections that occurred after the war was over.

CASE STUDY	*The Last Refuge* Revisited (Johnson et al., 2010)

Research question: Effective care for the elderly is a major issue in British society and one that engenders much debate. This study explored the state of residential care for older people in the UK addressing concerns about the management of residential care homes and their changing nature. The project took a longer-term view comparing the state in 2006 with that of almost 50 years previously, inspired by the ground-breaking research of Peter Townsend and his seminal book, *The Last Refuge* (1962).

Data used: In the late 1950s Peter Townsend conducted a major investigation of long-stay institutional care for old people in Britain questioning whether the institutions were still needed and, if so, whether improvements could be made in the nature of such provision. The study was groundbreaking in its use of qualitative research methods; in-depth interviews were conducted with numerous local authority chief welfare officers and with serving staff and residents of almost 200 institutions. The collection, available at the UK Data Service, also contains diaries kept by several of the residents and staff and a collection

(Continued)

(Continued)

of photographs of the buildings, facilities, staff and residents taken by Townsend (Townsend, 2011).

Methods used: The research team consulted the original data, findings and recommendations from Townsend's work as the foundation for a follow-up study and were encouraged and supported by Townsend himself. A tracing study recorded what had happened to the original institutions studied; while almost 40 of the 100 plus still existed as registered care homes, 20 formed the basis of a follow-up study. This methodology replicated as far as possible the approach taken by Townsend and his team when they conducted their original research in the late 1950s; visits to the homes were made over several days, interviewing managers and some residents. A survey of the building was undertaken, taking photographs and noting any changes and refurbishments.

Brief findings: The research found that there has been both change and continuity in the way the homes functioned in the past and currently. Legal regulations have resulted in improvements and refurbishments to the buildings and environment. There have been major changes in the varied ethnicity of the staff, with some homes now being staffed almost completely by individuals from abroad as well as by British Indians and Africans. Continuities included issues such as funding, freedom to make choices, activities and quality of care. More positively, voluntary homes were found to have retained their status today as they did in 1959 as comfortable, warm and welcoming.

Tips for Reusing Qualitative Data

With many different ways to reuse qualitative data, there cannot be any hard and fast rules about procedure. However, there are some steps common to most approaches (Irwin and Winterton, 2012):

- get familiar with the original research project by reading all documentation and metadata to answer questions such as why each type of data was collected;
- understand the multiple levels of context of the original data generation, from researcher-participant interaction through project rationale and design to the conditions in society at the time of the original study;
- build an understanding of the data; often the volume of data available is large, and reusers must find a 'way in' to the data. The best starting point is often summaries, such as case summaries or data inventories;
- develop analytical strategies, refining concepts by cross-collection comparisons or bringing cases and quantitative data together.

Case Studies of Linking Multiple Data Sources

We present two selected examples of research that have linked different data sources. Each has used a different approach to data linking, the first seeking to exploit the opportunities that openly available government data can provide, and the second case study used archived microdata sources from the UK Data Service (UK Data Service, 2013a).

| CASE STUDY | **Example Mashup: How Does Residential Energy Use Vary Across the USA? (National Renewable Energy Laboratory, 2010)** |

Research question: Experiment linking U.S. public energy data that are available online, to show how energy use varies across the U.S.

Data used: This experiment combined 'Electric Sales, Revenue and Average Price 2008' data from the Energy Information Administration (EIA), available on Data.gov; with data from OpenEI.org, the USA Census and SmartGrid.gov.

Methods used: In 2010, a mashup was created at the first Data.gov mashathon event, by the National Renewable Energy Laboratory, to compare energy use characteristics for seven cities with populations of just over half a million people. With differing electricity rates, median income levels, energy-related incentives and types of Smart Grid programmes being introduced, cities across the country are transitioning to a new energy marketplace in unique ways.

Brief findings: An online visualization map shows energy use statistics about each city, the local electric utility organization, rebates and financial incentive programmes and up-to-date information about local Smart Grid projects. Cities can be compared and contrasted to see how local utility rates, median income and other regional characteristics relate to average annual electricity use. The mashup evolves over time as energy data are added and updated.

| CASE STUDY | **Business Innovation and the Moving Workforce (Crescenzi And Gagliardi, 2012)** |

Research question: Innovation, or the successful use of new ideas that generate economic, social or environmental value, has been regarded as a key driver for Britain's economic growth. This research investigated what stimulates innovation and whether the mobility of knowledgeable, highly skilled workers has an impact on the local economies that attract them. The researchers hypothesized that knowledgeable individuals, such as inventors, with the flexibility to change geographical location, would positively impact the innovative behaviour of firms in the areas they moved to.

Data used: This research used the 2004 and 2007 years of the UK Innovation Survey series, the UK's segment of the Europe-wide Community Innovation Survey that provides the main source of information on the nation's business innovation (Department for Business, Innovation and Skills and Office for National Statistics, 2011). Topics include general business information, innovation activity, goods, services and process innovation, the context for innovation and general economic information. Anonymized postcodes in the surveys were linked with the reference numbers from the UK Inter-Departmental Business Register, available only via secure access. Data from the European Patent Office was also used and linked with the data.

(Continued)

(Continued)

Methods used: Data access and analysis was conducted on a secure remote-access server housed at the University of Essex. The key dependent variable was based on firms performing on any product of process innovation in the time period under investigation. The inflow of inventors into the local labour market was used as a proxy for the overall mobility of highly skilled 'innovative' individuals. By looking at inventors' mobility the research investigated the internal mobility of a very specific group of knowledgeable and 'innovative' agents, measured by taking into account their capability to participate in the generation of economically valuable innovation. The probability of firm innovation was carried out using econometric techniques of a Linear Probability Model and a Control Function Approach.

Brief findings: The results demonstrated that the relocation of the skilled individuals did not have a direct impact on the firms' innovation; a positive effect emerges only after controlling for the capability of local firms to exploit external sources of information, such as suppliers, clients and competitors. Only those firms who complemented their internal knowledge with external sources were able to benefit from the arrival of highly skilled individuals into the local labour market, improving their innovative performance.

Finding Data

Data archives and special collections offer online data catalogues with links to access data, supporting documentation and guidance on how to use these resources. Examples of data catalogues for social scientists include the UK Data Service, the Interuniversity Consortium for Political and Social Research (ICPSR) in the USA and various European countries' social data archives (ICPSR, 2013b; UK Data Service, 2013b). The Council for European Social Science Data Archives (CESSDA) hosts a federated catalogue that enables users to search for national survey data across a range of European countries (CESSDA, 2012). In the UK, more traditional archival collections found in universities' or museums' archives and special collections can be searched via the Archives Hub (Archives Hub, 2013). These catalogues make use of standardized ways of describing data collections, as discussed in Chapter 4.

Using the UK Data Service Discover catalogue as an example, users can search and browse by subject, type of data, data producer and date of data collection. An example of a search on the word 'drug use' is shown in Figure 10.1. As the catalogue records are indexed on search engines like Google, a Google search will also reliably locate datasets.

Once a user has identified an appropriate dataset the data can be ordered via a simple registration process. Registered authenticated users can download a complete survey data file, typically in SPSS, Stata or tab delimited formats, or explore a dataset with its questions, responses, frequencies and basic tabulations online via the UK Data Service's online data survey browser, Nesstar, as shown in Figure 10.2 (Nesstar, 2013). Using Nesstar a user can specify subsets and download data tables in a range of formats.

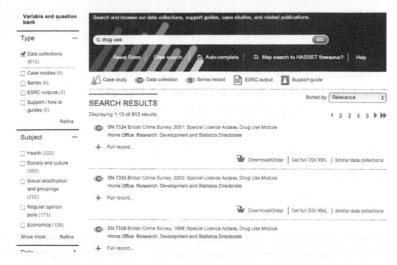

Figure 10.1   UK Data Service Discover search for 'Drug use'

Source: UK Data Service, 2013b

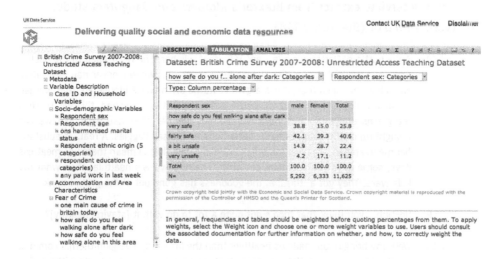

Figure 10.2   Nesstar online tabulation for the British Crime Survey, 2007–08

Source: Nesstar, 2013

In the USA, key archives such as ICPSR, the Roper Center and Harvard-MIT Data Centre have major holdings searchable via similar online catalogues.

As noted earlier, public data sources are being published on public websites as part of the open data agenda. The growing number of data repositories can be located via the Databib (2013) registry or the re3data.org (2013) registry. As institutional repositories come on stream holding local data, unified national portals are being developed. Research Data Australia is the most integrated portal for discovering hundreds of research data resources dispersed across Australia

(ANDS, 2013). Another example is NARCIS in the Netherlands, a portal for the discovery of datasets, people, organizations and publications (NARCIS, 2013).

> ### Exercise 10.1   Reusing data: Examining the value of context for qualitative data
>
> Read through the two following interview extracts. A data user would usually have accompanying context or biographical information for the interviewees. For this exercise, all context has been removed for you to reflect on its role and value.
>
> After reading the extracts:
>
> 1.   Identify one or two analytical points or research questions that these data might address.
> 2.   Consider which contextual information would help you to better understand the extracts.
> 3.   Explain why each item of context would be useful.
>
>
> #### Extract 1: Interview extract from Blaxter's *Mothers and Daughters* study, interview with G19 (Blaxter, 2008)
>
> G19:   An' a bottle o' Dettol wis aye... an' TCP.. that wis her. She niver gaed to the doctor. She wis a walkin' doctor. She didnae need a doctor... we wis never nae weel. Ken. We hidnae much clathes, it wis a gym costume an' a white blouse an' that woman brushed it doon every night wi' Dettol an' water... it wis brushed, this wis to keep the germs aff ye. It must have worked, cos we wis niver nae weel, but we wis brought up on, fit, soup, tatties... butter, eggs.. fit else? Veggies. A real... a substantial meal. I mean, we niver got steak an' things like that.. I mean there wis meatless days, some days you couldnae get meat. I believe we wis healthier than what my kids were. They got a' this... a' the goodness has gone oot o' the grub, I think.
>
> LP: Uh-huh... you think that food's got quite a lot to do with it [staying healthy]?
>
> G19:   Well, my bringin' up made us healthier than the brinin' up I've gien them... comin'... wi' the things we ate. Wi' the things that we was forced to eat or do withoot. But nowadays... baked rice... now, you got baked rice. It wis made wi' eggs an' there wis currants in it, an' this wis a luxury, mind?
>
> Husb: Nowadays, they'd sooner buy a tin.
>
> G19:   Nowadays they get a tin an' there's nae eggs in it an' the goodness is oot o' it. Like... have you ever had frozen stuff an' you've cooked it an' you feel as though it didnae taste right... efter ha'in a fresh bit o' steak an' onion. Ken fit I mean? The juice... there's nae the juice in it. Well, that's whit we find wi' the things nowadays an' a, the richt good is out o' them... the body-buildin' material.. afore you eat it.
>
>   I mean, tinned soup, I would niver hae it in the hoose unless it wis maybe Karen [daughter] comin' in an' I wis gaun away in a hurry an' gettin' a tin o' soup... I wouldnae gie it to him [husband]... we were nae brought up like that, we wis

brought up to get a' thing oot o' the groun' and intae a pot... My father grew a' thing. As I say we niver had the money that they've nowadays. My mother could have niver bought four tins, five tins of soup to pit in a pot. It would have cost her very little to put on a pot o' soup an' gettin' the full body o' that pot o' soup, ken?

Makin' toast at the fire wis a great thing... you niver tasted toast at the fire that you will in a grill, it's nae the same taste. An' baked tatties in a fire. Used to sit aoun' an' bake tatties, or bake chestnuts... it wis somethin'... we wis happy sittin' singin'... even when the kids were little we used to say 'Come on, kids, come on an' we'll hae a little concert'. We used to dress them up an' they used to sing an' dance. It wis great, ken... nowadays they'd think we was feel! And now, you see, when they're up we could sit an' speak about this an' laugh aboot it . what we used to dee, an' this an' that, an' dress them up an' mak' them sing an'... Isabel wis that fat, but she wis goin' to be a ballet dancer an' she wis gaun aboot Like an elephant! Ken. We all laugh aboot this nowadays. They were happy, days.

Kids are nae happy nowadays. They're gettin' too much. They're never deprived of onythin', they get it eventually. Even wi' the school... they're nae feart at their teachers the wey we were. The wey they were, we used to come hame... 'I got the strap' an' then get a punch up for gettin' the strap. Karen comes hame an' says to me 'I got the strap today'. I says 'Oh well, ging back an' get anither een'".. she thinks I should ging up an' say to the teacher 'Dinna strap my daughter'. Ken fit I mean? It's a difference... they're defiant wi' the strap they were feart at the strap. They come hame an' telt us they got the strap.. we wanted to know what for... an' then we got a punch up for... gettin' it.

Extract 2   Interview extract from Short's *Domestic Cooking and Cooking Skills in Late Twentieth Century England*, interview with LA (Short, 2007)

FS: ...can you think of any techniques you use when you're trying to eat a healthy diet?

LA: ...um...{thinks}...for a healthy diet well we don't...fry much...we...but then I've always grilled rather than fried stuff...for example sausages...it's the one sort of meat thing that we all quite like...and {L's older daughter} likes...we do have sausages...usually once a week...a nice quick meal...my liver and bacon equivalent...a kind of warm...easy to make meal and you've got nice gravy that goes into mashed potato...um so I would grill but I've always grilled...I don't think there's anything that I particularly change but then...

FS: ...um...

LA: ...I think also my mum was quite conscious of health even...twenty years...thirty years ago...she was quite advanced with that as a cook...to not fry...to grill most things...so it's more up-bringing I'd say then conscious healthy living...that has um...yeah I mean...you know with potatoes we're much more likely to have them mashed or boiled...we'll have the odd sort of...chips out of the freezer...but I'd never have a deep fat fryer and I'd never make chips...um I might do sliced fried potatoes with an omelette...I think that's a really nice combination...um...so...yeah...there's...the only concession is very little frying of food...

FS: ...um...

(Continued)

(Continued)

LA: …we don't have lots of meat but again that's…I mean that is healthy {?}…we don't particularly like a lot of meat…um…not much fat…semi-skimmed milk…can't think of anything else…

FS: …the last section…in Britain today…etc?

LA: I think it's brilliant…I think um…my grandmother who I was talking about earlier and who's had a lifetime of preparing food and sick of it…she's also nearly blind…and she came to stay with me when {L's younger daughter} was first born so that was about eight months ago…and she's never been round a big supermarket…she lives in Shropshire… um…and they've got quite a good shop that sells quite a variety of foods for where it is…

FS: …um…

LA: …but I took her over to the Sainsbury's in Haringey…and we walked up and down the aisle…and I had to tell her what was on the shelves because her eyesight isn't good enough…and we spent half an hour just in the fruit and veg section…pointing out all the different pears and all the different…all the exotic…star fruit and…and it was all too much for her in a way because you know she's eighty five or something and she's had meat and two veg all her life and yet she's still sort of young enough at heart to want to try these different things…so she had pasta for the first time…the first time she'd ever had pasta was here…and I was just thinking we take it so much for granted now…but things are so different now…I think it's brilliant…I wonder where we can go from here…I suppose there'll just be more and more influx of foreign foods and foreign recipes and I'm all in favour of it all…I think it's a good thing…

FS: What about prepared and semi-prepared foods?

LA   ….it's funny because this same Grandmother…if she knew the extent to which we buy ready prepared foods…she'd be absolutely horrified because of the war-time mental-ity…of everything must be…cooked…[edits] …and I…there's part of my background that tell me I shouldn't do it…

FS: …um…

LA: …but I also know that for today's living…it's impossible…[edits] I cannot think how they [mother and mother-in-law] managed it…but then I think our lives are different because we have a much bigger social like and…we're more house proud…we want to get our houses looking nice and…I always remember our house being the same for years and years…but my Mum was always cooking our food…plus obviously most women I know work…with kids, so… you know you're both out of the house…[edits] so all in all…I think it's…it's…there's so much a place for it and I wish in a way it wasn't because it's cheating…I still feel it's cheating…I think I said earlier…

FS: …um…

LA: [edits]…in fact my sister makes me laugh 'cos her and George are the epitomy [sic] of the kind of nineties could both working really long hours in trendy jobs…and she said cooking for her now is heating up some pasta…some sauce…she says they've 'cooked' if they've done that...most of the time they're either eating out or getting a takeaway...so it's like 'oh should we cook tonight' and then they get ready prepared food and yet deep down...she's got the same sort of thing as me...she comes from a background where cooking food was important...um...and you feel you're cheating...[edits] ...whereas because of the life I'm leading...you know at home with children...I've got more time here...more time to think about food and whatever...and more time to shop for it...but um..

FS: ...um...

LA: there's still a huge part of our lives with ready prepared food...and I can't see that going to change for a while...I just can't see...because as the kids get older and get more time for me I'll probably end up working more...I can't see that suddenly I'm going to have two hours every day...to create wonderful food...and I just think back and wonder how my Mum did it...I don't think she went out much...she didn't go out much... she didn't watch telly much...she didn't have hour long conversations on the phone with friends which I frequently have...I just think our lives are very different...I'm in favour of it I think.

Answers to Exercise 10.1

Below is the related contextual information provided for the two interview extracts you examined. After reading these pieces of contextual information, consider these additional questions:

1. How does the information provided fit, or not, with what you thought would be useful?
2. Reflecting now on the beginning of this exercise, were you able, even without context, to generate a research question from the data?
3. What value might there be in working with 'just the data'? Is it similar to any other phases of a research project?

Extract 1   Contextual Information for Blaxter's *Mothers And Daughters* Study

Background: The aim of Blaxter and Patterson's (1982) research was to study inter-generational transmission of deprivation using a sample of women in 58 three-generation families and was part of a larger ESRC programme on Transmitted Deprivation. Sampling was purposive: families that remained working class across two generations, grandmother–daughter co-location in a Scottish city, and continuing contact. The study addressed diverse factors, exploring whether health and social histories, attitudes, and health behaviours would affect the health experiences of the children and were possibly transmitted across generations. Nutrition was one of several topics addressed; others were orientations toward medicine, antenatal care, preventive behaviour, use of lay remedies, etc. The study used several types of data: information from longitudinal visits with the mothers, health visitor reports, etc. Other data, including the archived material archived, were semi-structured interviews that focused on attitudes and perceptions. The original study was intended to inform social policy.

A year after publishing their book, Blaxter and Patterson re-analysed their data to study the historical and moral significance of food. They reported on what constituted 'good food': specific foods were less important than a 'proper' meal, as contrasted with processed foods, or 'snackery'.

(Continued)

(Continued)

They also used their rich intergenerational data to compare the different attitudes and behaviours between grandmothers and their daughters.

Interviews were done by two educated, white women. Regular visits were made to the families by either Blaxter or Patterson. Patterson did the majority of the grandmother interviews; she was from the same area where the families lived. Blaxter praised her ability to gain rapport with the respondents. Mothers were interviewed at the end of the six-month study. The study was presented to respondents as being about child-rearing and child-rearing beliefs and practices across generations.

Biographical Information and Interviewer Notes for the Interview with G19 (Edited):

Date of interview: 1978; age of G19: 43.

Upstairs flat in drab block of 4. Untidy. Back garden overgrown grass. A daughter with baby living with parents. Doesn't appear to be married. Another daughter who is pregnant was also present. Not sure whether she is living there also. A teen aged daughter also lives at home. The two daughters present looked gaunt and ill. Son-in-law came in later and left granddaughter – seemed to be about 4 or 5. G19 seemed quite forthcoming despite the presence of all these people. But when I was leaving she showed me to the door and confided that she and [someone of her daughter's generation] were very different: 'Although she's a nice person, she was brought up on the good things of life. She likes to get out and enjoy herself, while I only thought of my family.'

Extract 2   Contextual Information for Short's *Domestic Cooking* Study

Background: This research was conducted as part of Frances Short's work toward completing a PhD in Food Policy in 2002 (Short, 2003). She also has a diploma from a recognized cooking school and has worked as a professional chef.

The aim of the research was to further understanding and debate by providing a systematically researched and theoretically-based way of thinking about cooking and cooking skills. The research took the form of a two-stage study. This data extract is from the first stage. Both stages were based around semi-structured interviews but the first also included the keeping of 'cooking diaries'.

In the first stage of fieldwork, couples aged between 30 and 50 from different social, financial and occupational backgrounds and household; two couples had very young children living with them; another couple had no children; and another a teenage daughter who came to stay at the weekends and so on. The interview schedule was designed around current areas of concern surrounding domestic food, eating and cooking practices but with sufficient room to allow exploration and points of interest develop. Topics discussed with the participants included: childhood experiences of cooking and eating; current cooking practices; the role of ready-meals; and 'typically British' food.

In both stages, participants were selected opportunistically for reasons of accessibility, coming mostly from the Greater London area. The interviews took place in the participants' own homes or workplaces and were recorded. All interviewees were given a shopping voucher worth fifteen pounds as a thank-you.

Biographical Information and Interviewer Notes for the Interview with LA

Interviewee description: Woman in her 30s, married with two daughters, white British, with polytechnic or university degree. She is not currently employed. Husband is a self-employed journalist. She receives over £500 per week in child benefits. She has lived with her husband for 7 years in an owned home, with a mortgage. Interview was done around 2001.

Interviewer notes: 'LA had a neat house, trendy but both she and her partner viewed their trendiness quite ironically and knowingly. I interviewed LA and her partner LB in turn on the same evening whilst they swapped over putting their daughters to bed.'

Further Discussion

Context operates at different levels, so think broadly about it. If you considered examples of only one level of context, for example, the interview encounter, consider the multiple levels of context discussed in Chapter 4. For example, how might this extract fit into the complete interview? At a broader level, how might the project topic shape the interviewees' responses? Would a study on health elicit different food narratives from a study about cooking? How could reusers take this into account when reusing these data?

The Blaxter interviews (as shown in Extract 1 above) were transcribed as spoken. Does this contextual information influence your reading? Would a glossary help for the Scottish words that might not be so familiar?

In the Short study extract on domestic cooking, would you need to know the employment status of the interviewee, and numbers and ages of any children living at home with her? If so, why? Is it to help answer a particular hypothesis or interest you might have?

It is very easy to list points of contextual information that 'might' be helpful to inform the data. What you might see as relevant context will depend on the research question you are asking. What about also considering context from the perspective of a data creator, who is very close to the data? In this exercise, you undertook a more distanced, objective view of data in which you have no personal investment. Recognize that research requires skills both of close-up examination of data, but also of distancing, analysing and comparing.

Finally, consider how historians might make use of archival materials that may have quite limited contextual information available to them. They often rely on gathering context creatively from independent formal records, such as published documents and reports or news items.

References

ANDS (2013) *Research Data Australia*, Australian National Data Service (ANDS). Available at: http://researchdata.ands.org.au/.

Archives Hub (2013) Available at: http://archiveshub.ac.uk/.

Birth to 20 Study (2012) *About Us. Birth to 20 Study*, Faculty of Health Science, University of Witwatersrand, Johannesburg. Available at: http://www.wits.ac.za/birthto20.

Bishop, L. (2009) 'Ethical sharing and re-use of qualitative data', *Australian Journal of Social Issues*, 44(3): 255–72. Available at: http://www.data-archive.ac.uk/media/249157/ajsi44bishop.pdf.

Bishop, L. (2012) 'Using archived qualitative data for teaching: Practical and ethical considerations', *International Journal of Social Research Methodology* [Special Issue: Perspectives on working with archived textual and visual material in social research], 15(4): 341–50. DOI: 10.1080/13645579.2012.688335.

Blaxter, M. (2008) *Mothers and Daughters: Accounts of Health in the Grandmother Generation*, 1945–1978 [computer file], Colchester, Essex: UK Data Archive [distributor], April. SN: 4943. Available at: http://dx.doi.org/10.5255/UKDA-SN-4943-1.

Blaxter, M. and Patterson, E. (1982) *Mothers and Daughters: A Three-generational Study of Health Attitudes and Behaviour.* London: Heinemann Educational Books.

Bonin, E., Stevens, M., Beecham, J., Byford, S. and Parsonage, M. (2011) 'Costs and longer-term savings of parenting programmes for the prevention of persistent conduct disorder: A modelling study', *BMC Public Health*, 11: 803. DOI: 10.1186/1471-2458-11-803.

Booth, Charles (1891–1902) *Life and Labour of the People in London.* London: Williams and Norgate/Macmillan.

Boyle, E.M., Poulsen, G., Field, D.J., Wolke, D., Alfirevic, Z. and Quiqley, M. (2012) 'Effects of gestational age at birth on health outcomes at age 3 and 5 years of age: Population based cohort study', *British Medical Journal.* 344. DOI: 10.1136/bmj.e896.

Brown, G. and Harris, T. (1978) *Social Origins of Depression: A Study of Psychiatric Disorder in Women.* London: Tavistock.

Bureau of Labor Statistics (2013) *Labor Force Statistics from the Current Population Survey*, Bureau of Labor Statistics. Available at: http://www.bls.gov/cps/.

Centre for Longitudinal Studies (2010a) *Millennium Cohort Study: First Survey, 2001–2003* [computer file], 9th edn, Colchester, Essex: UK Data Archive [distributor], April. SN: 4683. Available at: http://dx.doi.org/10.5255/UKDA-SN-4683-1.

Centre for Longitudinal Studies (2010b) *Millennium Cohort Study: Second Survey, 2003–2005* [computer file], 6th edn, Colchester, Essex: UK Data Archive [distributor], April. SN: 5350. Available at: http://dx.doi.org/10.5255/UKDA-SN-5350-1.

Centre for Longitudinal Studies (2010c) *Millennium Cohort Study: Third Survey, 2006* [computer file], 4th edn, Colchester, Essex: UK Data Archive [distributor], April. SN: 5795. Available at: http://dx.doi.org/10.5255/UKDA-SN-5795-1.

CESSDA (2012) *Member Organizations*, Council of European Social Science Data Archives. Available at: http://www.cessda.org/about/members/ (http://www.cessda.org/.

CLS (2013) *Home Page*, Centre for Longitudinal Studies. Available at: http://www.cls.ioe.ac.uk/.

Corti, L. and Bishop, L. (2005) 'Strategies in teaching secondary analysis of qualitative data', *Forum Qualitative Social Research*, 6(1). Available at: http://nbn-resolving.de/urn:nbn:de:0114-fqs0501470.

Corti, L. and Thompson, P. (2004) 'Secondary analysis of archived data' in C. Seale, G. Gobo, J. Gubrium and D. Silverman (eds), *Qualitative Research Practice.* London: Sage. pp. 327–43.

Crescenzi, R. and Gagliardi, L. (2012) 'Moving people with ideas: Does inventors' mobility make firms more innovative?', *UK Data Service Case Study*, UK Data Service, University of Essex. Available at: http://ukdataservice.ac.uk/use-data/data-in-use/case-study/?id=109.

Crow, G. and Edwards, R. (2012) (eds) 'Perspectives on working with archived textual and visual material in social research', *International Journal of Social Research Methods* [Special issue], 15(4). DOI: 10.1080/13645579.2012.688308.

Dale, A., Arber, S. and Proctor, M. (1988) *Doing Secondary Analysis*. London: Allen and Unwin.

Data.gov (2013) Available at: http://www.data.gov/.

Databib (2013) *Registry of Research Data Repositories*, Databib. Available at: http://databib.org/index.php.

DBPedia (2013) Available at: http://dbpedia.org.

Department for Business, Innovation and Skills and Office for National Statistics (2011) *UK Innovation Survey, 1996–2008: Secure Data Service Access* [computer file], Colchester, Essex: UK Data Archive [distributor], July. SN: 6699. Available at: http://dx.doi.org/10.5255/UKDA-SN-6699-1.

Dex. S. (ed.) (1991) *Life and Work History Analysis: Qualitative and Quantitative Developments*, Social Review Monograph, 37. London: Routledge.

DIW (2013) *German Socioeconomic Panel*, Deutsches Institut für Wirtschaftsforschung (DIW), Berlin. Available at: http://www.diw.de/english/soep/.

Elder, G. (1974) *Children of the Great Depression: Social Change in Life Experience*. Chicago: University of Chicago Press.

Elliot, J. and Marsh, C. (2008) *Exploring Data: An Introduction to Data Analysis for Social Scientists*, 2nd edn. Cambridge: Polity Press.

Felstead, A. and Green, F. (2012) *Changing Patterns in the Quality of Work*, UK Data Service Case Study, UK Data Service, University of Essex. Available at: http://ukdataservice.ac.uk/use-data/data-in-use/case-study/?id=100.

Fielding, N. and Fielding, J. (2000) 'Resistance and adaptation to criminal identity: Using secondary analysis to evaluate classic studies of crime and deviance', *Sociology*, 34(4): 671–89.

Gillies, V. and Edwards, R. (2012) 'Working with archived classic family and community studies: Illuminating past and present conventions around acceptable research practice', *International Journal of Social Research Methodology*, 15(4): 321–30. Available at: http://dx.doi.org/10.1080/13645579.2012.688323.

Hakim, C. (1982) *Secondary Analysis of Social Research*. London: Allen and Unwin.

Hammersley, M. (1997) 'Qualitative data archiving: Some reflections on its prospects and problems', *Sociology*, 31(1): 131–42.

Hammersley, M. (2010) 'Can we re-use qualitative data via secondary analysis? Notes on some terminological and substantive issues', *Sociological Research Online*, 15(1): 5. DOI:10.5153/sro.2076. Available at: http://www.socresonline.org.uk/15/1/5.html.

Haynes, J. (2010) *Getting Students to do Data Analysis in a 12-week Unit*, UK Data Service Case study, UK Data Service, University of Essex. Available at: http://ukdataservice.ac.uk/use-data/data-in-use/case-study/?id=22.

Home Office (2008) *Offending, Crime and Justice Survey, 2006* [computer file], 2nd edn. Colchester, Essex: UK Data Archive [distributor], December. SN: 6000. Available at: http://dx.doi.org/10.5255/UKDA-SN-6000-1.

Huby, M. (2010) *Social and Environmental Inequalities in Rural England, 2004–2009* [computer file], Colchester, Essex: UK Data Archive [distributor], July. SN: 6447. Available at: http://dx.doi.org/10.5255/UKDA-SN-6447-1.

Hyman, H. H. (1972) *Secondary Analysis of Sample Surveys*. New York: Wiley.

ICPSR (2009) *Age and Attitudes about the Rights of Homosexuals: A Data-Driven Learning Guide*, Inter-university Consortium for Political and Social Research, University of Michigan. Available at: http://dx.doi.org/10.3886/gayrights.

ICPSR (2013a) *Instructional Materials*, Inter-university Consortium for Political and Social Research, University of Michigan. Available at: http://www.icpsr.umich.edu/ icpsrweb/ICPSR/studies?geography%5B0%5D=United+States&geography%5B1%5D= Global&classification=ICPSR.X.A.*&keyword%5B0%5D=instructional+materials&pa ging.startRow=1.

ICPSR (2013b) Available at: http://www.icpsr.umich.edu.

Irwin, S., Bornat, J. and Winterton, M. (2012) 'Timescapes secondary analysis: Comparison, context and working across data sets', *Qualitative Research*, 12(1): 66–80. DOI: 10.1177/1468794111426234.

Irwin, S. and Winterton, M. (2012) *Qualitative Secondary Analysis: A Guide to Practice*, Timescapes Methods Guide No. 19. Available at: http://www.timescapes.leeds.ac.uk/ assets/files/methods-guides/timescapes-irwin-secondary-analysis.pdf.

ISER (2013) *British Household Panel Study (BHPS)*, Institute for Social and Economic Research, University of Essex. Available at: https://www.iser.essex.ac.uk/bhps.

ISR (2013) *The Panel Study of Income Dynamics (PSID)*, Institute for Social Research, University of Michigan. Available at: http://psidonline.isr.umich.edu.

Johnson, J., Rolph, S., and Smith, R. (2010) *Residential Care Transformed: Revisiting 'The Last Refuge'*. Basingstoke: Palgrave.

Klineberg, S.L. (2011) *Kinder Houston Area Survey, 1982–2010: Successive Representative Samples of Harris County Residents*, ICPSR 20428-v2, Ann Arbor, MI: Inter-university Consortium for Political and Social Research [distributor]. DOI:10.3886/ICPSR20428.v2.

Kynaston, D. (2005) 'The uses of sociology for real-time history', *Forum Qualitative Social Research* [Online], 6(1). Available at: http://www.qualitative-research.net/ index.php/fqs/article/view/503.

Llewellyn Smith, H. (1930–35) *The New Survey of London Life and Labour*. London: P.S King.

Marsh, C. (1982) *The Survey Method: The Contribution of Surveys to Sociological Explanation*. London: Allen and Unwin.

Mauthner, N. (2012) 'Accounting for our part of the entangled webs we weave: Ethical and moral issues in digital data sharing', in T. Miller, M. Birch, M. Mauthner and J. Jessop (eds), *Ethics in Qualitative Research*, 2nd edn. London: Sage. pp. 157–75.

McInnes, J. (2012) *ESRC Undergraduate Quantitative Methods Initiative List of Resources for Teachers*, National Centre for Research Methods. Available at: http://eprints.ncrm. ac.uk/779/.

McKee, D. and Vihjalmson, R. (1987) 'Life stress, vulnerability and depression: A methodological critique of Brown et al.', *Sociology*, 20(4): 589–99.

Moore, N. (2007) '(Re)Using qualitative data?', *Sociological Research Online*, 12(3): 1. Available at: http://www.socresonline.org.uk/12/3/1.html.

NARCIS (2013) *National Academic Research and Collaborations Information System*, Royal Netherlands Academy of Arts and Sciences. Available at: http://www.narcis.nl.

National Renewable Energy Laboratory (2010) *Data.gov Mashathon 2010: an Energy Mashup*, Open EI. Available at: http://en.openei.org/apps/mashathon2010/.

National Research Council (2005). *Expanding Access to Research Data: Reconciling Risks and Opportunities*. Washington, DC: The National Academies Press. Available at: http://www.nap.edu/catalog.php?record_id=11434.

Nesstar (2013) *Nesstar*, UK Data Service, University of Essex. Available at:(http:// ukdataservice.ac.uk/get-data/explore-online/nesstar/nesstar.aspx.

NORC (2013) *Bibliography, General Social Survey*, NORC, University of Chicago. Available at: http://www3.norc.org/GSS+Website/Publications/Bibliography/.

Nurses' Health Study (2012) *About the Nurse's Health Study (NHS)*, Channing Laboratory, Harvard School of Public Health. Available at: http://www.channing. harvard.edu/nhs/.

Office for National Statistics (2012) *Harmonized Concepts and Questions for Social Data Sources: Primary Standards. Long-lasting Health Conditions and Illnesses*, Office for National Statistics. Available at: http://www.ons.gov.uk/ons/guide-method/ harmonisation/primary-set-of-harmonised-concepts-and-questions/long-lasting-health-conditions-and-illnesses--impairments-and-disability.pdf.

Office for National Statistics (2013) *Labour Market Statistics, January 2013*, Office for National Statistics. Available at: http://www.ons.gov.uk/ons/publications/re-reference-tables.html?edition=tcm%3A77-222531.

re3data.org (2013) *Registry of Research Data Repositories*. Available at: http://www. re3data.org/.

Roper, M. (2009) *The Secret Battle. Emotional Survival in the Great War.* Manchester: Manchester University Press.

Rowntree, S. (1901) *Poverty. A Study of Town Life.* London: Macmillan.

Ruspini, E. (2002) *Introduction to Longitudinal Research.* London: Routledge.

Savage, M. (2010) *Identities and Change in Britain since 1940: The Politics of Method.* Oxford: Oxford University Press.

Short, F. (2003) 'Domestic cooking practices and cooking skills: Findings from an English study', *Food Service Technology*, 3(3–4): 177–85.

Short, F. (2007) *Domestic Cooking and Cooking Skills in Late Twentieth Century England, 1996–1997* [computer file], Colchester, Essex: UK Data Archive [distributor], August. SN: 5663. Available at: http://dx.doi.org/10.5255/UKDA-SN-5663-1.

Singer, J.D. and Willett, J.B. (2003) *Applied Longitudinal Data Analysis: Modelling Change and Event Occurrences.* Oxford: Oxford University Press.

Smith, E. (2008) *Using Secondary Data in Educational and Social Research.* Oxford: Oxford University Press.

Social Science Research Methods Centre (2012) *SSRMC Training Programme*, University of Cambridge. Available at: http://www.ssrmc.group.cam.ac.uk/ programme/.

The City of New York (2013) *NYC Open Data*, The City of New York. Available at: https://data.cityofnewyork.us/.

Thompson, P. (1975) *The Edwardians: The Remaking of British Society.* London: Weidenfeld and Nicolson.

Thompson, P. and Lummis, T. (2009) *Family Life and Work Experience Before 1918, 1870–1973* [computer file], 7th edn, Colchester, Essex: UK Data Archive [distributor], May. SN: 2000. Available at: http://dx.doi.org/10.5255/ UKDA-SN-2000-1.

Townsend, P. (1962) *The Last Refuge: A Survey of Residential Institutions and Homes for the Aged in England and Wales.* London: Routledge and Kegan Paul.

Townsend, P. (2011) *Last Refuge, 1958–1959* [computer file], 2nd edn, Colchester, Essex: UK Data Archive [distributor], August. SN: 4750. Available at: http://dx.doi. org/10.5255/UKDA-SN-4750-1.

UK Data Service (2013a) *Case Studies of Re-use*, UK Data Service, University of Essex. Available at: http://discover.ukdataservice.ac.uk/?sf=Case studies.

UK Data Service (2013b) *Discover*, Data catalogue, UK Data Service, University of Essex. Available at: http://discover.ukdataservice.ac.uk/?sf=Data catalogue.

Vaillant, G. (2012) *Triumphs of Experience: The Men of the Harvard Grant Study*. Cambridge: Belknap Press/Harvard University Press.

Webb, S. and Webb, B. (1920 [1894]) *History of Trade Unionism*. London: Longmans, Green.

Whitehall Study (2012) *Whitehall II History*, UCL Department of Epidemiology and Public Health. Available at: http://www.ucl.ac.uk/whitehallII/history.

ELEVEN
Publishing and Citing Research Data

While research data can be shared in informal ways with colleagues and trusted collaborators or made available upon request, formally publishing data brings many advantages. Data can be published through deposit with a data repository, or by publishing in a data journal or as supplementary materials to a journal publication. When data are published, their profile is increased by having a proper citation, so that reuse of data can be attributed and acknowledged, similar to citations of more traditional sources of information.

Methods for data citation have evolved rapidly in the last few years. Not only are data repositories offering permanent citation for their holdings, many publishing houses also recommend a format for citing data.

Publishing Data: Where and How

There is more than one avenue through which research data can be published:

- deposit in a specialist data centre, archive or thematic repository;
- deposit in an institutional repository;
- submitting to a journal to support a publication;
- publish in a data journal;
- dissemination via a project or institutional website;
- self-publishing via a cloud-based system such as figshare.

Options available to you vary according to your research discipline and country. Taking each option in turn, we will examine the pro and cons.

Data Centres and Specialist Archives

The digital archiving of social research data has a rich history dating back to the 1950s and its activities have been successfully professionalized over the years through internationally collaborative efforts. Recent developments in data archiving methods have built on this foundation and are enabling the take-up of digital data curation practices on a wider scale (Corti, 2012). Initial developments were largely driven by the foresight of a few key academics who were working on international efforts to facilitate access to social science data for cross-national and cross-cultural analysis. Prior to the 1960s survey archiving activity in Europe, earlier initiatives from the USA paved the way for the practices of data archiving. In 1945 Elmo Roper, one of the founders of survey research, gave the IBM punched cards from his 1930s opinion poll surveys to a university library in the USA. Shortly afterwards George Gallup, inventor of the Gallup Poll, followed his lead and a dedicated unit was set up to hold the data. This led to the formation of the Roper Center, which opened as an archive of international opinion polls in 1957 at the University of Connecticut (Scheuch, 2006).

The Central Archive for Empirical Social Research at the University of Cologne, Germany (Zentralarchiv für Empirische Sozialforschung ZA, now part of GESIS-Leibniz Institute for the Social Sciences) was the first survey data archive to be founded in Europe in 1960. The Inter-university Consortium for Political Research followed, set up in 1962 in Ann Arbor, Michigan. In 1967 the SSRC Data Bank (now the UK Data Archive) was established by the Social Sciences Research Council (SSRC) at the University of Essex in Colchester. Other research communities around the world followed these initiatives to preserve databases for future national and international research and teaching (Mochmann, 2008). Thus crucial survey data can be re-analysed by other researchers, and the money spent on research has become not only an immediate outlay but also an investment continuing to pay dividends well into the future.

Early international collaboration among these archives built data inventories and retrieval systems, created data archiving management practices and provided training in secondary analysis. The collaborative network built over 50 years ago, which brings together social science data archiving professionals from all across the world, is still thriving today, known as the International Association of Social Science Information Systems and Technology (IASSIST) (O'Neill Adams, 2006).

The first social science data archives collected data of specific interest to quantitative researchers, such as opinion polls or election data. As the trend for large-scale surveys grew in the late 1970s, archives began to acquire international comparative surveys, government surveys and censuses. Because of their large sample sizes and the richness of the information collected, these national and international surveys already used by governments for planning, policy and monitoring purposes represent major research resources for the social scientist.

Many of the digital data archives now accept a diverse range of digital data, from historical databases to qualitative interviews. The UK Data Archive, for example, integrated both the Essex-based Qualidata unit and specialist History Data Service, which broadly expanded its mainly survey-focused collection to include non-numeric, textual, image and mixed methods data collections.

Examples of Specialist UK-Based Research Data Centres

Antarctic Environmental Data Centre

Archaeology Data Service

Biomedical Informatics Research Network Data Repository

British Atmospheric Data Centre

British Library National Sound Archive

British Oceanographic Data Centre

Cambridge Crystallographic Data Centre

Endangered Languages Archive

Environmental Information Data Centre

ESRC UK Data Service

European Bioinformatics Institute

Geospatial Repository for Academic Deposit and Extraction

National Biodiversity Network

National Geoscience Data Centre

NERC Earth Observation Data Centre

NERC Environmental Bioinformatics Centre

Publishing Network for Geoscientific and Environmental Data (PANGAEA)

The Oxford Text Archive

UK Data Archive

UK Solar System Data Centre

Visual Arts Data Service

The advantages of depositing data with a specialist data centre may include:

- assurance that data meet set quality standards;
- long-term preservation of data in standard file formats, which can be upgraded when needed due to software upgrades or changes;
- safe-keeping of data in a secure environment with the ability to control access where this is required;
- regular data backups;
- online resource discovery of data through data catalogues;
- access to data in popular file formats;
- licensing arrangements to acknowledge data rights and appropriate handling of confidential data;
- standard citation mechanism to acknowledge data creation;
- promotion of data to many users;
- monitoring of the secondary usage of data;
- management of access to data and user queries on behalf of the data owner.

Data centres and archives can provide safekeeping with controlled access to sensitive data. However, data centres have collection development policies and priorities, and cannot necessarily accept all research data offered to them.

Throughout the world there are also innumerable more traditional archives that collect research papers, as well as sound and ethnographic archives. One of the earliest and perhaps best known sources in the UK is the collection of papers resulting from the 1930s social research organization 'Mass-Observation'. This was established as a public archive at the University of Sussex in the early 1970s and has since then attracted a steadily increasing number of researchers (Sheridan, 2000). This popular collection is being selectively digitized.

Oral history has a long tradition of preserving and making available data from oral history research projects. In the USA, Columbia University Library has run an oral history archive for over 40 years while in 1987 the oral history section of the British Library's National Sound Archive has accrued important collections of interviews with key people in various trades and professions (Thompson, 2000). Notable examples of oral history archives in the world are: the oral history archive of 'German Memory' based in Hagen, Germany, comprising some 1,500 life history interview recordings with witnesses of time periods from East and West Germany (Leh, 2000); and various collections of oral history testimonies relating to the Holocaust across the world, such as the expansive collection in the USA Holocaust Memorial Museum in Washington DC (United States Holocaust Memorial Museum, 2013).

Eminent scholars, on retirement, will often donate their papers, in many cases representing their entire academic career, to their local university archives. In addition to primary research data created by the investigator during the research process, administrative documents concerning the research, such as grant proposals, associated correspondence and the products of analyses, such as manuscripts, are often kept. Such collections may also contain secondary sources utilized for a particular research study, such as newspaper clippings, organizational or medical records. University archives therefore retain the cultural and material 'sedimentation' of both institutional, and theoretical or intellectual processes, for example the development of ideas within key social science departments (Hill, 1993).

For some smaller archives whose current focus is on curating non-digital materials, access to these special collections archives can be restrictive and their capacity to look after digital materials is limited. As a result they may not be the best place for a researcher to publish contemporary research data.

Institutional Data Repositories

Data sharing policies by research funders and publishers, combined with supporting technological initiatives have seen academic institutions begin to take more responsibility for supporting their research assets. This can be seen in the rise in institutional repositories (IRs), set up primarily to host materials such as journal articles, theses and dissertations, now attempting to preserve research data. These initiatives can provide wide-scale visibility for an institution's scholarly research. At the time of writing in 2013, institutional data repositories are still in a state of experimentation, testing procedures and tools for ingesting and curating their data assets. Across the disciplines, data are so vastly heterogeneous in nature that common solutions for archiving are challenging; perhaps the only common denominator being a top-level description of a defined collection, like a catalogue record. In time, we would expect some of the more mature IRs, to hold and provide access to social science data with rich metadata.

What we can probably expect in the future is a new richer data landscape where traditional social science data archives and IRs live together, with the former providing access to nationally acclaimed data and IRs holding locally created research data collections. Data archives have a responsibility, and are well-placed, to offer expert domain-specific guidance and capacity building for these local data enterprises (Green and Gutman, 2006). An institutional repository then can offer a place to store data but the suitability of its access conditions and preservation policy and the ability for other researchers to discover the collection need to be assessed before data are deposited there for sharing. The Databib (2013) and re3data.org (2013) registries provide an authoritative overview of existing data repositories.

CASE STUDY ┤ **IQSS Dataverse Network**

Dataverse can be used by an individual researcher, research group, institution or journal to create a 'dataverse' to hold and share their research data collections. This dataverse can be branded and embedded in a website. Over 500 dataverses have so far been released, making research data available for reuse, for example by various universities in the USA, the Ghana Centre for Democratic Development, the World Agroforestry Centre, the Bogor Agricultural University and the MacArthur Foundation. Examples of journals with a dataverse holding datasets that supplement published articles are *International Studies Quarterly, American Journal of Political Science, International Interactions* and *Review of Economic and Statistics* (IQSS, 2013).

Journals and Data Publishing

The digital revolution has caused a drive towards making information openly accessible, with the internet making information sharing fast, easy, powerful and empowering. Scholarly publishing has seen a strong move towards open access to increase the impact of research, with e-journals, open access journals and copyright policies enabling the deposit of outputs in open access repositories (RIN, 2010; Laakso et al., 2011). The same movement has also driven opportunities for enabling access to data and evidence underlying research publications. A growing number of journals require data underpinning research findings to be published. While some journals encourage data to be added as supplementary material, others mandate deposit and publishing in open access repositories when manuscripts are submitted. Providing access to underlying data is customary in some disciplines, but not others. Moreover, most journals even if they do recommend opening up related data, certainly do not enforce it. Chapter 1 provides more information on journals' data policies and mandates.

In the social and behavioural sciences, the discipline of psychology demands that research can be replicated. Psychology suffered an abuse of research etiquette in 2011 when a Dutch researcher was found to have faked data from a series of publications. This resulted in the withdrawal of publications from the *British Journal of Social Psychology* and *Basic and Applied Social Psychology* and an investigation into the fraud (Enserink, 2012a). Furthermore in 2012, another Netherlands-based social psychologist, specializing in consumer behaviour, had papers retracted and resigned after a panel found problems with the scientific integrity of his studies (Enserink, 2012b). The publishing and professional societies have rallied to address these embarrassing scandals by mandating data from experiments supporting key publications be more available, and from 2013 must be held for at least five years after publication, and made readily available upon request to other scientific practitioners. This applies to laboratory data, completed questionnaires, and audio and video recordings.

In economics, some journals require the uploading of datasets, but in sociology, research data are very rarely made available to peer reviewers or readers of the published article. In the life sciences, the practice is more common. As early as 2003, in the USA, the National Academies with the support of the National Cancer Institute, National Human Genome Research Institute, National Science Foundation and the Sloan Foundation published a detailed report and recommendations on data sharing in the biological sciences (National Research Council, 2003). A number of BioMed Central journals now encourage or require authors, as a condition of publication, to include a link to the data supporting the results reported in an article.

In the environmental sciences, dedicated data repositories have been set up to provide more robust support for journals. There are some good established examples of repositories formally supporting the management and sharing of data that underlie academic publications. Examples are Dryad, PANGAEA and DataONE as described in the 'Journals and Data Sharing' case study.

Emerging new formats of publishing are using hyperlinking to data within the article narrative itself. In an 'enhanced publication' the linear article in a paper journal is replaced by a multidimensional multimedia journey. The reader follows a research narrative with the opportunity to view text extracts from data or watch clips of film, listen to audio clips and so on (Dicks et al., 2004; Wouterson-Windhuwer, 2009). This requires data to be accessible and referenceable, down to the level of an interview extract.

| CASE STUDY | Journals and Data Sharing |

Dryad is an international data repository for the biosciences which serves to preserve data that underpin peer-reviewed publications. The vision of Dryad is to be a

> scholarly communication system in which learned societies, publishers, institutions of research and education, funding bodies and other stakeholders collaboratively sustain and promote the preservation and reuse of data underlying the scholarly literature. (Dryad, 2013)

By January 2013, Dryad contained more than 2,500 data packages and more than 7,000 data files associated with articles in almost 185 journals. Dryad has a number of partner repositories, which exchange data with Dryad and co-develop mechanisms for data submission and search functionality.

The Publishing Network for Geoscientific and Environmental Data (PANGAEA) is an open access repository hosting data to support various journals for earth and environmental science (PANGAEA, 2013). Data archived at PANGAEA are fully citable and can be cross-referenced with journal articles, for example with the publisher Elsevier.

The *Nature* family of journals has a policy that requires authors to make data and materials available to readers, as a condition of publication, preferably via public repositories (*Nature*, 2013). Appropriate discipline-specific repositories are suggested. Specifications regarding data standards, compliance or formats may also be provided. For example, for research on small molecule crystal structures, authors should submit the data and materials to the Cambridge Structural Database (CSD) as a Crystallographic Information File, a standard file structure for the archiving and distribution of crystallographic information. After publication of a manuscript, deposited structures are included in the CSD, from where bona fide researchers can retrieve them for free. CSD has similar deposition agreements with many other journals. Data Observation Network for Earth (DataONE) preserves and provides access to multi-discipline and multi-national science data offering open, persistent, and secure access to richly described Earth observational data. DataONE is funded by the National Science Foundation in the USA.

There has recently been a rise in the publishing of a 'data paper' or 'data article' which describes a dataset deposited in a repository, detailing data collection and processing methods relating to large-scale datasets. This gives credence to datasets as valuable publishable assets. Such data papers can be published in a specific data journal, or in regular journals.

The Ecological Society of America (ESA Publications, 2012) defines a data paper as:

> a unique type of article published in *Ecology*, used to present large or expansive datasets, accompanied by metadata which describes the content, context, quality, and structure of the data. Metadata may contain limited statistical analysis of the data; more detailed analysis of data sets could, however, form the core of a companion article. Data papers are subject to full peer-review; the review process will evaluate ecological significance and overall quality first, but data papers

will also undergo further technical review to ensure a high standard of usability, especially with respect to associated metadata.

One example is the *Earth System Science Data Journal* (ESSD) – an international and interdisciplinary journal for the publication of articles on original high quality research datasets for use by Earth system scientists. Similarly, the *Geoscience Data Journal* offers an open access platform where scientific data can be formally published and peer-reviewed. Featuring as an online-only journal, this journal publishes short data papers linked to, and citing, datasets that have been deposited in approved data centres with persistent identifiers. *GigaScience* is an open-access open-data journal that publishes 'big-data' studies from the entire spectrum of life and biomedical sciences. Others include the more recent *Journal of Open Public Health Data* and the *Journal of Open Psychology Data* by Ubiquity Press. The journals work with a charging model whereby the submitter pays a fixed fee to publish. Along similar lines, cohort studies in the population health sciences have a tradition of publishing a cohort profile in the *International Journal of Epidemiology*, describing the data collection in detail with its potential for new research. The data are typically held and made available by the research organization, rather than being deposited in a repository.

Project Websites and Linked Open Data

Project websites can provide easy immediate storage and simplified access to research data, but offer less, or no, sustainability for the longer-term. In addition, it may be difficult to control who is using data and how they are using them, unless administrative procedures are put in place. A project website holding data should always have a backup and exit plan for sharing data.

An increasing number of web-based services provide opportunities to publish data tables openly on the web to promote mashing and analysis of disparate information sources. Examples of using linked open data are provided in Chapter 10 on reuse. The website CKAN, known as the Data Hub, is a community-run website which in January 2013 listed some 5,000 open datasets available on the web (CKAN, 2013). The UK Government uses CKAN to run its data hub, data.gov. uk, which in January 2013 listed some 8,000 government datasets. It is possible for the Hub to host a copy of anyone's data in a database, and provide some basic visualization tools. However, as with web facilities, this should be viewed as a short-term impact-generating facility and not a long-term data storage solution.

The Value of Citing Data

Proper citation should be a significant feature of any publication that references anything created by someone else. In most cases this is referencing another academic publication, source of knowledge or fact, but it should also include references to any primary or secondary data sources used.

Making a data collection citable and encouraging users to cite it:

- acknowledges the author's sources;
- makes identifying data easier;
- promotes the reproduction of research results;
- makes it easier to find data;
- allows the impact of data to be tracked;
- provides a structure that recognizes and can reward data creators.

Chapter 4 shows how data citation and discovery depend on core structured and standardized metadata for a data collection, such as that specified in the DataCite metadata schema.

An innovative and unreproduceable data collection that has been expensive and time-consuming to create, prepare and document has value that needs to be recognized alongside more tradition academic outputs. Various final products of research projects such as videos, website resources and plays deserve to be recognized alongside traditional academic outputs in the domain of the social sciences and humanities. Data are close behind.

Piwowar et al. (2011) demonstrate that data sharing provides many potential benefits, including increased citation of articles related to the shared data, and reuse. While measuring the amount of actual data reused is impossible, Piwowar's study tracked the reuse of data from three data repositories, NCBI's Gene Expression Omnibus, PANGAEA and TreeBASE, and found that reuse of data was correlated with the number of citations to the article about the data collection.

Conventions in Citing Data

In the past, publishers have not always specified the methods by which data should be cited in their guidelines for publication, and typically users of data might informally acknowledge the data creator. Thus, the value of the published data could not readily be seen, such as via citation indices.

Fortunately key style manuals of some of the major publishing houses have started to provide guidance on and examples of citations for datasets. Both the *Publication Manual of the American Psychological Association* and the *Oxford Manual of Style* offer such guidance (APA, 2009; OUP, 2012). However, making the data citable is the harder challenge, as it requires a formal longer-term reference point for data, carrying an expectation that others can go to the reference at any time in the future.

Practices for citing data have taken a while to come on-stream despite data archives and special collections providing unique references for their archival collections.

In 2007, Altman and King, quantitative data experts based at Harvard, called for robust citation of data in the social sciences (Altman and King, 2007). They proposed:

a similar universal standard for citing quantitative data that retains the advantages of print citations, adds other components made possible by, and needed due to, the digital form and systematic nature of quantitative data sets.

They argued that making use of six components would enable parallels to print documents but also take into account the unique nature of the digital form. Author(s), title and publishing date of the dataset would provide the capability to browse and search, and a unique global identifier, a universal numeric fingerprint, and a bridge service would persist and identify the data even when the publishing technology or location changes.

Following this paper, a White Paper published by Green (2009) of the OECD further called for a recognized standard and proposed a working model which was taken up and used by the OECD for its own international data series and tables.

Unique and persistent identification of a digital document *on the internet* requires the use of a Uniform Resource Name (URN). Once assigned to a document, the identifier remains unchanged as long as the name and the contents of the document remain intact. The same identifier is never assigned to two different documents. The URN identifier is typically exploited as a persistent web address through some kind of registration procedure, via an organization set up to fulfil this role, such as a national library. Private individuals cannot register URN identifiers.

URN identifiers need a persistent web address that comprises the URN identifier prefixed with the address of the resolving service. Since the mid-2000s, a number of URN issuing and resolving services for data, each with their own naming conventions, have come into play. These include the Digital Object Identifier DOI system that was launched back in 2000 providing 'a social and technical infrastructure for the registration and use of persistent interoperable identifiers for use on digital networks' (IDF, 2012). A DOI is simply a string of characters that make up a digital identifier used to uniquely identify an object. Metadata about the object is stored together with the DOI name, which can include a web address, a uniform resource locator (URL), where the object can be located. The DOI for a document is permanent, whereas metadata could change and thus result in broken webpage links. By April 2013 more than 85 million DOI names had been assigned by some 9,500 organizations across the world.

A number of data archives and data centres have adopted the DOI system for their data collections, making use of a registration agency to provide unique DOIs, rather like an International Standard Book Number (ISBN), used for books. They choose how to assign DOIs to various published objects in their collections, often following a similar methodology (Callaghan et. al, 2012; ESRC, 2012).

There are other systems in use to assign and resolve URNs, such as the German system, URN:NBN, initiated by the German National Library and acting as a URN resolving service for Germany, Austria and Switzerland (Deutsche National Bibliotek, 2013); and Archival Resource Key (ARK), which is a multi-purpose identifier created by the California Digital Library and used to assign URNs by a number of national organizations, such as the Bibliothèque Nationale de France and the USA National Library of Medicine (California Digital Library, 2013).

The case study below demonstrates how data citation using DOIs works at the UK Data Archive and shows what a working DOI looks like.

CASE STUDY ⊣ **Making Data Citable at the UK Data Archive**

A citation for a data collection should include enough information so that the exact version of the data being cited can be located, but does not include information on the sponsor or copyright ownership. Any acknowledgement, which is a general statement giving credit to sponsors or distributors, should not be a replacement for a proper citation.

The UK Data Archive provides a recommended citation for use of a data collection in the 'Study information and citation' file, available for every data collection from the study's online documentation table via the relevant catalogue record, as shown in Figure 11.1.

Health Survey for England, 2009
UKDA study number:6732

Principal Investigators
National Centre for Social Research
University College London. Department of Epidemiology and Public Health

Sponsor
Information Centre for Health and Social Care

Distributed by
UK Data Archive, University of Essex, Colchester.
July 2011 (2nd Edition)

Bibliographic Citation
All works which use or refer to these materials should acknowledge these sources by means of bibliographic citation. To ensure that such source attributions are captured for bibliographic indexes, citations must appear in footnotes or in the reference section of publications. The bibliographic citation for this data collection is:

National Centre for Social Research and University College London. Department of Epidemiology and Public Health, *Health Survey for England, 2009* [computer file]. *2nd Edition*. Colchester, Essex: UK Data Archive [distributor], July 2011. SN: 6732, http://dx.doi.org/10.5255/UKDA-SN-6732-1

Acknowledgement
Any publication, whether printed, electronic or broadcast, based wholly or in part on these materials, should acknowledge the original data creators, depositors or copyright holders, the funders of the Data Collections (if different) and the UK Data Archive, and to acknowledge Crown copyright where appropriate.

Any publication, whether printed, electronic or broadcast, based wholly or in part on these materials should carry a statement that the original data creators, depositors or copyright holders, the funders of the Data Collections (if different) and the UK Data Archive bear no responsibility for their further analysis or interpretation.

(Continued)

(Continued)

Figure 11.1 Citation for a survey data collection at the UK Data Archive

Source: UK Data Service, 2013

Note that the data citation contains:

- author and affiliation;
- data collection title or study title;
- year of publication;
- edition or version;
- publisher, being the UK Data Archive where the data are housed;
- access information, such as a persistent identifier, in this case, a DOI specified as a URL.

Note that a DOI is always included in the citation. In the case of the UK Data Archive, a DOI relates to the catalogue record for that data collection, but not to individual data files. This ensures that even if the location of the data changes, the DOI will always link to the description of the data collection being referenced.

A new DOI is assigned only when significant or high-impact changes are made to a data collection. Examples of such changes for a social survey at the UK Data Archive might be:

- a new variable is added;
- new labels or value codes are added;
- weighting variables are reconstructed;
- the wrong data have been supplied;
- data have been mis-coded, for example if 'Don't know/Refused' in responses have been confused;
- changes in format are made, for example, file migration;
- significant changes in documentation are made;
- changes in access conditions have been assigned.

The UK Data Archive **DOIs** are provided by the British Library's DataCite organization whereby the **URL** contains the root **URL** 'http://dx.doi.org/' followed by a string of unique numbers identifying the data publisher, the resource and the version (DataCite, 2012). For the
UK Data Archive, the structure of the **DOI** is easy to understand, as can be seen in the
example in Figure 11.2 which indicates a reference to the UK Data Archive (UKDA) Study
Number (SN) 6732, version 1:

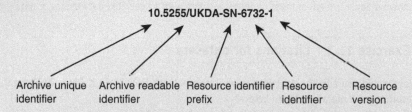

10.5255/UKDA-SN-6732-1

| Archive unique identifier | Archive readable identifier | Resource identifier prefix | Resource identifier | Resource version |

Figure 11.2   A DOI for a study at the UK Data Archive

Source: UK Data Service, 2013

By entering the **DOI** into a search engine, like Google, all references to that data collection can be picked up rapidly, allowing usage to be tracked efficiently.

A number of organizations around the world are making real efforts to promote data citation. Examples are the Australian National Data Service with their
Data Citation Awareness Guide (ANDS, 2011); the Economic and Social
Research Council's *Data Citation: What you Need to Know* (ESRC, 2012); and
initiatives on data citation and a related Special Interest Group coordinated by
the International Association of Social Science Information and Services and
Technology (IASSIST, 2013).

Permanent Identifiers for Researchers

Researchers have a unique identity and some consideration has been given to
providing a unique referencing system for individuals and organizations around
the world. Various organizations have made efforts to provide identification
services.

The Open Researcher and Contributor ID (**ORCID**) system presents a solution to the challenges of distinguishing one's own research activities from those
of others with similar names, by keeping a single record of one's profile in various research information systems. **ORCID** is an open, non-profit, community-
based effort to create and maintain a registry of unique researcher identifiers
that can be linked to research activities and outputs, and can cooperate with
other identifier systems (ORCID, 2013). An **ORCID** record holds non-sensitive
information such as name, email, organization name, and research activities, and
individuals are able to control levels of privacy. The International Standard

Name Identifier (**ISNI**) is an **ISO** certified global standard number for identifying contributors to creative works and their distributers. This includes artists, writers, performers, producers and researchers (ISNI, 2013).

At the time of writing, both systems are still in early phases of development.

Exercise 11.1 Depositing data with a data centre

Write down at least five advantages of depositing data with a specialist data centre or data archive.

Exercise 11.2 Citations for datasets

1. How would you cite the following quantitative dataset from the UK Data Service using the recommended metadata listed below?
   http://discover.ukdataservice.ac.uk/catalogue/?sn=6627

   (a) Author
   (b) Title
   (c) Publication date
   (d) Publisher
   (e) Identifier/location.

2. How would you cite the following qualitative data collection from the UK Data Service using the recommended metadata listed below?
   http://discover.ukdataservice.ac.uk/catalogue/?sn=5407

   (a) Author
   (b) Title
   (c) Publication date
   (d) Publisher
   (e) Identifier/location.

3. How would you cite the following quantitative dataset from ICPSR in the USA using the recommended metadata listed below?
   http://www.icpsr.umich.edu/icpsrweb/ICPSR/studies/32445

   (a) Author
   (b) Title
   (c) Publication date
   (d) Publisher
   (e) Identifier/location.

Answer to Exercise 11.1

Here are some of the advantages of publishing data with a professional data centre:

- Your data will be safely stored for the longer-term in a secure environment.
- Your data will be regularly backed up and its future usability is likely to be ensured.
- The intellectual property rights and licensing of your data will be managed.

- Your data will be included in online catalogues and hence can be discovered by internet search engines and, where appropriate, could even be actively promoted.
- Access to your data can be administered and its future usage monitored.
- Your data will likely be assigned a persistent digital identifier and can be reliably cited.

Answers to Exercise 11.2

1. The following quantitative dataset from the UK Data Service has the following metadata: http://discover.ukdataservice.ac.uk/catalogue/?sn=6627

    (a) Author – Home Office. Research, Development and Statistics Directorate BMRB. Social Research. Note that the 'Author' may be one or more corporate entities. In this case It is the Government Department and the fieldwork agency.

    (b) Title – *British Crime Survey, 2009–2010*. Note that the dates are part of the title as this crime Survey is part of a series and is carried out on a regular basis, dating back to 1984.

    (c) Publication date – 2012. Note that there has been more than one version of this dataset and that the latest available one is the 2012 version, which is the 2nd edition.

    (d) Publisher – Colchester, Essex: UK Data Archive.

    (e) Identifier/location – 10.5255/UKDA-SN-6627-2. It is better to use the DOI rather than the local dataset identifier (UKDA SN number) or the URL.

2. The following qualitative data collection from the UK Data Service has the following metadata: http://discover.ukdataservice.ac.uk/catalogue/?sn=5407

    (a) Author – Mort, M., Lancaster University, Institute for Health Research. Note that it is Principle Investigators who are referenced and not depositors or sponsors.

    (b) Title – *Health and Social Consequences of the Foot and Mouth Disease Epidemic in North Cumbria, 2001–2003*.

    (c) Publication date – 2006.

    (d) Publisher – Colchester, Essex: UK Data Archive.

    (e) Identifier/location – http://dx.doi.org/10.5255/UKDA-SN-5407-1. It is better to use the DOI rather than the local dataset identifier (UKDA SN number) or the URL.

3. The following quantitative data collection from ICPSR in the USA has the following metadata: http://www.icpsr.umich.edu/icpsrweb/ICPSR/studies/32445

    (a) Author – University of Michigan, Survey Research Center, Economic Behavior Program. Note that the 'Author' may be an academic centre, and in this case the programme is specified.

    (b) Title – *Survey of Consumer Attitudes and Behavior, April 2003*. Note that the date and month is part of the title as this survey is part of a series and is carried out on a regular basis, dating back to 1994.

    (c) Publication date – 2012. Note that there has been more than one version of this dataset and that the latest available one is the 2012 version. The note says that the data collection was updated to be consistent in processing standards across the Surveys of Consumers for 2003.

    (d) Publisher – Ann Arbor, MI: Inter-university Consortium for Political and Social Research.

    (e) Identifier/location – http://dx.doi.org/10.3886/ICPSR32445.v1. It is better to use the DOI rather than the local dataset identifier, such as ICPSR study number, or the URL.

References

Altman, M. and King, G. (2007) 'A proposed standard for the scholarly citation of quantitative data', *D-Lib Magazine*, 13(3/4). DOI: 10.1045/march2007-altman.

ANDS (2011) *Data Citation Awareness*, ANDS Guide, Australian National Data Service. Available at: http://www.ands.org.au/guides/data-citation-awareness.html.

APA (2009) *Publication Manual of the American Psychological Association*, 6th edn, American Psychological Association. Washington: APA.

California Digital Library (2013) *ARK (Archival Resource Key) Identifiers*, California Digital Library. Available at: https://confluence.ucop.edu/display/Curation/ARK.

Callaghan, S., Donegan, S., Peplar, S. et al. (2012) 'Making data a first class scientific output: Data citation and publication by NERC's Environmental Data Centres', *International Journal of Digital Curation*, 7(1): 107–13. Available at: http://www.ijdc.net/index.php/ijdc/article/view/208.

CKAN (2013) *CKAN*, The Data Hub. Available at: http://datahub.io.

Corti, L. (2012) 'Recent developments in archiving social research', *International Journal of Social Research Methods*, 14(4): 281–90. DOI:10.1080/13645579.2012.688310.

Databib (2013) *Registry of Research Data Repositories*, Databib. Available at: http://databib.org/index.php.

Datacite (2012) *About Datacite*, Datacite. Available at: http://www.datacite.org/.

Deutsche National Bibliotek (2013) *URN Service*, Deutsche National Bibliotek. Available at: http://www.dnb.de/EN/Netzpublikationen/URNService/urnservice_node.html.

Dicks, B., Mason, B., Atkinson, P. and Coffee, A. (2004) *The Production of Hypermedia Ethnography*. London: Sage.

Dryad (2013) *Dryad Data Repository*. Available at: http://datadryad.org/.

Enserink, M. (2012a) 'Diederik Stapel under investigation by Dutch prosecutors', *Science*, 2 October, American Association for the Advancement of Science. Available at: http://news.sciencemag.org/scienceinsider/2012/10/diederik-stapel-under-investigat.html.

Enserink, M. (2012b) 'Rotterdam marketing psychologist resigns after university investigates his data', *Science*, 25 June, American Association for the Advancement of Science. Available at: http://news.sciencemag.org/scienceinsider/2012/06/rotterdam-marketing-psychologist.html.

ESA Publications (2012) *Instructions for Data Papers*, Ecological Archives. Available at: http://esapubs.org/archive/instruct_d.htm.

ESRC (2012) *Data Citation: What You Need To Know*, Economic and Social Research Council. Available at: http://www.esrc.ac.uk/_images/Data_citation_booklet_tcm8-21453.pdf.

Green, A. and Gutman, M. (2006) 'Building partnerships among social science researchers, institution-based repositories and domain specific data archives', *OCLC Systems and Services: International Digital Library Perspectives*, 23: 35–53. Available at: http://deepblue.lib.umich.edu/handle/2027.42/41214.

Green, T. (2009) *We Need Publishing Standards for Datasets and Data Tables*, OECD Publishing White Paper, Organisation for Economic Co-operation and Development. Available at: http://dx.doi.org/10.1787/603233448430.

Hill, M. (1993) *Archival Strategies and Techniques*, Qualitative Research Methods Series, Thousand Oaks, California: Sage.

IASSIST (2013) International Association for Social Science Information Science and Technology. Available at: http://www.iassistdata.org/.

IDF (2012) *The DOI system*, International DOI Foundation. Available at: www.doi.org.

IQSS (2013) *IQSS Dataverse Network*, The Institute of Quantitative Social Science, Harvard University. Available at: http://dvn.iq.harvard.edu/dvn/.

ISNI (2013) *International Standard Name Identifier (ISO 27729)*, The INSI Organization. Available at: http://www.isni.org/.

Laakso, M., Welling, P., Bukvova, H., Nyman, L. and Björk, B-C. (2011) 'The development of open access journal publishing from 1993 to 2009', *PLoS ONE*, 6(6): e20961. DOI:10.1371/journal.pone.0020961.

Leh, A. (2000) 'Problems of archiving oral history interviews: The example of the archive "German Memory"', *Forum Qualitative Sociology*, 1(3). Available at: http://www.qualitative-research.net/index.php/fqs/article/view/1025.

Mochmann, E. (2008) 'Improving the evidence base for international comparative research', *International Social Science Journal*, 59 (193–94): 489–506.

National Research Council (2003) *Sharing Publication-related Data and Materials: Responsibilities of Authorship in the Life Sciences*. Washington, DC: The National Academies Press.

Nature (2013) *Availability of Data and Materials*, Nature Publishing Group. Available at: http://www.nature.com/authors/policies/availability.html.

O'Neill Adams, M. (2006) 'The origins and early years of IASSIST', *IASSIST Quarterly*, 5(14): 5–13. Available at: http://www.iassistdata.org/downloads/iqvol303adams.pdf.

ORCID (2013) ORCID: *Connecting Research and Researchers*, ORCID. Available at: http://about.orcid.org/.

OUP (2012) *New Oxford Style Manual* (Reference). Oxford: OUP.

PANGAEA (2013) *PANGAEA Data Publisher for Earth & Environmental Science*. Available at: http://www.pangaea.de/.

Piwowar, H., Carlson, J. and Vision, T. (2011) 'Beginning to track 1000 datasets from public repositories into the published literature', *Proceedings of the American Society for Information Science and Technology*, 48(1). Available at: http://doi.wiley.com/10.1002/meet.2011.14504801337.

Re3data.org (2013) *Registry of Research Data Repositories*. Available at: http://www.re3data.org/.

RIN (2010) *An Introduction to Open Access*, Research Information Network. Available at: http://www.rin.ac.uk/system/files/attachments/open_access_booklet_screen_0.pdf.

Scheuch, E.K. (2006) 'History and visions for the development of data services for the social sciences', *International Social Science Journal*, 53(4): 384–99.

Sheridan, D. (2000) 'Reviewing mass-observation: The archive and its researchers thirty years on', *Forum Qualitative Sociology*, 1(3). Available at: http://www.qualitativeresearch.net/index.php/fqs/article/view/1043/2255.

Thompson, P. (2000) *The Voice of the Past: Oral History*. Oxford: Oxford University Press.

UK Data Service (2013) Study Information and Citation in catalogue record for SN 6732. Available at: http://discover.ukdataservice.ac.uk/catalogue/?sn=6732.

United States Holocaust Memorial Museum (2013) *Oral History Collection*, United States Holocaust Memorial Museum, Washington DC. Available at: http://www.ushmm.org/research/collections/oralhistory/.

Wouterson-Windhuwer, S. (2009) *Linking Publications and Research Data in Digital Repositories*, SURF, Netherlands. Available at: www.surf.nl/en/publicaties/Pages/EnhancedPublications.aspx.

Conclusion

Science is forever changing. Innovation arises from both looking forward towards new discoveries and opportunities, and from looking back to learn from the past. As researchers we drive change through our own innovations in research and in research methodologies and through our increasing knowledge. Research practices are continually evolving and building on the work of others.

To promote this evolution, we also need to embrace the exciting potential that new technologies offer and exploit them appropriately. The internet, the World Wide Web, social media and exponentially developing technologies accelerate the availability of information and the exchange of knowledge. The mechanisms by which information is accessed, especially in developing countries, in resource-restricted institutions or under oppressive regimes, is transforming society. Easy access to online information resources transgresses the traditional boundaries of economic or political restrictions.

Improvements in society are also engendered by the free flow of quality information, and this has been recognized by governments across the world. As researchers are one of the core producers of data, their responsibilities towards their research data is set to change across all domains of scientific endeavour. Research funders are increasingly mandating open access to research data, governments internationally are demanding transparency in research, the economic climate is requiring much greater reuse of data, yet fear of data misuse and loss calls for more robust information security practices.

All these developments call on researchers to improve, enhance and professionalize their research data management skills to meet the challenge of producing the highest quality research outputs in a responsible and efficient way, and with the ability to share and reuse such outputs. The promotion of these skills offers a strategic contribution to the UK's and other countries' research capacity building programme.

While many hurdles remain over sharing and easy, open and free access to research data, such as ethical concerns, commercial sensitivities, or researchers' personal concerns over career progression, we also have an ethical responsibility towards humanity to apply data to the advancement of science. Just as in the vision of sustainable development we have a responsibility to take the well-being of future generations into account, so we also have a duty towards future generations to harness the opportunities provided by this digital era to open up research and data for new, more and better science.

We believe that this book will play a role in better science. Written by and for researchers, it guides researchers through key topics which are important for ensuring that research data are sustainable, high quality, and can be (re)used in a wide range of scientific pursuits, by current and future generations of scientists. At the same time we have showcased practical applications and real research cases, with interactive exercises and discussions so readers can practise and develop their data skills.

This is an exciting time for data users and creators. With rapidly evolving technological, infrastructure and policy progress, both in the international arena as well as locally, opportunities for enhanced data sharing arise and are growing fast. Our best practice guidance will keep pace with those developments. Consult our web resources accompanying this book, to stay informed of new advances (http://ukdataservice.ac.uk/manage-data/handbook.aspx). And please share your research data.

Glossary of Abbreviations

ASCII	American Standard Code for Information Interchange
ASR	Automatic Speech Recognition
CAQDAS	Computer Assisted Qualitative Data Analysis Software
CD-RW	Compact Disk-ReWritable
CSV	Comma-Separated Variables
DDI	Data Documentation Initiative
DIN	German Institute for Standardization
DOI	Digital Object Identifier
DPA	Data Protection Act
DVD-RW	Digital Versatile Disc-ReWritable
FLAC	Free Lossless Audio Codec
FOI	Freedom of Information
FTP	File Transfer Protocol
GIS	Geographic Information System
IP	Intellectual Property
IRB	Institutional Review Board
ISAD(G)	General International Standard Archival Description
ISBN	International Standard Book Number
ISNI	International Standard Name Identifier
ISO	International Organization for Standardization
ISSP	International Social Survey Programme
JPEG	Joint Photographic Experts Group
JPEG 2000	Joint Photographic Experts Group 2000
MD5	Message-Digest 5 algorithm

METS	Metadata Encoding and Transmission Standard
MP3	MPEG-1 Audio Layer-3
MPEG	Moving Pictures Expert Group
NDNS	National Diet and Nutrition Survey
OAI-PMH	The Open Archives Initiative Protocol for Metadata Harvesting
OAIS	Open Archival Information System
OCR	Optical Character Recognition
ODF	Open Document Format
ORCID	Open Researcher and Contributor ID
PDA	Personal Digital Assistant
PDF	Portable Document Format
PDF/A	Portable Document Format (Archival)
RAM	Random Access Memory
REC	Research Ethics Committee
RTF	Rich Text Format
SBML	Systems Biology Mark-up Language
SDC	Statistical Disclosure Control
SOA	Service-Oriented Architecture
TEI	Text Encoding Initiative
TIFF	Tagged Image File Format
UPS	Uninterruptable Power Supply
URL	Uniform Resource Locator
URN	Uniform Resource Name
USB	Universal Serial Bus
VPN	Virtual Private Network
VRE	Virtual Research Environment
WAV	Waveform Audio File Format
XML	Extensible Mark-up Language

Index